ARGENTINA'S MISSING BONES

VIOLENCE IN LATIN AMERICAN HISTORY

Edited by Pablo Piccato, Federico Finchelstein, and Paul Gillingham

ARGENTINA'S MISSING BONES

Revisiting the History of the Dirty War

———

James P. Brennan

Photographs by Mercedes Ferreyra

UNIVERSITY OF CALIFORNIA PRESS

University of California Press, one of the most distinguished university presses in the United States, enriches lives around the world by advancing scholarship in the humanities, social sciences, and natural sciences. Its activities are supported by the UC Press Foundation and by philanthropic contributions from individuals and institutions. For more information, visit www.ucpress.edu.

University of California Press
Oakland, California

Library of Congress Cataloging-in-Publication Data

Names: Brennan, James P., 1955– author. | Ferreyra, Mercedes, photographer.
Title: Argentina's missing bones : revisiting the history of the dirty war / James P. Brennan; photographs by Mercedes Ferreyra.
Description: Oakland, California : University of California Press, [2018] | Series: Violence in Latin American history ; 6 | Includes bibliographical references and index. |
Identifiers: LCCN 2017050752 (print) | LCCN 2017052779 (ebook) | ISBN 9780520970076 (ebook) | ISBN 9780520297913 (cloth : alk. paper) | ISBN 9780520297937 (pbk. : alk. paper)
Subjects: LCSH: Argentina—History—Dirty War, 1976–1983. | Córdoba (Argentina)—History—20th century—Case studies. | Trials (Crimes against humanity)—Argentina.
Classification: LCC F2849.2 (ebook) | LCC F2849.2 .B743 2018 (print) | DDC 982—dc23
LC record available at https://lccn.loc.gov/2017050752

Manufactured in the United States of America

26   25   24   23   22   21   20   19   18

10   9   8   7   6   5   4   3   2   1

For Córdoba's disappeared and their families

CONTENTS

ACKNOWLEDGMENTS

Sometimes books are the result of an opportunity. The changes in human rights policies under the government of Nestor and Cristina Kirchner (2003–2015) made feasible undertaking serious historical research on the state terrorism of Argentina's last military dictatorship. Previously, the obstacles were daunting. The systematic destruction of the military's records on its conduct during the so-called dirty war, an attempted erasure of all incriminating evidence, seemed to preclude research beyond oral histories, most notably those of the victims. The Kirchners revived the human rights issue and made it a central component of a governing strategy, repealing the previous amnesty laws, resuming trials and on an unprecedented scale of those accused of crimes during the dictatorship, establishing monuments and "memory sites" to memorialize its victims, even assembling archives for purposes of litigation if not historical research. I could not have written this book without these fortuitous changes.

Beyond favorable circumstances in Argentina, I have benefited from the support of various institutions and individuals. A research fellowship from the National Endowment for the Humanities permitted a year of research (2010–2011) in Argentina and a visiting fellowship the following year at the Woodrow Wilson International Center for Scholars in Washington, DC, allowed some additional research and preliminary writing on the subject. I am grateful to the staff at the latter and especially the director of the Latin America program there, Cynthia Arnson, for their support and for creating such a stimulating environment to share my research and learn from that of other fellows. In Argentina, my debts are many but I would like to thank especially the staff of the Archivo Provincial de la Memoria in Córdoba for their efforts to assist me in multiple research visits to the archive at a time of enormous activity for them with the trials and the human rights issue generally in the city. Despite hectic schedules and multiple demands on their resources, they found time to answer my questions and search for materials, and accommodated me with a working space as well as facilitated contacts in the local human rights movement. The staffs at the two *sitios de memoria* in Córdoba, La Perla, and the Campo de la Ribera likewise were generous with their time, and my multiple visits to both former detention centers informed in a very personal way my interpretation of the crimes committed there. In California, the interlibrary loan staff of Tomás Rivera Library at UC Riverside patiently and efficiently handled my repeated requests for materials. To all, I am deeply grateful.

My greatest debt is to the many individuals who in diverse and crucial ways contributed to this project. Darío Olmo, the former head of the Equipo Argentino de Antropología Forense and at the time of this research the undersecretary for human rights in Córdoba, made available to me the forensic team's reports and offered his personal assessment on the peculiar conditions that existed in Córdoba during the dictatorship. Juan Martín Zanotti and Agostina Parisi were eager and tenacious research assistants. Mercedes Ferreyra provided the book's photographs, which offer remarkable and instructive images not easily conveyed by mere words. Bill Nelson provided the cartography expertise for the city map of Córdoba. The manuscript was read and I received excellent criticisms from John Bawden, Federico Finkelstein, Mark Healey, and David Pion-Berlin, which greatly improved the book. A talk at the University of Chicago's Latin American history workshop likewise offered an opportunity to present some of the preliminary conclusions that I had reached and to receive excellent feedback from faculty and a group of very able graduate students. In Argentina, Raúl García Heras, Mónica Gordillo, Vicente Palermo, Marcelo Rougier, Carol Solis, and Juan Carlos Torre all encouraged me to write this book and offered helpful advice along the way.

I owe a very great debt to Fernando Reati. By sheer chance I was in the courtroom in 2010 when Fernando gave his gripping, detailed testimony of his incarceration and torments in the UP1 penitentiary. In the afternoon proceedings, an empty seat beside me was occupied just as another witness was to begin his testimony. It was Fernando who sat next to me. We struck up a conversation about his testimony and the trial and since then have maintained a correspondence. Fernando read the manuscript with great care, offered trenchant criticisms, but not so harsh as to discourage me from publishing. Fernando most likely will not agree with all my arguments in the book, but I do hope he agrees with most of them. A chance encounter with him at the 2010 UP1 trials allowed me to make a friend of someone whose personal history in these terrible events served to deepen my understanding of the human cost of the military's crimes.

My wife, Olga Ventura, and daughter, Nadine Brennan, became almost as engrossed in this history over the past seven years as I have been. They pored over the numbers with me of the thousand-plus victims of the state terrorism in Córdoba, and helped me track down the dates and sites of their abductions and uncover the precise circumstances of their fates. In the process we all became more than familiar with many of the victims, and felt a personal bond with them and a moral responsibility to get this history right. Hopefully, we have succeeded.

INTRODUCTION

In December 2002, the Argentine Forensic Anthropology Team (Equipo Argentino de Antropología Forense or EAAF) discovered a gruesome legacy of the country's so-called dirty war. After months of preliminary preparations, the team located a large common grave in Córdoba's San Vicente cemetery, in the city's gritty eastern neighborhoods. A subsequent analysis of genetic material of the remains matched blood samples taken from family members who had claimed missing relatives, confirming accusations of mass murder perpetrated by the former military government. Forensic evidence also revealed violent death for most, mainly by gunshot.[1]

Established in 1984 under the tutelage of American forensic anthropologist Clyde Snow, the EAAF had emerged as a protagonist in the human rights cause since the early days of Argentina's restored democracy that followed more than seven years (1976–83) of military rule. During the government of Raúl Alfonsín (1983–89) it enjoyed a period of official tolerance if not outright support. The EAAF had earned its spurs in the search for the remains of the victims of the country's state terrorism in the 1980s, uncovering some large, ghastly sites. Then EAAF gained international notoriety as the premier forensic anthropological team in the world with expeditions to Guatemala, East Timor, Croatia, Bosnia, and elsewhere, including a successful search for the remains of fellow Argentine, Che Guevara, in Bolivia. As the human rights issue faded in their country under the government of Carlos Menem (1989–99), the EAAF developed new techniques, acquired additional experience, and trained a core of seasoned forensic anthropologists who lent their services to locate and document the many victims of the twentieth century's genocides and crimes against humanity.[2]

The election of Peronist Nestor Kirchner to the presidency in 2003 revived the human rights issue movement that had remained active at the societal level through the 1990s, which was a decade of official indifference. The Kirchner administration's resuscitation of human rights as state policy led to a period of renewed activity for the EAAF. One of the major areas of interest in this second round of activity was the industrial city of Córdoba, the site of thunderous social protests and political violence in the years preceding military rule. Córdoba had suffered grievously under the dictatorship. In the regime's notorious clandestine detention centers (CDCs), including the largest in the country's interior, La Perla, the military had detained, tortured, and murdered many thousands, and nearly a thousand in Córdoba alone.[3] Yet unlike in other parts of the country, human rights groups and family members there had been unable to locate the remains of the *desaparecidos* (disappeared). Great hope therefore surrounded the arrival of the EAAF team, especially following the discovery and excavation in the San Vicente cemetery.

This early success was not destined to continue. Despite strong suspicions of the existence of a mass grave near the La Perla detention center, the EAAF failed in subsequent years to locate such remains. After years of searching, the forensic team made an important but modest discovery in late 2014 and early 2015 of the remains of several disappeared students and members of the Juventud Universitaria Peronista (JUP), located in a crude crematorium on the grounds of La Perla. Such findings nonetheless paled in comparison to the scale of the violence and the numbers of those actually murdered. The missing bones of Córdoba's experience with dictatorship and state terrorism would undoubtedly have provided valuable evidence to document precisely both the identities of the victims and the methods employed by the military dictatorship in their disappearance.[4] In their stead, other methods and different kinds of evidence were needed to reconstruct the history of state terrorism in the city and the fate of the disappeared.

In September 2010 I attended in Córdoba the trials of the military and security forces accused of human rights violations during the dictatorship. Among the defendants were General Rafael Videla, the army commander and president of the country from 1976 to 1981, and General Luciano Benjamín Menéndez, commander of the army's Third Corps with its headquarters in Córdoba, who was responsible for undertaking the "war against subversion" in Córdoba and elsewhere in the country's interior. This was the third of such trials for Menéndez, all of which would lead to guilty verdicts and life sentences for him. This particular trial involved an especially terrible incident: the summary execution of some thirty political prisoners at the federal penitentiary there, under the direct orders of President Videla. The dynamics of the trial were themselves revealing. The defendants were all, save one accused woman police officer, old men now "withered and implausible avatars of their earlier selves" as defendants in such trials, often held years after their crimes, tend to be.[5] Some were doddering now and unsteady on their feet. They sat in rows in a hierarchy, intended or not, of authority and degree of culpability. In the front row sat the highest-ranking military officers, with Videla and Menéndez side by side, only rarely speaking to one another and never offering so much as a word to the police and junior officers seated behind them, undoubtedly regarded by the former military commanders as second-class underlings, former subordinates, not worthy of sharing the courtroom with them. In 2015 I returned for the fifth of what might be termed the Menéndez trials, the former commander of the Third Army Corps a defendant in each. This trial, one including Menéndez and some of the defendants from the 2010 trial but also new ones, involved charges of unlawful abduction and murder at the city's two largest detention centers, La Perla and the Campo de la Ribera. The trial proved to be the longest and most anguishing of the five, the numbers of victims unprecedented and the graphic testimony stretching out over a period of four years. These trials, the subject of chapter 6, revealed much about the military government's brutal methods in Córdoba but left as many questions unanswered, including the precise motivations and rationale compelling the state terrorism there.

Books on the so-called dirty war are legion but fail to address underlying causes for human rights abuses on such a scale. Only Peronism rivals the dirty war as a subject of inquiry in modern Argentine history. Yet unlike the case of the great populist movement, research and scholarship on the subject has been thin, the violence and human drama of those years more the preserve of investigative journalism than historical scholarship.[6] In Argentina, only recently have historians begun to conduct research and publish on the period, producing a handful of studies based on archival and other evidence.[7] Scholars of other disciplines such as anthropology and sociology have produced a substantial literature on memory, drawing largely on the oral testimonies of the victims of state terrorism and their families.[8] Yet even the best of this nascent scholarship has focused more on questions of societal trauma and memory than on causation and methods. A provocative exception to the victim-centric literature is *Argentina's "Dirty War"* by Anglo-Argentine Trotskyist Donald Hodges. Hodges takes seriously the military's history, its strategic calculations and belief that Argentina had been converted into a battleground in a global war, albeit an unconventional and undeclared war. In his lengthy narrative on the history of the revolutionary Left, he argues that the armed Left's relatively small numbers were compensated by its verve and cultural influence, that it in effect constituted a formidable adversary to Argentina's armed forces, though he summarily rejects the military's outlandish claims of Argentina as a battleground of World War III. Hodges also sees at least as strong an influence of Catholic nationalism as Cold War ideologies and related geopolitical thinking on the Argentine officer corps.[9]

The very term *guerra sucia* ("dirty war") is roundly rejected now by all human rights groups in Argentina as morally indefensible, of lending credence to the military's assertion that it was indeed waging a war and therefore its crimes were mere acts of war and legitimate. Yet the military did not hold a monopoly on the use of such terminology and the Left itself routinely referred to a "revolutionary war" being waged at the time against the reactionary forces, public and private. I employ the term *dirty war* for several reasons. First, since a major objective of this book is to examine the perpetrators of the violence and not just its victims, it is necessary to understand the military government's understanding of what constituted war and its applicability to conditions in Argentina. Aside from some passing references in often obscure, both right-wing ultranationalist and leftist publications to a "dirty war" being waged against the left during the 1973–76 Peronist government, it was the military that most appropriated the term but only belatedly, in the final stages of the dictatorship and early days of the reestablished democracy, to describe the methods employed in its campaign against the Left and then its defense of such tactics in criminal proceedings to defeat the so-called subversion. It did so publicly for the first time during the brief government of General Reynaldo Bignone (1982–83), the last of the military juntas, in a press conference given by Bignone, followed by letters to the editor of various newspapers, written by retired officers invoking the experience of the French in Algeria and French theories of counterrevolutionary war as a justification for its methods (methods now being severely questioned by society) and a besieged military regime in the wake of the Falklands-Malvinas conflict. The Argentine press soon appropriated the dirty war characterization and popularized it. I also employ the term because the current preferred term in Argentina, *the repression*, is both imprecise and contains its own assumptions about culpability and causation. Moreover, its very blandness makes it unlikely to replace the term *dirty war* widely used elsewhere in the world and likely enshrined for posterity in histories of Argentina dealing with the period. Even from a strictly juridical and moral point of view, the term *war* does not exonerate. There are rules in war, and those states, governments, and individuals that violate them can and should be held accountable. Indeed, during the clandestine so-called antisubversive campaign the military government deliberately avoided the term *war* since to acknowledge it as such it would have conferred certain rights on the belligerents (guerrillas) as defined by the Geneva convention. It employed the term only after the fall of the dictatorship as a defense of its actions. The human rights movement itself did not always reject the term, and the Permanent Assembly on Human Rights used it in its 1988 report ("Las cifras de la guerra sucia") on the numbers of disappeared, with a prologue written by journalist and human rights activist Horacio Verbitsky.

Why Córdoba? Águila's study of the dictatorship in Rosario demonstrated the significance of regional variations in the heretofore rather monochromatic story of the state terrorism of those years. The peculiarity of the experience of provinces like Chaco and Neuquén has also been noted, where the dictatorship attempted to claim the mantle of protector of indigenous peoples' rights through a program of modernization and a "commodification of indigenous identity" marketing souvenirs and other supposed artifacts of indigenous culture at the same time it promoted Catholicism to better integrate the Toba, Mataco, Mapuche, and other tribes into the national community.[10] Such policies were contemporary with a murderous campaign of state terrorism directed against the Left in those provinces.

The case of Córdoba in the pursuit of the regional dimension of the dirty war is particularly urgent since it loomed as one the worst sites of repression, a place not only that contributed a large number of the disappeared and many others unlawfully detained, tortured, and murdered but also where the military sought to erase an entire sociocultural milieu. Massive social protests in 1969 and 1971, a militant and in some sectors radicalized labor movement, site of an active Third World Priests movement, and contributor of many youthful recruits drawn from the city's large university population to guerrilla organizations such as the Montoneros and the Ejército Revolucionario del Pueblo (ERP), Córdoba seemed to incarnate in a single place all those supposedly corrosive influences that the military hierarchy wished to extirpate. The military was well positioned to undertake such a campaign. Not only was the army's Third Corps based in Córdoba, so too were other military units including air force, paratrooper, intelligence, and artillery brigades as well as one of the three regional headquarters of the federal constabulary (Gendarmería Nacional) subordinate to the army command. The dictatorship thus brought with it not only state terrorism and detention centers but also a thorough militarization of public administration and the judicial system, key components in the repressive architecture. A study of the dirty war in Córdoba, however, cannot be a mere exercise in regional history. Córdoba's experience with state terrorism goes beyond Córdoba itself, extending to French counterinsurgency theories essayed in Algeria, to Cold War strategies devised in Washington, to secret military cabals held in Buenos Aires to coordinate a national campaign against the Left, even to Mexico where an exile community was closely monitored by both the Argentine embassy and an obliging Mexican government.[11]

The regime that terrorized Córdoba and Argentina perpetrated one of the twentieth century's many dirty wars—war in the dark, murderous yet deniable. War before the twentieth century lacked such qualities and was rather the confrontation on the battlefield of armies advancing the interests of kings, empires, and states, "the extension of politics by other means" to use Clausewitz's famous maxim. Even partisan guerrilla warfare produced dead bodies. In the twentieth century, the nature of war changed. It sometimes now involved not large armies but small groups of men, operating secretly, employing the most violent methods including torture to annihilate, demoralize, and defeat not only an enemy but an entire society, ethnic or religious group, or political sect deemed to have engendered such enemies. Its victims were as much ideas and cultures as flesh-and-blood human beings. These wars too were Clausewitz's extension of politics by other means, but they were the politics of antipolitics, to dissemble, to expel, and to erase. The road to Argentina's experience with such a war is littered with the missing bones of Kenyans, Algerians, and others who had lived under similar regimes. One of the first such wars was the brutal British counterinsurgency in Ireland in the 1920s, much of it directed against the civilian population, complete with abductions and murders.[12] The Nazis took such tactics to new depths with their tactics, after Hitler's December 1941 "Nacht und Nebel" decree authorized the army and Gestapo to make underground resistance fighters disappear into the "night and fog," a chilling prequel to Argentina's dirty war.[13] In Algeria, the French refined the techniques of mass detention, torture, and psychological warfare against a colonial people fighting for their independence.[14] The British responded to an anticolonial struggle in Kenya with similar tactics.[15] Argentina's experience departs from all these in the small number of combatants involved, and that the vast majority of the dirty war's victims were unarmed political and union activists. If Argentina suffered a war, it was above all a war of extermination of defenseless civilians.

In the dreary catalogue of twentieth-century genocides and crimes against humanity, Argentina's dirty war certainly ranks small. Not millions, not even hundreds of thousands died in the death camps of the dictatorship. The state terrorism in Argentina lasted but a few years, its victims numbered at most 30,000 and almost certainly a far smaller number.[16] Yet it occupies a special place in the pantheon of the last century's horrors given the circumstances surrounding it. Argentina had not passed through the disruptions of prolonged war or anticolonial struggle; it had no serious ethnic, racial, or religious divisions; nor was it experiencing a particularly difficult economic conjuncture when the state terrorism occurred. Neither was it animated by a struggle over scarce resources such as land or aggravated by famine.[17] Argentina was no stranger to military rule, but the turn to state terrorism was unprecedented, an apparent aberration in the military's culture and certainly that of the country generally. The violence of the 1970s therefore cannot be traced to some intrinsic national ethos, or Argentina's societal complexion, or an episodic cataclysm. The dirty war's explanation lies in the realm of history, of deep, unresolved conflicts of some kind. This book seeks to explain precisely which ones, at least in one particular place.

Argentina's dirty war, of course, forms part of the larger story of the global Cold War. Washington trained and financed repressive military governments throughout the hemisphere, and indeed Latin America provided a "workshop" of theories and practices applied elsewhere in the world by the United States before, during, and after its confrontation with the socialist bloc.[18] The dirty war, however, cannot be reduced simply to Cold War dynamics, and indeed the Cold War in Latin America revealed a great diversity of influences, tactics, and methods. Too often the story has been told as a simple imposition of American power, with the Latin

American militaries as passive recipients of its indoctrination and training, overlooking the precise national contexts in which the violence occurred and the independent agency of the perpetrators of its crimes.[19] In Argentina, the clandestine
state terrorism with its death camps, black market in children, and bureaucratic-
juridical scaffolding differed greatly from the more conventional counterinsurgency tactics implemented in Southeast Asia and even the Central American
monte. Its ideological underpinnings were similarly an amalgam of influences,
drawn from Argentina's history and the military's own institutional culture as well
as diverse foreign sources.

I have long wanted to write this book. In the mid-1980s, while conducting dis-
sertation research on a previous period in Córdoba's history, I heard many accounts
of the recent experience of life under terror there. In many ways, with dictatorship
having just ended, memories were fresher and the need to engage in reflection on
that experience far greater than the period I was actually studying, which the traumatic experience of dictatorship almost seemed to have erased. These were the
very days of the discovery of the first mass gravesites of the *desaparecidos*, of the
Alfonsín government's trials of the fallen junta, of a furious, seditious military that
staged several unsuccessful military rebellions against that same government.
Unfolding events such as these were not yet the subject of history. Now, more than
three decades later, they certainly seem to be.

THREATS

Apostles of the New Order

To combat day and night until annihilating these subversive criminals who want to subjugate the still standing Argentina to the bloody dictates of foreign regimes.

—GENERAL LUCIANO BENJAMÍN MENÉNDEZ

The military government that assumed power on March 24, 1976, did so with a determination to both transform the country and neutralize, indeed to annihilate, those who, so they believed, held radical agendas of their own that threatened Argentina's sovereignty and its national traditions, its cultural identity. A brutal dictatorship emerged in response to years of social mobilization and popular protest, but even more menacing, also of a Left confident of its ascendance within the working class, influential if not dominant in the new youth culture, and prepared to employ extreme measures to fashion a new society.[1] Antonius Robben has characterized the military's violence and the state terrorism of these years as a "cultural war," a war on an ensemble of ideas, beliefs, and ideologies that the military, forged in its own culture of *integralista* Catholic nationalism, found repugnant and destructive. The dirty war was certainly partly a cultural war, but it was also much more. The threats operated on levels beyond the ideational and eventual, were immediate, visible, and present in multiple sites. The armed Left encroached on the military's monopoly of violence and therefore threatened its institutional integrity. The Catholic Church posed another threat, a Church wracked by internal rifts caused by the Left's ascendance and in its growing influence in social spaces formerly the sole preserve of the secular Left. Working-class militancy in the workplace and outside of it threatened powerful business interests and Argentine capitalism itself. A revolution of the kind the Left envisioned jeopardized Argentina's international alliances and the web of interests tied to those alliances, everything from its links to international financial institutions to those strictly related to hemispheric defense.[2]

Political violence in Córdoba, even state-sanctioned terrorism, did not begin with the 1976 coup and the military government that followed. It had occurred periodically in the city since the establishment of the dictatorship of Gen. Juan Carlos Onganía in 1966, flaring up especially in moments of social protest and labor agitation, and became endemic in the final years of the 1973–76 Peronist government. Its perpetrators were the military, police, union thugs, and paramilitary organizations with shadowy links to the security forces, governments, and local business groups. The infamous right-wing death squads of Peronist government minister José López Rega, the Alianza Anticomunista Argentina (AAA), independent of the army and targeting largely enemies within the Peronist movement, had less influence in Córdoba than a paramilitary organization, the Comando Libertadores de América, under the army's direct command and targeting the entire Left, Peronist and otherwise.

Violence, however, had not been a monopoly of the Right. The Left had practiced it as well, though violence of a different character and certainly with other objectives. Particularly after the 1969 *Cordobazo*, a massive social protest against the Onganía dictatorship, various leftist organizations had accepted violent tactics including armed struggle and targeted assassinations as legitimate responses to right-wing provocations as well as part of a broad revolutionary strategy. Virtually every leftist organization with a presence in Córdoba, with the exception of the Communist Party, had sanctioned it to some degree. Sympathy for violence as an appropriate, even necessary response to class inequalities, dictatorship, and censorship also flourished among the university students and within the youth culture generally. In Córdoba, perhaps as in nowhere else in Argentina given its large university student population, "*la juventud*" was a sociopolitical and cultural category, not simply a biological stage. To be young in these years meant much more than nonconformist, even rebellious behavior. It meant embracing a new ethic and assuming the cost of a new political activism, including the possibility of violent death, one's own and that of another.[3]

Though the leftist influences in the city's youth culture were manifested in other sites, in working-class neighborhoods and in the factories among others, it was above all in the university where revolutionary ideas and the sanctioning of violence flourished. Córdoba's large public university, the Universidad Nacional de Córdoba, was not only the country's oldest university but also the most politicized. Drawing on its history as the site of the historic 1918 university reform movement, the university had occupied a central place in Córdoba's civic life in subsequent decades. During the government of Juan Domingo Perón (1946–55), Córdoba's overwhelmingly Catholic and then largely middle-class student body had comprised a bulwark of opposition to the regime. After Perón's fall, the country's entire public university system experienced a thorough revamping. The first expression of such reform was the recovery of university autonomy, an academic independence greatly compromised during Perón's government. The purging of Peronist faculty and administrators was itself a highly political act and did not respond to purely academic criteria as claimed by the new public authorities, nor did the return of faculty forced to abandon the university during the Perón years always represent a triumph of academic qualifications over political sympathies.[4] The ten years that followed witnessed large student mobilizations to protest university policies as well as a growing radicalization as the Cuban Revolution penetrated deep into student identity and reformist ideas ceded to revolutionary solutions.

The subsequent decade would prove tumultuous. Nationally, this new stage was inaugurated by an ominous event: the 1966 attack on university professors in Buenos Aires by police, an event known as the "Noche de los Bastones Largos." In Córdoba, university politics moved largely underground with the military's assumption of power that same year and the government's interdiction of the university that followed. Occasional acts of state violence became routine with the onset of the Juan Carlos Onganía dictatorship (1966–70). These mostly took the form of unlawful arrests and abusive police interrogations, excessive force by the military and police alike in suppressing strike actions by local unions and student protests, and a few violent deaths at the hands of security forces, such as the shooting of autoworker Máximo Mena, an event that triggered the 1969 *Cordobazo*, which marked a turning point in the escalation of violence in the city by public authorities. The mass arrest of protesters, the ignoring of writs of habeas corpus and lengthy prison sentences swiftly imposed by military tribunals, as well as accusations of police and army abuse of prisoners ushered in a decade of intimidation, terror, and torture. Army occupation of the Fiat factories in 1971, one of the largest industrial complexes in the city, was followed by a terror campaign against the deposed leadership of the *clasista* unions there. The frequent arrests of union leader Agustín Tosco and harsh treatment of student activists and protesters in these years formed part of an established pattern now of interpreting any acts of civil disobedience and legitimate protest as unlawful, to be met with a summary, decisive response and indifferent to due process and established legal procedures.[5] The military government in power at the time of the *Cordobazo* ignored both the social underpinnings of the uprising and the reports on its causes by the local military commanders responsible for suppressing the protest, attributing it strictly to the work of "extremist organizations" and, what was soon to become a favorite characterization, "subversive groups," providing the military henceforth with its institutional interpretation of the events of May 1969 that would greatly influence its subsequent behavior.[6]

Contemporary with its repressive policies, the military established the legislative scaffolding authorizing its tactics. In 1970 the military government decreed a law (ley 18.670) that made certain crimes exempt from appeal, and the following year penalties were increased for crimes that would have fallen under the vague rubric of "subversion" while establishing a new legal body, the Cámara Federal, with jurisdiction over such crimes. In June of that year, a revised version of the

1966 Ley de Defensa Nacional from the Onganía dictatorship authorized the executive to employ the armed forces to investigate, prevent, and combat subversion during declared states of siege, and the following year a newly decreed law actually passed jurisdiction for certain crimes to military courts.[7] Onganía's Ley de Defensa Nacional would not be repealed until the Alfonsín presidency (1983–89) and other "antisubversive" legislation from the 1966–73 military governments, though briefly repealed with the return of Peronism to power in 1973, would in piecemeal fashion be resuscitated with Perón's 1974 assumption of the presidency and then under his widow and successor, Isabel Perón.

Such severe reactions deepened sympathy for equally violent responses. Following the *Cordobazo*, a marked shift took place toward political radicalism and a popular sanctioning of violence occurred, both sentiments particularly potent within the ranks of Córdoba's youth. Revolutionary organizations that supported armed struggle and had existed before the *Cordobazo*, such as the Fuerzas Armadas Revolucionarias (FAR) and the Fuerzas Armadas Peronistas (FAP), redoubled their commitment to direct, violent confrontation with the government and with so-called counterrevolutionary forces, while new ones equally convinced of the legitimacy of violent tactics, such as the Ejército Revolucionario del Pueblo (ERP) and the Montoneros, emerged in the wake of the *Cordobazo*. The onset of the 1973–76 Peronist government escalated the situation as Peronism experienced a rancorous and bloody internal struggle for control of the movement. By now violence had become a talisman, viewed as a legitimate and indeed ineluctable way of confronting adversaries now more than just the public authorities and security forces. The eruption of guerrilla violence following the *Cordobazo* in the form of the Montoneros and the ERP signaled a qualitative change in the political culture, nationally and locally. Nationally, the Peronist Left's rhetoric and actions invoked revolutionary war to both purge Peronism of traitorous elements from within its ranks in the form of union bureaucrats and fascistic nationalists and for an assault on state power. The Montoneros' public statements, broadsides, and publications are replete with a language exalting war, a popular army, military strategy, and martyrdom.[8] A Montonero training manual from 1974, complete with illustrations, gave precise instructions on the use of firearms, bomb making, propaganda work, and how to organize a street demonstration, and detailed a Spartan code of expected comportment from the Montonero militant. The formation of a "Montonero army" and this army's "Montonero militias" were invoked as a legitimate use of violence, sanctioned, it was said, by Perón himself.[9]

Born of the long history of fraudulent elections, the proscription of Peronism, as well as manifold intellectual and cultural influences, some domestic and others foreign in origin, the revolutionary Left of both Peronist and Marxist tendencies won recruits and in the beginning enjoyed considerable popular support. Its tactics in these and subsequent years ranged from kidnappings to targeted assassinations to urban and rural guerrilla warfare. The largest attempt at armed struggle was that of the ERP in the mountains of Tucumán province, where an estimated five hundred to six hundred *erpistas* launched a guerrilla war, heavily influenced by the Cuban example, in the final months of the restored Peronist government. With the restoration of civilian rule and ascension to power in 1973 of the FREJULI electoral alliance dominated by the Peronists, popular support for the Left's violent tactics flagged among some sectors but remained potent among others, especially university students and, to a lesser extent, working-class youth. The Cámpora government's May 1973 release from prison of Montonero, ERP, and other leftist militants, who in most cases immediately resumed their activism, in many ways marked the high point of their influence, though the amnesty also enraged the military, galvanized its resolve to purge the country of its various leftist factions and influences, and undoubtedly contributed to the extreme tactic of the death camps and disappearances that would follow the 1976 coup. It convinced the military that legal procedures and civilian government could not be entrusted with responsibility for neutralizing the "subversives."

Repression of the Left did not have to wait for military rule. With Perón's return to power in late 1973, the Peronist government undertook a sustained, brutal campaign against it, one that included the military, police, and a separately organized death squad, the AAA, run out of the offices of the Social Welfare Ministry. Both Perón and his successor to the presidency, his wife Isabel, passed a cluster of laws intended to legitimize harsh government measures, including broad powers to arrest, in the name of national security and extirpating subversion. In November 1974 the Peronist government declared a state of siege, greatly curtailing civil liberties and leading to an exponential growth in arrests and imprisonment, a state of siege that would continue under the military government and not be lifted until the restoration of democracy in 1983. A November 1975 proposed bill, supported by the country's major political parties, essentially ceded all control to the military in the "war against subversion" including powers to decree edicts that would circumvent the legislature and the establishment of military tribunals of the kind employed in the aftermath of the *Cordobazo* with broad powers that overrode those of the civil courts.[10] Only procedural chaos in the final months of Isabel Perón's government prevented the bill from becoming law, but the draconian terms revealed the extent to which a full-scale assault on the Left had intensified under the Peronist government. By the time of the 1976 coup, the revolutionary Left had been gravely wounded, its ranks depleted, morale low, and much of the remaining leadership living clandestinely or in exile, though it retained some capacity for another year.[11]

In Córdoba this story played out dramatically. The Left there had a most complicated history. Initially, the Montoneros and ERP both had replicated the militarization of their organizations and supported violent strategies, though they were at least as active in the city in other ways. Despite ample available targets among the leadership of the local Peronist *ortodoxo* union leadership, the Montoneros in Córdoba did not adopt the tactics of targeted assassinations of so-called union bureaucrats that were common in Buenos Aires. They did engage frequently in other violent acts such as bank robberies and kidnappings, and indeed the first public act by the Montoneros anywhere in the country took place outside the city in the small town of La Calera, the July 1970 abortive raid on a local police station and bank robbery, culminating in a shootout and the death of local Montonero leader Emilio Maza. La Calera was the first of many armed actions perpetrated by the Peronist Left in and around Córdoba, not just the Montoneros but also FAR and FAP. The ERP in Córdoba was even more prone to such tactics, and there were some notorious examples of assassinations of businessmen and military and police officers.

Yet the revolutionary threat represented by the Peronist and Marxist Left cannot be reduced simply to "redemptive and retributive" violence, as one anthropologist has described it.[12] The militarization of the Left was a reality, but sole focus on its violent tactics simplifies and distorts its history, both as an actor and perceptions of it by the military. In Córdoba, as a new scholarship has demonstrated in the case of other urban areas, both the Peronist and Marxist Left expended greater efforts to recruit among university students, workers, and in the city's poorest neighborhood and employed strategies in the city that were more political than military in nature. The Montoneros' surface organization and political wing, the Juventud Peronista (JP) was especially active in the university and in the city's slums or *villas miserias*. Often working in tandem with activist priests drawn from the Third World Priests (Sacerdotes del Tercer Mundo) movement, rather than firefights with the army and police, they engaged in such unglamorous behavior as running literacy campaigns and soup kitchens.[13] The ERP's political wing, the Partido Revolucionario de los Trabajadores (PRT), also was active in the university and won a large following there, but concentrated more than the JP/Montoneros on political recruitment among the city's large working-class population, especially in its large automotive complexes. Other leftist groups (the Partido Comunista Revolucionario [PCR], Peronismo de Base [PB], Vanguardia Comunista [VC], Poder Obrero [Organización Comunista Poder Obrero or OCPO]), stronger in Córdoba than in other urban centers, also concentrated on gaining working-class followers. To reduce their activities to violence underestimates the complexity of their revolutionary praxis and also the perceived threat that their actions represented to the military. Therein lay part of the explanation why the state terrorism continued long after the Left's armed contingents had been defeated and its leadership dead or in exile.

In Córdoba, the Peronist Left, the largest of the country's leftist factions, demonstrated this complexity of the threats it posed and of the Left's revolutionary praxis better than any other. After the disastrous and abortive armed action in La Calera, the local branch of the Montoneros undertook a period of reflection and self-criticism. The result was the formation in late 1972 of the "Montoneros-Columna José Sabino Navarro," named for an autoworker and former SMATA (autoworkers union) shop steward who had joined the Montoneros and perished in an armed confrontation with security forces. Local Montonero dissidence with the national leadership and that leadership's emphasis on strategies of armed struggle was reflected months later in the abandonment of the word *Montoneros* altogether and self-appellation as the Columna José Sabino Navarro. In the early 1970s, the Sabinos were the largest contingent of the Peronist Left in Córdoba and concentrated, much like the PB, on grassroots work in the city's shantytowns, factories, and universities. With their Catholic origins in the Movimiento Universitario Cristo Obrero (MUCO), the Sabinos garnered considerable support among the city's large student population whose efforts focused more on political organization, indoctrination, literacy campaigns, and soup kitchens in the city's poor neighborhoods than armed struggle. Such efforts were intended for consciousness-raising and mass protest tactics of the kind Córdoba had already dramatically demonstrated its aptitude for in the 1969 *Cordobazo* and 1971 *viborazo*. In many ways, it was the Left's diverse revolutionary praxis coming from youth with traditional Catholic backgrounds that so alarmed the country's military leaders and made "subversion" perceived as an assault on the national culture, more than just an adversary in counterinsurgent war.[14]

A return to violent tactics and armed struggle within student ranks eclipsed the Sabinos' influence only with the return of Peronism to power in 1973 and the unleashing of paramilitary violence against the Left. Though often at cross-purposes in the early 1970s, with the Montoneros agitating for the return to power of Perón and the ERP pursuing more conventional revolutionary strategies and indifferent to bourgeois politics, their combined actions had served to weaken military rule and allow elections to take place, this time with proscription of the Peronists, though not yet Perón, lifted. In Córdoba, the 1973 election brought to power figures closely associated with the Peronist Left, governor Ricardo Obregón Cano and vice-governor Atilio López, a Peronist union leader opposed to the national labor bureaucracy and its local representatives in the *ortodoxo* faction. Despite the fact that once in power the provincial government followed rather centrist policies, Cordoban business groups and the army commanders in the nearby Third Corps regarded the Obregón Cano-López government as little more than a JP-Montonero front, a realization of their worst fears about the ascendancy of the Left and the city's increasing radicalization. Perón, back from exile and elected president in special elections held in September 1973, apparently shared those suspicions.

In his government's campaign to purge the Peronist Left from its ranks, Córdoba became a notorious target. Within months of Perón's election, Córdoba, along with other provincial governments associated with Peronist Left tendencies, came under assault. Obregón Cano and Lopez were removed from office forcibly in March 1974 in a putsch by the local police with the support of several military officers, an event that came to be known as the *Navarrazo*, named for the local police chief, Antonio Domingo Navarro, who led the putsch. The *Navarrazo* was partly due to the attempt by the provincial government to restructure the Cordoban police force, including allowing the readmission of police officers cashiered in an anti-Peronist purge in 1955, but more deeply was the product of growing political tensions emanating from Buenos Aires, with Perón himself denouncing the "foco de infección" that was Córdoba. Perón and the Peronist government's sanction of a blatantly illegal act that forced the resignation of two democratically elected officials, fellow Peronists moreover, marked a further deterioration of the rule of law in Córdoba, making possible the utter lawlessness of the state terrorism that was soon to follow.[15]

After months of uncertainty and unrest, Córdoba came under dictatorial rule by Air Force Brigadier Gen. Raúl Oscar Lacabanne in September 1974, named "interventor" by Isabel Perón's government, and the so-called antisubversive campaign began in earnest in the city long before the March 1976 coup.[16] With a long list of names provided by the police intelligence service, the Departamento de Informaciones de la Policía de la Provincia de Córdoba (the so-called D-2), and shielded by the national government's declaration of a state of siege in late 1974, Lacabanne undertook arrests of political, union, and student leaders. A longtime ally of Perón and therefore with little real influence within the largely anti-Peronist air force, Lacabanne unleashed this first phase of state terrorism in tandem with federal and provincial police, under the command of Héctor García Rey, the ex-chief of police of Tucumán accused of human rights abuses. Lacabanne also carried out an "ideological cleansing" of the public administration, sacking hundreds of employees who failed to meet the "moral requirements and qualifications for government service."[17] Abductions, torture, and killings, though certainly not on the scale of what would happen during the first years of the military dictatorship, also occurred in the final two years of the Peronist government. The Comando de Libertadores de América, a private death squad but with direct ties to the army's Third Corps, was responsible for much of the terror in these years. It would be disbanded within weeks of the March 1976 coup when full responsibility for the dirty war passed to the military.[18] In late 1974, the Peronist union bureaucracy also interdicted militant union locals and removed their leadership. Arrest warrants were issued for union leaders Agustín Tosco, René Salamanca, and several others, while large firings of university administrators and professors as well as purges within the public bureaucracy took place. Prominent public figures such as labor lawyer Alfredo Curutchet and deposed vice-governor Atilio López were both murdered. On October 6, 1975, the government signed decree 2772 ordering the armed forces to eradicate the "subversive" organizations. By late 1975 occurred the first instances of large numbers of disappearances while the army organized the first of the detention centers, Campo de La Ribera, near the San Vicente cemetery where the EAAF forensic team would later locate the large mass grave. The EAAF itself estimated that nationally some five hundred people were "disappeared," now a transitive verb, in 1975. A large number of these took place in Córdoba.[19]

In Córdoba, most menacing for the military was the insertion of the revolutionary Left in the local labor movement and the workplace. Córdoba's Left was a uniquely diverse and successful one in the Argentine context, with not only the Peronist Left in its manifold expressions and the ERP-PRT enjoying influence but even small Maoist and Trotskyist groups gaining a following. The 1972 electoral victory of the *lista marrón* slate, a coalition of left-of-center activists headed by a Maoist leadership, in the local autoworkers union—the SMATA, the largest and most influential in the city—was only one of many examples of this ideological and political pluralism.[20] The military, business, and Peronist trade union bureaucracy responded to the Left's growing presence on the factory floor with charges of "industrial and factory guerrillas," with Córdoba the prime example. The three conspired to destroy these so-called *clasista* movements, a policy they would extend to other parts of the country where similar left-wing activism appeared in the unions and in the workplace.[21]

Though hardly industrial and factory "guerrillas," the Left did undoubtedly develop a revolutionary praxis that combined effective rank-and-file representation with a larger project of a fundamental transformation of Argentine society, with the working class its major protagonist. Following the *Cordobazo*, the city witnessed factory occupations, wildcat strikes, and street protests on an unprecedented scale. The Left assumed a prominent and deliberate sponsorship of what were largely workplace-driven conflicts and spontaneous grassroots, rank-and-file agitation to challenge the *ortodoxo* Peronist trade union leadership in many industries and workplaces. The two Maoist parties, the PCR and the VC, inserted party activists and recruited young workers on the shop floor to serve as a nucleus of union insurgencies against the entrenched *ortodoxo* leadership, most notably in the form of *comisiones obreras*, factory committees meant to address workplace issues while also raising political consciousness. Breakaway Peronist factions, of whom the most important in Córdoba was the PB, adopted similar tactics. The PRT, the ERP's surface organization, adopted similar tactics, with less notable results than it experienced in other parts of the country such as the Rosario industrial belt and in Tucumán's sugar mills, but still gaining a sizable shop floor presence and recruiting some committed working-class activists as party members. Smaller left-wing organizations such as OCPO likewise adopted a strategy of *entrismo*, of inserting themselves into the city's many factories and workplaces, including the white-collar government bureaucracies and the bank and teachers' unions, and linking revolutionary strategies to broader working-class demands and struggles.[22]

Collectively, these *clasista* movements challenged important local, national, and even foreign interests, a number of them interlocking. Italian capital in particular felt threatened. Fiat was in many ways the dominant foreign enterprise in Córdoba, a major employer with its massive automotive complex on the city's outskirts in Ferreyra but also with ties to sundry other local enterprises, the provider of the turbines to the public provincial power company, EPEC, for example, and with prominent presence in the city's cultural life. The *clasista* movements in the Fiat plants in the early 1970s marked a turning point in the company's increased contacts with local right-wing groups and especially the military, represented locally by the Third Army Corps with its headquarters in Córdoba. The strikes, factory occupations, and hostage taking in Fiat's Córdoba plants, culminating in the 1972 murder by the ERP of Fiat general manager Oberdán Sallustro, had led to serious financial losses in the Italian company's most important Latin American operations. Shortly thereafter, the Italian Masonic lodge Propaganda Due (P-2) began to fund the right-wing death squad, the AAA, most active in Buenos Aires and during the 1976–83 military dictatorship, which became a major investor in the banking, publishing, and other industries as Italy emerged as Argentina's major economic partner. The Italian government for its part was silent on the human rights issue, refused to grant Argentine exiles (many of them of Italian descent) asylum, forcing them to rely on tourist visas and adopting a circumspect position towards Argentina's military authorities so as not to damage Italian business interests.[23]

The radicalization of at least sectors of the Catholic Church perhaps disturbed the deeply Catholic military commanders in Córdoba more than any other. The officers of the Third Army Corps adhered stubbornly, defiantly to an "antisecular" Catholicism, opposed to Vatican II and the Church's engagement with the modern world as embodied in those "committed" Catholics who stressed public engagement with the poor.[24] The socially progressive, activist current in Córdoba's Catholicism was represented most famously in the Sacerdotes del Tercer Mundo movement, but was not confined to it. Catholic activists, lay and clergy alike, appeared with increasing frequency in the city's working-class and poor neighborhoods through the 1960s and into the early 1970s, inspired by changes and initiatives coming from the Vatican and the Latin American Church such as the 1968 Latin American Bishop's Conference in Medellín. In Córdoba, the sites of Catholic social activism were many: the Catholic University, *integralista* student groups in the public university, neighborhood parishes, and informal Catholic study circles. Córdoba developed the so-called *cursillos* (Short Courses on Christianity) in the form of three-day retreats, an important innovation to reinvigorate the city's Catholic culture with its new social doctrines and the formative experience for many future Catholic activists in the city.[25]

Córdoba distilled the radical, and in the military's eyes "subversive," forces at work in the country more than anywhere else: a highly politicized youth culture, a socially activist Catholic Church, and a militant, combative, even radicalized trade union movement. Nor did these threats exist in isolation from one another. A synergy between this triad increased the radical tendencies within each. Committed Catholics and activist priests worked sedulously in the city's poor and working-class neighborhoods. Young party militants from the city's universities attended worker mobilizations and even entered the factory as worker-activists. Unions called solidarity strikes in support of the student struggles and its victims. An organization such as the Juventud Trabajadora Peronista (JTP) counted committed Catholics in its ranks as it sought to recruit young workers in the city's factories to a revolutionary Peronism. Such actors existed in other parts of the country, but the size of each and especially their collective influence in the political and cultural life of the city made Córdoba in many ways unique. The priority given to Córdoba by the military regime and the brutal nature of the dirty war there were not by chance.

2

DICTATORSHIP

Terrorizing Córdoba

I say again that this war, like all wars, is total. One loses the war that one does not wage in a total way.

—GENERAL LUCIANO BENJAMÍN MENÉNDEZ

On March 24, 1976, the Argentine armed forces overthrew the government of Isabel Perón and assumed power with every intention of wielding it indefinitely. The military junta immediately issued an edict that superseded the national constitution giving the military sweeping new powers, prohibiting public demonstrations, suspending collective bargaining, and interdicting numerous organizations associated with the former Peronist government. The latter included the Peronist trade union confederation, the Confederación General del Trabajo (CGT), and the Confederación General Económica (CGE), the business association that adhered most to nationalist economic policies and one generally supportive of Peronist governments. Mass firings of public employees followed suit, a draconian censorship was imposed, the national congress and provincial legislatures shut down, and a series of labor laws were repealed.[1]

Yet Argentines had seen this drama before. What was novel, and most characteristic of this new experience with military dictatorship, was not its hostility to civilian rule, its union-busting tactics or even efforts to muzzle any expression of dissent and free speech. It was the scale of violence and terror that accompanied such policies. The regime initially directed most of its fury against the by now gravely wounded and tottering but still active Left. At its most benign, the junta proscribed all the country's left-of-center parties, and froze their bank accounts and impounded their assets. At its most murderous, the already outlawed Montoneros and Ejército Revolucionario del Pueblo (ERP) faced an underground war of extermination, while lists of *subversivos* were drawn up and kidnappings and disappearances reached unprecedented levels.[2] Not even the worst years of the fallen Peronist government had witnessed state terrorism on this scale. The junta attempted to invest a patina of legality on its repressive policies via a series of laws that ranged from criminalizing the dissemination of partisan political literature to mere assembly and even the display of political insignias. The death penalty was also reintroduced though never applied since the preferred methods of abductions and disappearances were by their very nature clandestine and illegal. Formal trials rarely occurred. The junta also built institutional scaffolding that included the application of military law to civilians via the newly created special Consejos de Guerra (War Councils) though again actual trials were few in number. The Ministry of the Interior, a veritable appendage of the Defense Ministry under the military regime, held jurisdiction over all matters relating to political prisoners.

All this represented the public face of the dictatorship, but not its true, essential character. What did was a terrible triptych: disappearance, detention, and death. People were generally abducted by small bands of civilian-dressed masked men, *patotas* (gangs) as they were known in the Argentine vernacular, comprised of both military and civilian individuals. Abduction typically though not always took place at night. Abductions occurred throughout neighborhoods in and around the city: none were spared, though working-class neighborhoods such as Ferreyra, San Vicente, and Yapeyú; poorer ones like the northern periphery of Alta Córdoba with its *villas miserias* (shantytowns); and traditional student enclaves such as Barrio Alberdi and the Ciudad Universitaria in the city's southern districts were special targets (Map 1).

Abductions took place most frequently in private homes but also in the streets (en *la vía pública* was a common claimed point of disappearance) and even at factory gates. Detention then followed, sometimes prolonged but more often brief, a matter of days or weeks, a torment of torture and interrogation that made captivity seem much longer than it really was. For the vast majority, death followed, generally in Córdoba by gunshot. Bodies of the disappeared throughout the country were disposed one of four ways: dumping them from airplanes (sometimes drugged and alive) into the sea, buried as N. N. (*Ningún Nombre* or "Without Name") in municipal cemeteries, cremated, or buried in clandestine, often mass graves.[3] Such violence was calculated in its purpose, not merely for intimidation and certainly not for "spectacle" but to annihilate what the military perceived as the subversive threat.[4] First to acquire the intelligence needed to defeat the armed Left while it still posed a legitimate threat and then to eliminate any sympathizers who remained in society at large, and ultimately to erase entirely the Left's cultural influence. The military government perhaps adopted the precise method of the disappearance to create a culture of fear, but more tangibly to insulate it from foreign scrutiny and possible criticisms, even sanctions, that would result from a less concealed state violence. Disappearances rather than mass executions were the chosen method to prevent such consequences.[5] The decision to eliminate an initial estimate of six to seven thousand "subversives" had been taken at the highest levels

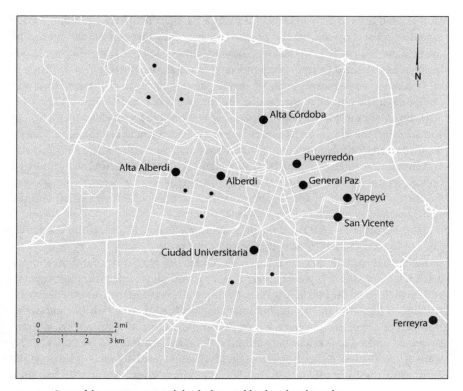

MAP 1. Sites of disappearances and deaths by neighborhood and number.

of the military leadership in the immediate aftermath of the coup. The failure of the court system to prosecute and punish such individuals during the 1973–76 Peronist government persuaded the military to adopt the practice of the disappearances, a "final disposition" for such individuals at the national level.[6] The junta's general policy of a violent, clandestine campaign to eradicate the so-called subversive threat nonetheless was decentralized in its application, with local commanders given near complete freedom on the precise tactics on how to wage it and even the ultimate decision of how to dispose of bodies that were to disappear without a trace, whether to cast them into the sea, to be buried in a secret sites, or cremated in ovens.[7]

The military government's attempts to terrorize and purge Córdoba of all its perceived radical elements, indeed to transform it socially, politically, and culturally, became apparent at the outset, as did the role that the army's Third Corps would play in the effort.[8] Plans were laid for undertaking a violent campaign against the "subversives" months before the March 1976 coup. The military's so-called

Comunidad Informativa met weekly in Córdoba, each Thursday, for months prior to and after the coup to work out precise tactics and assign responsibilities for conducting the *guerra sucia* in the city. These meetings took place at either the headquarters of the Third Corps, commanded by General Menéndez, or the IV Brigada de Infantería Aerotransportada, the principal combat unit in the province and the Third Corps' operative wing under the command of General Juan Sasiaiñ. Also attending were the commanders of all those responsible for intelligence gathering and security: the Third Corps' Destacamento de Inteligencia 141, the Secretaría de Seguridad de Córdoba, the Gendarmería Nacional, the Servicio de Inteligencia de la Aeronáutica, Inteligencia de la Agrupación Escuela de Aviación, the provincial police's Jefatura de Inteligencia (D-2), the Estado Mayor del Tercer Cuerpo, and Córdoba's delegations of the Secretaría de Inteligencia del Estado (SIDE) and the Policía Federal.[9]

Documents recovered from the delegation of the Policía Federal on the activities of the Comunidad Informativa revealed the precise methodology of the state terrorism before and after the coup. A December 20, 1975, memorandum showed Menéndez creating a separate interrogating group and conferring interrogation responsibilities to the police. The memorandum emphasized the continued responsibilities assigned to the police, but only in coordination and with the authorization of the army. In keeping with the future violation of legal norms, current prisoners under the presidential authority of the Poder Ejecutivo Nacional (PEN) were to be denied judicial proceedings that might lead to their release, while another of the Comunidad Informativa's memoranda just weeks after the coup asserted Menéndez's authority over the removal or hiring of individuals in the public administration while determining a "background check" of those abducted in operations and determination of arrest or "elimination" (*aniquilamiento*). Most interestingly, an assessment of the Montoneros calculated their operative capacity at 90 percent and of the ERP at 70 percent, well above what is generally believed to be their fighting strength by the time of the coup.[10]

Immediately following the coup, the second in command of the Third Corps, General José Vaquero, was named "interventor" of the province, thereby giving him unlimited executive powers. Several weeks later, General Carlos Chasseing replaced Vaquero as a designated "military governor." Both were in reality subordinate to the individual who would wield real power and oversee zealously, with maniacal resolve, the antisubversive campaign in Córdoba: commander of the Third Corps, General Luciano Benjamín Menéndez. Menéndez's biography is inseparable from that of the story of state terrorism in Córdoba, indeed has become the very symbol of its crimes and excesses. Menéndez emerged as a prominent national figure in the very first days of the dictatorship when he gave the personal order for the public burning of banned books in Córdoba. Subversive influences in Menéndez's Córdoba had their broadest meaning of anywhere in the country. Menéndez forbade even the teaching of modern mathematics in Córdoba's high schools and universities for its relativism and its corrosive questioning of axiomatic logic and therefore, it can be assumed, accepted, eternal truths.[11]

Born in 1927 to a military family, Menéndez had graduated both from the Colegio Militar and the Escuela Superior de Guerra (ESG), thus anointed for a future distinguished military career. Menéndez entered the ESG as part of the same class as Jorge Rafael Videla and other future key members of the military dictatorship such as Roberto Viola, Ramón Díaz Bessone, and Albano Harguindeguy, among others. After a series of desk jobs, Menéndez finally received a field assignment in 1970, appointed second in command of the Fifth Brigade of Infantry of the army's Third Corps stationed in Tucumán province, replacing Videla in that post. The assignment was fortuitous. The recently established ERP had just begun planning and preliminary training for a rural insurgency in Tucumán. Two years later in December 1972, Menéndez received his promotion to general and assignment as commander of the brigade. Not long after he began a full-fledged campaign against the ERP in the province.

The Tucumán campaign comprised two facets. The army undertook sweeps through the countryside to search out and destroy the ERP *focos* at the same time that, in tandem with the Tucumán provincial police firmly under his authority, Menéndez targeted political and union activists in the provincial capital viewed as the urban cells supporting the rural insurgency. At first military operations proved improvised and took place in competition with the actions of the Federal Police. In December 1974 this changed with the secret plan known as Operación Independencia, in which the army asserted full control of the military operations in Tucumán, but that same month Menéndez was transferred to Buenos Aires as a member of the Estado Mayor (Chiefs of Staff). Six months later in May 1975, he was appointed second in command of the army's Third Corps based in Córdoba, and in August promoted to commander-in-chief.

Within weeks of his new assignment, Menéndez had authorized the Intelligence Battalion 141 and the D-2 provincial police force to undertake clandestine operations in the city, leading to the detention, torture, and murder of dozens of political and union activists. Beginning in October 1975, six months before the March 1976 coup, the practice of the disappearances was already being implemented. In that month, Menéndez centralized all the intelligence service of the military and police in the Comunidad de Inteligencia, which worked out of the offices of the Destacamento de Inteligencia 141 in the Parque Sarmiento.[12] The following month, Menéndez opened the first of the two major detention centers in the city, the Campo de la Ribera, a former military prison built in 1945 and converted to a clandestine detention center. Prisoners began arriving there soon thereafter. At the same time, as commander of the Third Corps, Menéndez had ongoing responsibility for waging the counterinsurgency war in Tucumán, where he employed similar methods. By the time of the coup, the Left's ranks in both Córdoba and Tucumán had suffered enormous, irreparable losses.

Under Menéndez's iron hand, a thorough militarization of Córdoba took place following the coup. Military personnel and individuals with close links to the Third Corps colonized university administration, the public bureaucracy, judiciary, even the local media. Despite the repression and state-sanctioned violence that accompanied the final years of the Peronist government, civil society maintained enough resilience, and intimidation was not yet so absolute, that the local press still denounced such arbitrary acts and covered public protests by unions and student groups that continued to take place. That was not the case after the 1976 coup. Newspapers were strictly censored and Córdoba's main television channel, Channel 10, transmitted with relentless monotony images and disseminated ideas glorifying the armed forces, urging adherence to the regime, and excoriating all those believed unwilling to offer it. Public ritual involving the military such as parades, flag and memorial ceremonies, and speeches on patriotic holidays became routine throughout the year. In the annual Día del Ejército, made a national holiday, in the city's largest park, the Parque Sarmiento, children could stroll the grounds and visit exhibits of weapons and army equipment.[13] At the same time Menéndez oversaw the secret creation and administration of six major clandestine detention centers in and around the city. In addition to the Campo de la Ribera, a detention center already in operation and under the command of General Juan Bautista Sasiaiñ, five additional centers were established: the premises of the police intelligence service's (D-2) "Office of Information" located in the *cabildo* in the town center facing the city's imposing colonial cathedral staffed by the police but under the command of the army, serving as a temporary processing and torture center through which a steady stream of political prisoners passed through between 1974 and 1979; La Perla, the main detention center just twelve kilometers outside the city on the main and well-traveled highway to the Cordoban sierras; a much smaller nearby center called La Perla Chica (also Malagueño, from the name of the small hamlet where it was located); the offices of the "Dirección Provincial de Hidráulica" administered directly by the police of the D-2 rather than the army. Located on the shores of the San Roque dam, this camp provided a convenient place to dispose of evidence (and perhaps bodies) by casting them into the dam's waters. Southeast of the city, in Pilar, a former trucker's stop turned detention center held small numbers of prisoners, almost none of whom survived (Map 2).

Prisoners were also held, processed, and murdered in numerous smaller places such as police commissaries and local jails and prisons. The federal penitentiary system was fully integrated into the repressive apparatus. Unidad Penitenciaria No. 1 (UP1), the site of an execution of some thirty prisoners discussed in chapter 6, held many political prisoners, as did the women's prison, the Buen Pastor, in the city center.

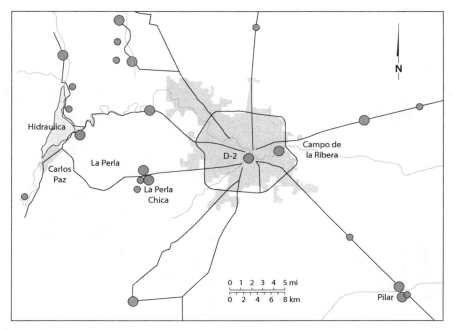

MAP 2. Clandestine detention centers in Córdoba.

FIGURE 1. Buen Pastor (Good Shepherd) women's prison, street view.

Within the map:

Hidraulica

Carlos
Paz

La Perla

La Perla
Chica

D-2

Campo de
la Ribera

Pilar

N

0 1 2 3 4 5 mi
0 2 4 6 8 km

FIGURE 2. Buen Pastor women's prison, front entrance.

FIGURE 3. Buen Pastor women's prison, columns with photos of *desaparecidas*.

Generally, prisoners held in federal penitentiaries enjoyed some privileges denied to those held in the clandestine death camps, such as conjugal and visitation rights. But their freedom was limited, and wardens were given precise instructions on the treatment of all prisoners arrested for "subversive behavior."[14] Prisoners were segregated according to their perceived degree of importance, or rather their level of political militancy, a characteristic of practices in other federal prisons intended to isolate the influence of the militants on those prisoners deemed *recuperables* ("salvageable").[15]

The architecture of state terrorism mirrored that found elsewhere in the country. Menéndez described the military's tactics as "low-intensity warfare," in other words an intelligence war with carefully targeted victims, not random violence, though in practice either the intelligence did not prove precise enough or the execution of its operations was so sloppy that random victims did occur. Special task forces (*fuerzas de tareas*) divided into operational task forces (*grupos de tarea*) undertook their actions separate from the larger contingent of the Third Corps conscripts. Menéndez and a select group of officers oversaw this parallel force with its specialized military intelligence personnel and the local police well integrated into its structure. It was this parallel force that most actively perpetrated the dirty war in Córdoba. Regular army troops were employed in guard and sentry duties in the camps, but not involved in the urban abductions.

The "mode of destruction" in Córdoba also resembled that found in other parts of the country, but with some distinguishing peculiarities.[16] Córdoba's delegation in the truth commission charged with investigating the crimes of the dictatorship, the CONADEP (Comisión Nacional sobre la Desaparición de Personas), published a separate report on human rights violations there, benefited by the unique good fortune of actually acquiring some military files on the prisoners held in several of the detention centers. These and the oral testimonies of survivors relate over and over again the same pattern of nighttime raids, unmarked police cars, masked gangs, ransacking, abductions, detentions, and torture. For those who did not live to tell their tale, violent death was the final stage. Some of the disappeared such as the trade union leader and close collaborator of Tosco in the local light and power workers union, Tomás Di Toffino, and SMATA secretary-general René Salamanca, were prominent figures. Most were anonymous workers, students, lawyers, university professors, and others with suspected left-wing ties. The demographic profile of the disappeared in Córdoba resembled that of other parts of the country but with some variations peculiar to the province. One was the scale of the terror relative to its size. The CONADEP report placed Córdoba third, some 9 percent, in the total number of *desaparecidos* nationally, trailing only the more populous province of Buenos Aires and the federal capital.[17] As in the rest of the country, males comprised the majority of the disappeared, but females were almost a third and the victims were overwhelmingly young. Over 70 percent were between the ages of twenty and forty, and of those 54 percent were between the ages of twenty and thirty. However, workers comprised the largest socioeconomic category of the disappeared, almost 42 percent, while students were the second largest, making up nearly 31 percent.[18]

Calculation of the numbers of victims in Córdoba and their identities has grown more precise over time. The first rigorous attempt to compile a list of Argentina's disappeared along with dates of disappearance and national identity card numbers, as well as fragmentary information on age, profession, and believed place of detention, was a 1982 report by the Comité de Defensa de Derechos Humanos en el Cono Sur. Based in São Paulo, the committee received testimony from Argentine exiles and visitors, former political prisoners among them, on the fate of the thousands of disappeared. The report compiled a list of 7,291 names with a subsequent supplementary report comprising an additional 494 names, not only of the disappeared, but also those who it was believed continued to be detained and others released from detention. Córdoba's share of that 7,785 total figure, confined to those arrested strictly in the provincial capital and its environs, numbered approximately 457. The information revealed that of this number, more than half, some 250, disappeared in the first six months following the March 24, 1976, coup and another thirty-eight in the subsequent six months leading up to the first anniversary of the coup. Perhaps most surprising at the time was the large number, an estimated sixty-one, who disappeared in the six months prior to the coup. Though many of these were to disappear in the weeks preceding the coup, the remainder disappeared months and in some cases even as much as a year before the March 1976 military takeover. This confirms that the death squads were already in full operation in Córdoba and had adopted the practice of the disappearance in the final stages of the 1973–76 Peronist government. The military merely intensified the practice. Information on age in the report was more fragmentary, but of those with a recorded age, a clear majority were between the ages of eighteen and twenty-five, figures in line with the subsequent CONADEP estimates, confirming that the victims of the dirty war, in Córdoba and elsewhere, were overwhelming young. University students and young workers of both sexes were the dirty war's victims.[19]

The university, viewed as the breeding ground of subversion, became a target on multiple levels. Even before the coup, the *interventor*, Air Force general Raúl Oscar Lacabanne, had demanded quarterly lists with the personal information on professors and students for surveillance purposes.[20] During the dictatorship, the university hosted on several occasions representatives of the military government, such as the minister of planning and one of the chief advocates within the military for the antisubversive campaign, General Ramón Genaro Díaz Bessone, for the inauguration of a Plan de Desarrollo para Córdoba (PLANSECOR) while its philosophy and history departments promoted liberal thought, the critical and Marxist perspectives once dominant completely silenced. A thousand university faculty of the now thoroughly purged public university even sent a letter to the U.S. embassy protesting the Carter administration's human rights policies and criticisms of Argentina.[21] The replacement of civilian authorities by military personnel to administer the university, the massive purge of professors, even the requirement of a certificate of good conduct by the police for admission to the university, all testified to the university as a favored site of the dictatorship's so-called Process of National Reorganization.[22]

The terror in Córdoba was not confined to just physical violence. Psychological terror was a deliberate outcome of the abductions and disappearances, one that affected far more people in the city than the victims of the task forces and political prisoners of the detention centers. Though many, in Córdoba and elsewhere, were totally oblivious to the state terrorism destroying lives all around them, others were fully aware. For every individual so directly touched by the violence, there were friends, family members, work mates, and others who were also affected. One of Menéndez's particular obsessions and special targets was the local Jewish community. Due to the popularity of Jacobo Timerman wrenching narrative of his imprisonment, *Prisoner without a Name, Cell without a Number*, as well as Argentina's reputation as a Nazi haven, perceptions outside of Argentina were often that the dirty war was animated largely by anti-Semitism. Though an exaggerated description generally, anti-Semitism did inflect state terrorism and was a prominent facet of the repression in Córdoba, probably more than anywhere else in the country. Despite the muzzling of the left-wing press, anti-Semitic publications such as the venomous *El Caudillo* encountered no censorship and circulated freely in the city under the dictatorship. In addition to Timerman memoir, accounts abound of unusually cruel torments inflicted on Jewish prisoners.[23]

Anti-Semitism was not simply ethnic or religious prejudice. It was interwoven with long-standing nativist strains in Argentine culture and more urgently with the association of the subversive threat with Marxism, and therefore the logic went, the country's Jewish population, with prominent Jews such as Timerman and businessmen José Ber Gelbard and David Gravier suspected of financing left-wing groups, especially the Montoneros. Anti-Semitism among the military hierarchy took on perhaps its most bizarre, paranoid manifestation in the widespread belief of a Zionist plot with the full collaboration of Argentina's Jewish population, to create a second Jewish homeland in the Patagonia, stoking fears of a larger Zionist conspiracy to dismember Argentina, an obsession that dovetailed neatly with the Cold War concerns of the internal enemy, threats to an idealized "ser nacional" and the country's territorial integrity.[24] More real were the large number of Jewish victims of the state terrorism. The precise meaning of the generally accepted figure of 10 percent of the disappeared out of a Jewish population that numbered roughly 1 percent of the national total is difficult to decipher. Anti-Semitism as an independent variable in the disappearances is almost impossible to prove. The large representation of Jews had much to do with their higher than average presence in leftist organizations and parties as well as in professions such as psychiatry and journalism, and certain academic disciplines such as sociology, targeted by the military. Various Jewish organizations, both international and national, have nonetheless insisted on Jewishness as an independent variable in the high percentage of Jews among the disappeared.[25] Testimonies alleging Nazi swastikas in the torture chambers of detention centers and of insults hurled at Jewish prisoners nonetheless do not prove a systematic anti-Semitism at work in the state terrorism. Yet given the visceral ultramontane Catholicism so ingrained in the military and longstanding anti-Semitism within its ranks, neither can it be dismissed completely.

In Córdoba, accusations of anti-Semitism emerged early, as in the September 1976 U.S. congressional hearings on human rights violations in Argentina.[26] Such well-publicized incidents as the arrest of the leader of Córdoba's Jewish community, Jaime Pompas, in the first months of the dictatorship signaled the presence of anti-Semitism in Córdoba's experience with state terrorism. Yet another example was Menéndez's impounding of the assets of Mackentor, one of the leading construction companies in the country. Menéndez accused the company's leading stockholder, Natalio Kejner, of financing leftist groups. Kejner's status as a Jew with suspected left-wing sympathies made him a target for Menéndez's obsessions with the idea of an international sinarchy, a fantastical alliance of capitalists, Jews, and communists. The army arrested some twenty-nine members of the company's executive board, in Córdoba but also in branch offices in Buenos Aires and other parts of the country, while passing control of the company to various military officers, part of a pattern of spoliation of Jewish-owned firms that would occur elsewhere during the dictatorship.[27]

A 1980 human rights report on Argentina by the Organization of American States (OAS) mentioned a similar case of a local Jewish businessman, Jaime Lockman, arrested on the personal orders of Menéndez the day of the coup and still held prisoner at the time of the OAS investigation.[28] Prominent Jewish lawyer Mario Zareceansky was ordered by Menéndez while a prisoner to write a report on Córdoba's Jewish community and suffered tortures for a report that failed to meet the anti-Semitic general's expectations of detail and names.[29] Perhaps the most notorious example of Menéndez's anti-Semitism was the kidnapping and imprisonment in La Perla of an entire Jewish family, the Deutsch family, whose plight came to the attention of the U.S. embassy and later B'nai B'rith, becoming an international cause célebre with coverage in the *New York Times*, prompting Videla to demand their release from a reluctant Menéndez and eventual exile for the family in the United States.[30]

The degree of complicity in these and other crimes stretched all the way to the top, to the government ministries and leading figures of the regime. The mechanism of deceit and denial became formulaic. During the worst years of the terror, from 1976 through 1978, individuals with missing family members wrote to the Ministry of Interior, requesting, often pleading, for information about their loved ones. In Córdoba, after reaching the ministry, such petitions would be remitted back to provincial authorities and have to pass through series of bureaucratic steps: first to the province's Ministerio del Gobierno, then to the Jefe del Departamento Operaciones Policiales (D3), then to police's Departamento de Inteligencia (D2), moving on to Jefatura de Policia de la Provincia, then to the Secretaría de Estado de Seguridad, and finally back to the Ministerio de Gobierno, at which point the Ministerio de Gobierno would remit a response back to Ministry of the Interior who would then inform the petitioner that the person in question was not in custody and the government had no knowledge of the individual. The Jefatura de Policía was the point at which official denial of knowledge of the prisoner's whereabouts would begin. This bureaucratic maze allowed both for the fragmentation of responsibility and a belabored, drawn-out process meant to exhaust the petitioner and discourage continued inquiries. It also maintained the regime's fiction of legality and rule of law. The final response was almost always the same, indeed employed identical language, effectively a canned response denying knowledge and any responsibility for the petitioner's family member or loved one.[31]

Since these letters date from late 1975 to late 1977, they do indicate the degree to which, in the very worst years of the disappearances and state terrorism, many were as yet unaware how extensive the state terrorist apparatus was and how complicit in it were the local police and provincial government authorities. A number of these same petitioners also submitted writs of habeas corpus to the local courts. The dictatorship oversaw a dismantling of constitutional guarantees of all sorts and, through decree, passed new laws in accordance with its antisubversive fixation, facilitated by an obliging judiciary. Among the most egregious abuses pertaining to the law was the systematic disregard of the right of habeas corpus. In courts all over the country, the judiciary cravenly accepted the military's denial of knowledge of the individuals named in such writs and frequently resorted to procedural and jurisdictional excuses when a simple denial of knowledge of the individual in question was not sufficient. In other instances, the Supreme Court remitted cases to lower courts where they died a labyrinthine death in a jurisdictional buck passing that ultimately left the habeas corpus writs unattended.[32] Such behavior contrasted with the courage of human rights lawyers who often paid with their lives for filing these writs and for their advocacy for political prisoners in general.[33]

Córdoba's press was similarly cowed if not actually collaborative. The city's leading newspaper, La Voz del Interior, parroted the language of the junta in the first days of the new military government and published the Third Corps' communiqués as if they were mere news stories, neither questioned nor criticized by the newspaper's editors. To mention just one example, the death, just days after the coup, of Mario Andrés Osatinsky, the eighteen-year-old son of Montonero leader Marcos Osatinsky, in nearby Alta Gracia, was reported as that of "extremists" killed while "trying to flee."[34] The dubious veracity in the rendering of this particular incident becomes even more suspect with the content of news reporting in the weeks after the coup in which "extremists" invariably died in shootouts with the army and the brazen denial of abductions, at a time when Córdoba's prisons and detention centers were overflowing with political prisoners. References to "guerrillas" gradually vanished from the newspaper's pages to be replaced by terms such as "subversive delinquents" and "terrorists."[35] In subsequent months, the newspaper failed to mention the abductions and disappearances and was silent on all matters related to the state terrorism, as was virtually all of the national press.

The repressive apparatus stretched into the city's oldest institution, one closely associated with its very culture and history. In Córdoba, as perhaps in nowhere else in the country, the complicity of the local Catholic Church, its hierarchy specifically, was deep and ongoing. Córdoba's Catholic Church was wracked by internal factions in the years prior to the 1976 coup. The emergence of the powerful Third World Priests movement, which adhered to the positions of Vatican II, engaged in grassroots community work and maintained friendly relations with the Left, enraging the older, more conservative members of the local Church hierarchy, a number of whom were drawn from the ranks of Córdoba's patrician families. That some of these activist priests were foreigners added nativist resentment to the generational and class one. The victims of state terrorism included priests and seminarians drawn from these progressive sectors of the church. The establishment of the Studium Teologicum in 1968, which gathered professors and seminary students from all the dioceses in the province of Córdoba, looms as a turning point. With a curriculum aligned with the spirit of the Second Vatican Council, it offered classes in contemporary history, psychology, and sociology, among other subjects.[36]

One individual in particular, Archbishop Raúl Primatesta, stands as a key if controversial figure in the Church's history in Córdoba during the dictatorship. Videla noted an early suspicion by the military government of Primatesta as a "progressive" prelate turned out to be inaccurate and the dictator eventually viewed the bishop a "reasonable man."[37] Sociologist and Jesuit scholar of Córdoba's Catholic Church Gustavo Morello has argued that Primatesta's accommodation with the military regime was the result of fear rather than sympathy and moreover more apparent than real, and that privately he interceded on a number of occasions on behalf of Christian leaders in danger from Menéndez.[38] Such an interpretation is, however, a largely solitary one. As Morello himself notes, between 1972 and 1975 Primatesta restructured the curriculum of the Studium Teologicum away from subjects that might provoke the military's suspicion. Even more damning, Primatesta appeared to forge a close personal relationship with Menéndez, defended the military government publicly on several occasions, and, as ample oral histories and witness testimony at the human rights trials insist, refused repeatedly to intercede on behalf of families seeking information on disappeared family members. Other priests, most of them military chaplains and priests associated with the Third Army Corps, were identified by former prisoners at the La Perla detention center as frequent visitors to the death camp, some reputedly even hearing confessions shortly before prisoners were executed.[39] The heroic defiance of the dictatorship by other Catholic churchmen such as Enrique Angelelli, the bishop of La Rioja, or Jaime de Nevares, the bishop of Neuquén, had no counterpart in Córdoba. Whatever Primatesta's interest is in keeping the Church neutral and equidistant from both the revolutionaries and the repressors, his actions belied such neutrality during the dictatorship. He may have simply been afraid, but his fear overwhelmed his sacred oath.

More difficult to corroborate is the degree of complicity of local business groups. Business was virtually unanimous in its support for the coup and showered the country's new military leaders with fulsome praise. Given the social upheavals of preceding years, the two *Cordobazos*, the presence of the country's most militant unions, a greatly radicalized local student population, and the recent emergence of the guerrilla organizations, it is not hard to imagine why military rule was accepted enthusiastically by some, with relief by many. Outright collaboration in the terror is not as clear. For other parts of the country, some have argued that management in some of the country's leading industrial firms actively aided and abetted the military in identifying union militants, facilitating their abduction and murder.[40] The evidence offered for such a serious charge, one that would seem to warrant judicial proceedings and convictions against the individuals if not the firms involved, is largely circumstantial, mostly confined to the oral testimonies of workers in the plants, but compelling.[41] The unhindered abduction of workers on company grounds, management's providing of personnel files and home addresses of workers later abducted and disappeared, the cooperation between the plant security forces and the military happened so frequently that the only reasonable conclusion is collaboration by the companies. That the country's leading firms had an interest in ridding themselves of union militants among an increasingly combative and in some cases politically radicalized working class, and took advantage of the new situation to remove bumptious individuals within their labor forces, there now seems little doubt.

In the case of Córdoba's leading industry, the auto terminals, the evidence is even stronger of close collaboration between the company and state terrorism. Major Ernesto Barreiro, one of the principal figures in the dirty war in Córdoba, asserted the willing collaboration of politicians, student and professor informants from the local university, and business leaders in drawing up the lists of "subversives," with an especially active participation by Fiat managers, a company that had seen a number of its executives kidnapped by various leftist organizations.[42] A team of researchers has documented carefully Barreiro's claims and made a compelling case for company collaboration in the dirty war. In the Fiat plants, the harsh repression of the *clasista* SITRAC-SITRAM unions between 1971 and 1976 was followed by a targeting of Fiat workers by the military. Some fifty Fiat workers, mostly union or political activists, were disappeared and an even larger number were arrested and passed through one of the city's many detention centers. The close links between Fiat management and the local security forces, including regular, ongoing consultations and even shared personnel, help explain the particularly grim fate suffered by the Fiat workers.[43]

The lack of research in other Cordoban firms nonetheless does not prevent acknowledging the widespread belief among the local working class that such collaboration was real and widespread, and the consequences deadly.[44] The accuracy of the testimonies is impossible to verify with company or military sources, but they do point to an essential characteristic of the dictatorship in Córdoba: a perception of its brutal tactics as a response to Córdoba's previous history as a center of social and union mobilization and political radicalism. The final years of the 1973–76 Peronist government had been particularly volatile in Córdoba. Labor unrest added to the activities of the armed Left made the city a horror in the eyes of the Argentine bourgeoisie generally and that in Córdoba in particular. Its initial tactic was to adhere to the Peronist program of the so-called Social Pact, an agreement with at least the dominant Peronist sectors of the labor movement to defuse tensions in the workplace and to establish a mechanism to control wages and prices simultaneously. Such a labor-capital truce it was hoped would weaken the appeal of the more radical, militant currents within the local unions as well as isolate the armed Left from union matters, in which it had an increasing tendency to coordinate actions in response to workplace conflicts. The failure of the Social Pact was especially felt among Córdoba's bourgeoisie, perhaps because expectations were so high given the volatile nature and indeed escalating violence surrounding management's relations with its labor forces.[45] With expectations dashed, business supported a frontal onslaught against the unions including the interdiction of the more militant unions and arrest warrants for union leaders such as Agustín Tosco and René Salamanca. Given such behavior, it is not all surprising that local business interests would not only sympathize with the military's harsh tactics, but perhaps even participated actively in them. Repression of the unions and especially union activists also complemented the military government macroeconomic policies, which sought to concentrate economic assets, shatter former political alliances, and particularly reduce of the power of the labor movement, in the broader political economy as well as in the workplace, something it achieved with notable results. Tosco's powerful Light and Power unions, one of the main protagonists of the *Cordobazo* that had also achieved a notable degree of union worker participation in its industry, not only suffered large numbers of arrests and disappearances but also witnessed a wholesale dismantling of wages, working conditions, and union influence in management decisions, including planning for Córdoba's power industry.[46]

The fate of the small Perkins factory illustrates the antiworker animus of the military authorities in Córdoba. Perkins, a British manufacturer of diesel engines, experienced a shop floor rebellion of the kind that became so common in the city in the aftermath of the *Cordobazo*. Union rebellions in Perkins and in other factories in the city often revolved around issues of union affiliation, not as a trivial bureaucratic matter but one tied to effective rank-and-file representation. In the case of Perkins, workers widely regarded the company union established by the British firm as a mere appendage of management with contracts rubber-stamped and bereft of any genuine collective bargaining. In the social ferment and factory mobilizations following the *Cordobazo*, young workers, some with party affiliations and some not, occupied the Perkins plant demanding the ouster of the entrenched company union leadership and affiliation with SMATA, the national autoworkers' union. Effective union representation and revolutionary politics merged in yet another *clasista* movement and culminated in a 1973 affiliation with SMATA, now under the leadership of an alliance of Maoist and other left-wing party members.[47] Following the coup, the military occupied the factory, abducted the more prominent union and political activists Pedro Ventura Flores and Adolfo Ricardo Luján, and murdered them and other Perkins workers. Perkins management lodged no protests against the security forces in the brutal treatment of its labor force, before and after the coup.

Yet in the end, the cravenness and even collaboration of the courts, the complicity or at least silence of the Catholic Church hierarchy and the involvement of business groups notwithstanding, it was the security forces themselves, controlled and coordinated by the Third Army Corps, that perpetrated the violence and carried out the dirty war. The death squads, detentions, and disappearances took place at their hands. These formed part of a well-oiled and organized apparatus, cogs in a deliberate plan unrelenting in its implementation, devised by the military hierarchy and executed by subordinates throughout the country, though with considerable room for regional variations given local conditions and the composition of the local military commanders and their subordinates. One characteristic of Córdoba's experience with state terrorism did resemble that of the rest of the country: the chances for survival in the city's detention centers were slight. In Córdoba, detention almost automatically translated to death. The testimony of the few survivors of the detention centers, especially La Perla, offers a unique glimpse into the terrifying world there but also the dreadful mechanisms of repression that existed in Córdoba and the role of the detention center–turned–death camp in the dirty war.

DEATH CAMP

La Perla

La Perla, did it exist? Yes. It was a meeting place for the prisoners, not a secret prison . . . the subversives were there but in the protection of each other's company.
—GENERAL LUCIANO BENJAMÍN MENÉNDEZ

From the highway, the former death camp known as La Perla is barely visible, just as it was at the height of the dirty war. One of a number of the death camps from the dictatorship converted into *sitios de memoria*. La Perla functions now as an education center, a museum, and a memorial to the victims of state terrorism.[1] It is a place where schoolchildren and the occasional curious tourist can wander the large hall where political prisoners were once held, view the nearby *sala de tortura* (torture chamber) where men and women, some mere adolescents, were subject to electric shocks and beatings, terrorized, humiliated, and threateningly questioned, and now listen to the young guides laconically offer lurid details and anecdotes about the camp's sinister history. Pictures of the victims with their names and date of disappearance, articles of clothing and jewelry left behind, writings scribbled to while away the long periods of boredom, crude rosary beads created from whatever materials were at hand, fragments of lives suspended from reality awaiting death, are among the museum's displays. The bucolic setting, on a hillock overlooking a sloping field, and the relaxed atmosphere found there now can almost make one forget its history as a site of terror, torment, and death. The vast majority who rode in unmarked police cars or military vehicles up the winding driveway, blindfolded and handcuffed, never made the return journey. Some died under torture; most died in mass executions, their remains burned or buried in graves still never located.

During the dictatorship, La Perla functioned as an integral piece of the repressive apparatus that waged the dirty war in Córdoba. With the official name of "Lugar de Reunión de Detenidos por el Destacamento de Inteligencia General. Iribarren del III Cuerpo de Ejército" (Meeting Place of those Arrested by Intelligence Task Force General Iribarren Third Army Corps), it occupied a position of dubious

FIGURE 4. La Perla death camp as seen from Highway 20.

distinction as one of the largest of the death camps and the most important in the country's interior.[2] The detention center converted to death camp was one of the distinguishing characteristics of the dictatorship. Most like La Perla were active only in the first years of the regime, with relatively few still in operation after 1980. While functioning, they replicated the military chain of command and hierarchy though all personnel, from the camp commander to lowly conscript, were expected to participate in its activities, in varying intensity and degrees to be sure, in a system that created a shared responsibility and unified ranks behind the *guerra sucia*. At the apex of the death camps were the commanders, followed by a middle rank of intelligence officers and operatives who planned and executed the kidnappings, below them a larger group responsible for sentry and maintenance duties of the camps themselves. All participated to some degree in the torture and execution of prisoners, in a rotating system, a "blood pact" system later adopted throughout the country but reputedly first adopted by Menéndez in Córdoba.[3]

Kidnapping and holding such large numbers of prisoners, and their subsequent mass executions and disposal of the bodies, required a complex internal structure and even a bureaucratic process. The military's systematic destruction of its archives related to the dirty war deprives historians of ever fully reconstructing this essential

FIGURE 5. Entry gate to La Perla death camp.

component of its history and deciphering all its meanings but the recollections of formers prisoners, court testimony, and fragmentary information from military sources of various kinds give some idea of both the conditions in and functioning of the camp. Disappearances in Córdoba followed the general pattern found elsewhere in the country of abductions, torture, and death. Upon arrival, prisoners were assigned a number and subject to extensive interrogations with extensive files with personal data compiled for each. A torture session was invariably a prisoner's introduction to the camp, but unlike the case of the Escuela Mecánica de la Armada (ESMA) and many other camps, in La Perla torture sessions would often be repeated after initial interrogation, if it was discovered that a prisoner withheld information or had been uncooperative.[4] In other aspects, greater similarities existed with large camps such as ESMA, including a deliberate, purposeful approach to the torture, a search for useful information and intelligence rather than simply the sadistic infliction of pain, though wanton cruelty was certainly not unknown. To goad the tortured into compliance, the torturers would often hold out the possibility of survival in return for information, even introducing them before the torture sessions to militants who were presumed dead by their comrades outside the camp but whose continued existence was proof of the possibilities of survival in return for cooperation.[5]

La Perla stands as one of the most notorious of these detention centers turned death camps. The only such camp in the country's interior, it held during its roughly three years of operation, between 1976 and 1979, some 1,000 prisoners. The vast majority of those detained there were murdered and entered the ranks of the disappeared, but more than one hundred survived.[6] In the months leading up to the 1976 coup, the army's Servicio de Inteligencia (SIE) under the command of captain Héctor Pedro Vergez, a shady character later to be involved in the contraband of prisoners' personal property and with close ties to the right-wing death squad the Comando de Libertadores de América, worked with the military police (Gendarmería Nacional) in identifying so-called subversives.[7] Lists were drawn up, individuals were subject to surveillance, and abductions were set in motion. Menéndez made the decision to convert La Perla into a detention center and move some prisoners there from the Campo de La Ribera camp already in existence, largely due to the notoriety Campo de La Ribera had acquired by the end of the Peronist government and requests from the International Red Cross to inspect its premises. Henceforth, Campo de La Ribera, nicknamed La Escuelita (Little School) by the military, would function as a temporary detention center, either as a prelude for transfer to La Perla or to process prisoners regarded as less dangerous and whose status was to be legalized and their captive status formally recognized, by transfer to one of the federal penitentiaries, including the local UP1. Legal status also on very rare occasions could imply a formal trial by a military tribunal, a guarantee of a conviction and a prison sentence but certainly preferable to the alternative of assignment to the La Perla death camp.

Though some deaths did occur at Campo de la Ribera, generally detention in La Escuelita versus La Universidad (La Perla) served as a transit point. Incarceration in La Perla usually meant death. The army already had a small administrative building on the site that Menéndez had hurriedly constructed in the first months of 1976, built by a private contractor, Carusso S.A., a more elaborate compound whose specific purpose was to hold, torture, and murder political prisoners. Surrounded by several smaller buildings with offices and living accommodations for the military personnel stood the *cuadra* or stable, a long rectangular building measuring fifteen by forty meters with a height of approximately four to five meters, flanked by toilets and shower stalls at one end and offices for military personnel at the other. There the prisoners slept side by side on straw-filled mattresses.[8] Prisoners were held there, never more than one hundred at a time, most for relatively short periods of time—days, weeks, at most at several months—at which point they would be executed and a new contingent arrived.

Adjacent to the *cuadra* was a large patio where the prisoners ate. Nearby were two large sheds that served as garages for military vehicles as well as those stolen from the prisoners in the raids on their homes. In one of these was the small room, dubbed by the military captors as the "intensive therapy ward," in which the prisoners were

FIGURE 6. The *cuadra*, where prisoners were held in the La Perla death camp.

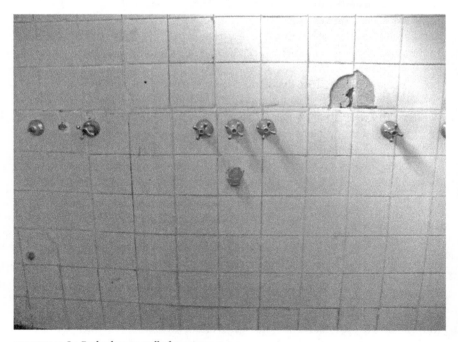

FIGURE 7. La Perla shower stalls for prisoners.

FIGURE 8. La Perla former torture chamber.

tortured with the so-called *margarita*, the electric generator and prod used by the torturers to apply electric shocks to the prisoners. The entire compound was surrounded by barbed wire, with sentries posted on its perimeter, a duty facilitated by the open surrounding fields that provided maximum visibility from the hill's crest.[9]

As with other camps, La Perla had its collection of particularly brutal torturers, usually known by the nom de guerre and nicknames they had adopted to hide their true identity, such as a sergeant, it was later learned, with the name of Elpidio Rosario Tejeda, known in the camp as "Texas." The Contepomis' memoir of life in the camp relates the horrors of Texas's torture session, blows with a paddle applied with methodical efficiency to the body's extremities and most sensitive parts. Found there was another torturer known as the "Priest" with a predilection for torturing radical clergymen from the Third World Priests movement, and yet another, "Uncle," a balding, middle-aged torturer obsessed with the excrement and stench of the torture room that he attempted to camouflage with flowers and aromatic herbs, as well as prints to cover the blood-stained walls.[10] There was camp commandant Menéndez himself, who went by the moniker of "Mutt" for his hound-dog face, given to outbursts of rage and also the organizer of strange, solemn ceremonies before the removal and execution of the prisoners, executions in which Menéndez on a number of occasions personally took part. False surnames

FIGURE 9. La Perla sentry tower.

were also used: Major Ernesto Barreiro, a member of the Destacamento 141 de Inteligencia del Tercer Cuerpo assigned to the camp and a figure of great authority there in its early months, had several nicknames (Nabo, Rubio, Gringo) and also went by the false surname of Hernández.[11] Anonymity was an obsession among the torturers.

The Contepomis' memoir relates other details about the camp: rivalries between the military police and regular army personnel in which the prisoners found themselves in the middle, suffering the consequences; the state of being permanently blindfolded and prohibited from standing erect save at mealtimes; the continuous psychological terror and mental anguish of being the next in line for the "truck," a death ride to one's execution; the unexpected occasional acts of kindness by their captors, followed by equally unexpected acts of cruelty, adding to the sense of vulnerability and unreality in La Perla.[12] There were also moments of solidarity, compassion, and even heroism: a shared cigarette, the furtive embrace of comrade or friend, the female prisoner who insisted in accompanying her son and daughter-in-law to a final execution, thereby ensuring her own. Mostly there was just boredom, punctuated by moments of terror and torment. The mass executions generally coincided with the *cuadra* reaching its maximum number of prisoners, thereby providing the prisoners some degree of predictability of the moment of the final, in the death camp jargon, *traslado* (transfer). The military's macabre jargon offered two kinds of transfer: *traslado por izquierda* (transfer to the left), for the vast majority, meant execution; the *traslado por derecha* (transfer to the right), for a lucky few, meant transfer to a federal penitentiary or perhaps another detention center, and very exceptionally outright release, though subject to constant vigilance and even house arrest.[13]

Lists of those selected for execution were drawn up by the local military commanders. The guards were assigned responsibility for lining up the victims, dubbed the *paquetes* (packages) in the sinister camp jargon, for the short delivery to the execution site.[14] The *traslados* generally occurred in the late afternoon at the hour of the siesta, and the truck's sound, different from that of other military vehicles on the death camp's grounds, was immediately recognizable to the prisoners as it parked alongside the barrack's wall. In the first year the executions were massive; once the *cuadra* became full, large numbers of prisoners would be removed for execution. The trucks transferring the prisoners would return in the space of fifteen to twenty minutes, indicating that the *pozo* (pit) where the bodies were buried was relatively close to the camp. Only a small number of prisoners avoided this grim fate. The some 150 survivors of the camp, according to the Contepomis, were of an upper-middle- and middle-class background, mostly university students. Few or none of the working-class prisoners would survive, apparently believed to be beyond redemption due to their class status by the commanding officers who made the final decisions on life and death, or perhaps simply detested because of it, to be dealt with only through their annihilation.[15]

La Perla functioned as part of a tightly woven apparatus under the authority of Menéndez and the Third Army Corps but with specific responsibilities assigned to each of its bureaucratic layers. Intelligence Task Force 141 (Destacamento de Inteligencia 141) worked as an appendage of the army's 141st battalion stationed in the Sarmiento Park, in the city itself, with separate "political" and "street" sections responsible for the investigation of political activities and for surveillance respectively. The Tercera Sección de Operaciones Especiales (OP-3) was assigned responsibility for the abductions, interrogation and execution of all the prisoners in La Perla, though in its ranks in the so-called *grupos de tarea* (task forces) were found not only military men but an assortment of off-duty policemen, hired thugs, and even common criminals involved only for the booty provided by the raids. A separate detachment handled the maintenance of the autos used in all the abductions, including scrapping them in one of the garages of La Perla transformed into a giant chop shop, after too many operations might make the vehicles recognizable on the street.[16] The provincial police and city police operated in a supportive capacity.[17] The city police participated in the abductions through coordinated police withdrawals from neighborhoods selected for raids, holding prisoners temporarily in jails before their transfer to the camps and engaging in torture and interrogation sessions of the prisoners in the police commissaries. The military police (Gendarmería), technically a border patrol but under the army's command and called upon periodically to quell social disturbances, had guard duties in and around the camps. Death camp cooperation by government agencies other than the security forces undoubtedly must have also taken place, such as with the publicly owned telephone company, ENTEL, necessary for phone tapping and surveillance or with the local power company, EPEC, to extend electrical service to the camp.

The names of the vast majority of La Perla's prisoners are now well known to us. The Contepomis' memoir gave us a preliminary list of slightly more than two hundred prisoners that they had personally seen or had knowledge of, along with the approximate dates of their arrest and, in the case of many, personal information regarding their background and ultimate fate. The list was slightly weighted to those who were released rather than disappeared, since such individuals were more likely than not to come forward and confirm their imprisonment. The permanent staff at the La Perla museum and the organization HIJOS (Hijos e Hijas por la Identidad y la Justicia contra el Olvido y el Silencio) completed the list. As with the case of former prisoners studied for other detention centers, capturing the experience of life in the camps is limited to the voices of the detainees themselves. Other sources that would provide invaluable information, such as the registries of prisoners maintained by the military, were either destroyed deliberately or lost, either way unavailable to the historian.[18] Since the local military commanders and their subordinates gave most of their orders verbally, neither is there a written record of most of their actions. We rely on their memories likewise for a fragmentary understanding of their role.

As in the case of other death camps, in La Perla the web of relationships and panoply of emotions between the torturers and the tortured was fraught with all kinds of contradictions, occasionally reaching the level of absurd. Coerced sexual relations were predictably a part of camp life, cruelty in all forms was rife, but so too were, albeit exceptionally, apparently genuine feelings of guilt, repulsion, and occasionally even remorse. Yet such contradictory feelings seemed to be confined to a small number of individuals. Most of the military personnel displayed no such doubts and the prisoners encountered pitiless treatment. The La Perla torturers may have referred to their infliction of pain and torment as "work," but by all accounts it was a job they performed with great zeal and conviction.[19] The methods of torture were those found elsewhere: the electric prod, the "submarine" (near suffocation with the head submerged in water), the "airplane" (suspending a blindfolded and handcuffed prisoners upside down and beating them), and other torments. Though a bureaucratic apparatus for the repression existed in and outside of La Perla, by all accounts, the prisoners' captors themselves did not comprise the cold, detached bureaucracy that characterized the Nazi concentration camps, the impersonal administrator of death incarnated in a figure such as Adolf Eichmann, but rather were willing and even enthusiastic participants in the undertaking. As Hugo Vazzetti has remarked, "At the heart of state terrorism that was employed in the abductions and terror there reigned the power of the *patota* rather than the technical bureaucracy."[20]

Former prisoner Graciela Geuna provided several lengthy testimonies to CONADEP (Comisión Nacional sobre la Desaparición de Personas) and various human rights organizations that left a rich corpus of information on conditions in La Perla. Geuna's recollections have been cited often in books on the dictatorship and her voice is one of the few we have that distills the nature of the torments and terror there. She describes the humiliation and the sense of powerlessness that cruelty imposed in the camp, but also the peculiar logic that characterized the torturers. In one frequently cited recollection, she described the attitude of Major Ernesto Barreiro, the direct subordinate of Menéndez at La Perla: "Barreiro was a good representative of the torturers because he was a lucid and conscious participant in the repressive acts. His logic was circular in that sense: he transferred his own personal responsibility to the activists and especially their leadership. That is to say, confronted with such people's resistance, torture was necessary. If people did not resist, he did not have to torture."[21] In another revealing recollection, she conversely also demonstrated her captors' vulnerability, such as when the feared torturer Texas was killed in an armed confrontation during an attempted abduction, deeply affecting the camp personnel because "in reality they all feared their own death. They were afraid, a legend had died, therefore they could too."[22] Geuna also corrects the image of the camp's ironclad discipline and internal order, relating bitter conflicts there between the military police and the army.[23]

Daily life in the camp consisted of hours lying helpless on the straw-filled mattresses that lined the *cuadra* on both sides. Prisoners were blindfolded (*tabicado*) and forbidden to speak, though the guards' vigilance was not absolute and whispered conversations and furtive gestures took place. Crude showers with leaky plumbing at the end of the *cuadra* allowed the prisoners to bathe, in the first months with cold water while later a water heater provided at least lukewarm showers.[24] The abduction and introduction to the camp followed a similar pattern for the prisoners. María Victoria Roca, a twenty-year-old member of the Juventud Guevarista, recounted the details of her baptism into the horrors of La Perla:

> They blindfolded me and put me into the back seat of a car. I could not see but I had heard of the supposed existence of a place called La Perla and I assumed they were taking me there. . . . after applying electric shocks to me while on a metallic bed . . . nearby me, in the same room I heard another group of military personnel torture Enrique Luis Mopty, a man that had been abducted in Buenos Aires and would later be executed by firing squad along with his sister to "commemorate" the Día del

Ejército. They applied electric shocks to him savagely while he, to gather strength, recited the Our Father. The military mocked his pleas and with cruelty tortured further.[25]

Entire families could be kidnapped, as in the case of the Deutsch family, an incident that received international attention due to the intervention of both B'nai B'rith and the U.S. government, including a personal inquiry by President Carter during Videla's state visit to the United States. The family's August 1977 arrest stemmed from the attempted abduction of the son, Daniel Deutsch, whose membership in the PCR made him a target. His escape led Menéndez to order the arrest of the entire family to use as ransom. Such prominent outside intervention was unusual, but in the case of the Deutsch family did lead to a transfer to the federal penitentiary UP1 and a legalization of their detained status, thereby assuring survival.[26] Other kidnapped families were not so fortunate, such as David and Eva Goldman and their daughter Marina, who joined the ranks of the *desaparecidos*, or the Espeche family, mother María Zulema and her son Rodolfo and daughter-in-law, the latter two activists in the Poder Obrero. When her son and daughter-in-law were called for the *traslado*, she insisted with her captors on accompanying them. The three remain *desaparecidos*.[27]

Tensions at the camp within the army's ranks themselves were commonplace, and not unknown were those between the various branches, specifically with the air force, reputedly resented by the army officers for its perceived lack of direct participation in the repression.[28] Yet in the repressive mission, more consensus than dissent prevailed. No political distinction seems to have been made among the prisoners, unlike the case of another notorious death camp, ESMA, where the hypernationalist Montoneros were sometimes regarded as "salvageable" by their military captors and therefore candidates for a less harsh treatment than members of the Ejército Revolucionario del Pueblo–Partido Revolucionario de los Trabajadores (ERP-PRT) or other Marxist organizations, invariably fated for disappearance and death. Rehabilitation in La Perla in these terms seemed to be a foreign concept. Neither was there the marked division of labor among the branch services, the army having a recognized and near exclusive responsibility for the dirty war in Córdoba.[29] Nor were interservice rivalries responsible for the survival of prisoners, as apparently was the case in ESMA, sparing some prisoners strictly for purposes of staking out authority in the rivalries between the military branches that so characterized the dirty war elsewhere.[30]

Survivor testimony concurs on the heavy presence of working-class prisoners in La Perla, union leaders, shop floor delegates, and political activists. The longest and richest human rights trial in terms of witness testimony was the fifth and final of the "Menéndez trials" held in Córdoba. The proceedings involved the fate of 416 former La Perla prisoners, among whom there were 253 listed as murdered or disappeared.

Of these, only fifty-five are names that can faithfully be linked to the local workers' movement, a fact due most likely to the greater reluctance of working-class families to participate in legal proceedings in a local court system that had rarely protected their interests. Though small in numbers, the names and the histories of the fifty-five stood out. They included the leading figures in the unions and some of the most notorious cases of the *desaparecidos* such as René Salamanca, the former secretary-general of SMATA, the autoworkers' union, the city's largest and most powerful union, as well as much lesser known figures. They were people like Hugo Francisco Casas, a construction worker and union delegate abducted at a construction site on August 19, 1976, or Ramón Roque Castillo, a former shop steward in the IKA-Renault auto plants kidnapped on July 26, 1976, in the *vía pública*, or Eduardo Raúl Requena, prominent in the local teachers' union, dragged from a bar in downtown Córdoba on May 12, 1976. The shared characteristics of these working-class victims of La Perla was that they were primarily young males with an active participation in union affairs; a sizable number also engaged in political militancy with one or another of the myriad Peronist and left-wing political organizations active in the city.[31]

The survival of only a small number of prisoners, some 150 out of a total of approximately 1,000 detained at the camp, was one of the defining characteristics of La Perla. At the country's largest and most notorious death camp, ESMA, located in the federal capital, a similar slim chance for survival is attributed, in large part, to the presence of former *guerrilleros* either willing or terrorized into collaborating with their captors, including identifying fellow militants on the street and even participating in torture sessions. Navy commander Emilio Massera reputedly singled out in particular Montoneros for special treatment, believing in the possibility of their rehabilitation because of their nationalist credentials and allowing a contingent of them to survive, a decision also in line with his political aspirations and attempts to build bridges to the Peronist movement.[32] In La Perla, there were considerations also at work at ESMA: the usefulness of certain prisoners to the workings of the camp, including but not confined to the willingness of some detainees to provide intelligence. There were also other factors. The camp was also a living albeit decomposing organism, at least for some prisoners a working community that benefitted from the skills and expertise they possessed, necessary to keep the detention center running efficiently. At times, prisoners were even taken to the private homes of their captors to perform chores such as carpentry, plumbing, and masonry work.[33] Some of those who survived managed to do so because of their usefulness in ordinary maintenance tasks, while for others there may been the right political connections, perhaps even a timely bribe or just sheer luck.

As many have argued, the death camp was the dictatorship's most emblematic institution, one that distinguished it from other military regimes at the time in Latin America and that incarnated the particular obsessions, objectives, and methods of the *Proceso*.[34] This proposition needs further refinement, however. The camps demonstrated significant differences, ones that corresponded certainly to the personalities of the camp commandants but also to the particular circumstances found in the areas where the camps were located and the characteristics of the population and societal context from which the prison population was drawn. In the case of La Perla, Córdoba's tumultuous decade that preceded the camp's establishment, the unusually high degree of social mobilization, political radicalization, and class polarization all influenced the death camp's practices and the very nature of prison life there. The larger number of prisoners who were workers and the few of them who managed to survive was perhaps the most obvious manifestation of La Perla's class character and counterrevolutionary purpose, a purpose heightened to a terrifying degree by the maniacal temperament of camp commandant Menéndez but that cannot be reduced to that admittedly raving, rabid individual.

La Perla's victims were selected carefully in deliberations by the intelligence services. There was nothing improvised or indiscriminate in the abductions. The overwhelming majority of the prisoners had histories of union or political activism. Certainly from the military's perspective, political involvement covered a broad array of activities. Ricardo Mora became suspect for creating a physicians' union, was imprisoned in La Perla and later transferred to the UP1 and La Plata federal penitentiaries, and, upon release, was fired from his position at Rawson Hospital.[35] Yet few were the victims of circumstance who have entered the folklore of Argentina's disappeared. Torture had a purpose. The military first sought valuable intelligence on activists' whereabouts, political associates, and activities. Then it sought to erase Córdoba's nonconformist culture through abductions and deaths. The camp implemented a brutal, destructive regimen intended to control the prisoners, break their will to resist, and facilitate their final removal. The executions were methodical, as was the disposal of the corpses.

La Perla would be the first of the camps to be visited by the CONADEP truth commission following the fall of the military government. The new commander of the Third Corps, General Mansilla, refused the delegation entry to the former detention center, converted by then into a military barracks, though eventually was forced to relent. Mansilla would subsequently head an abortive military uprising in Córdoba to protest CONADEP's investigation.[36] The general had good reason to object to CONADEP's inquiries. There were regular executions over a two-year period, from 1976 to 1978, with Menéndez often presiding, as many as fifty people at a time falling to firing squads, and large graves where the bodies were thrown.[37] La Perla, more than any of the other detention centers, seems to have functioned with a single-minded purpose: to eradicate the entire gamut of Córdoba's Left, from its leadership to the working-class activists and young students who comprised the vast majority of its recruits. Camp commandant Menéndez made no distinction between the heterogeneous Left's ideology or its praxis. The bookish, doctrinaire, cautious Communist Party members as much as swashbuckling, menacing, gun-wielding Montoneros were slated for a grim fate. Rehabilitation was unthinkable, annihilation the only possible solution. General Mansilla had good reason to wish that its history, along with its victims, lay buried, hidden and forgotten.

The 1985 trials of the military junta gave the first glimpse of the horror that was La Perla. Among the most cited testimonies of those trials was that of José Julian Solanille. Solanille worked as a herdsman and farm laborer in the fields adjacent to La Perla. His eyewitness account stands as unique given the clandestine nature of the dirty war and the paucity of eyewitness accounts of the fate of the disappeared. The estate Solanille worked on (called Loma El Torito) actually belonged to the Third Corps but was then rented out and privately being worked at the time of the coup. The property's semimilitary status gave Solanille a unique if grim opportunity, a special vantage point, to witness firsthand the methods of the dirty war and the practices of the La Perla death camp. At the trials, he recounted seeing young girls being flung from helicopters, his shepherd dogs bringing human remains to his work site, of seeing Menéndez leading a contingent of military trucks and later hearing gunshots. The most woeful part of Solanille's testimony was his claim to have witnessed large executions and mass graves—graves that years later he unsuccessfully attempted to relocate for the CONADEP delegation. They had been removed and covered over in the interim, leaving no trace of the remains he claimed to have once stumbled on. The waves of prisoners that Solanille saw mowed down testified to a site of horrendous cruelty and terrifying crimes.[38]

Testimony at the 1985 trials of the juntas revealed other peculiarities of state terrorism in Córdoba and the La Perla death camp. Court testimony verified the absence in Córdoba of a black market in babies with pregnant captives giving birth and the newborn sold to others, including military families, a practice so common elsewhere in the country. The trafficking of babies and later attempts by families to recover the children of loved ones became one of the defining features of the dirty war. Gustavo Contepomi testified that pregnant prisoners tended to be spared (the case of his own wife) while Margarita Elgoghen recounted her own experience with giving birth while a prisoner with the infant passed to the family for its care.[39] Contepomi's recollections notwithstanding, accusations of pregnant detainees being executed at La Perla are plentiful. The relative absence of a demand, with only one verified case, that of twenty-year-old Silvina Parodi, for the restitution of children by the local human rights movement and as an issue in the trials between 2007 and 2016 give credence to such claims.

La Perla functioned from the beginning of the dirty war in Córdoba to its end as the final stage in the abducted, interrogated, and tortured detainee's torment, the gallows for the vast majority of Córdoba's *desaparecidos*. It formed part of a national network of detention centers and death camps whose organization had been carefully planned by the military years before the March 1976 coup. Despite

Menéndez's later outlandish claims, the detainees were not held there for their own protection or to await trial, but to be interrogated and then eliminated. The dirty war in essence was a carefully orchestrated campaign designed to murder those individuals—women, adolescents, middle-aged professionals, no distinction was made—identified as the leadership and followers of the "subversion" that the military sought to erase. Death in La Perla was its deliberate purpose; to survive it was something miraculous.

4

INSTITUTIONAL DYNAMICS

The Third Army Corps

The armed subversives have been totally annihilated.
—GENERAL LUCIANO BENJAMÍN MENÉNDEZ

The history of the dirty war in Córdoba is inseparable from that of the institution charged by the country's ruling junta to wage it: the army's Third Corps. Years before the 1976 coup, the Third Corps had assumed a prominent role in the city in quelling social disturbances and repressing any signs of so-called subversive behavior. Within the ranks of the local army commanders, the idea of the internal enemy long antedated the dirty war. The mass arrests and military trials of union leaders following the May 1969 *Cordobazo* was the Third Corps' introduction into local protest and social ferment. Similarly, in 1971 following the *viborazo*, a second massive working-class protest, troops from the Third Corps forcibly entered the grounds of the city's Archbishopric to dislodge and arrest over one hundred activist priests and their supporters who had occupied it in protest.[1] Army troops on several occasions occupied the Fiat and other factories, arresting union activists and imposing a military discipline on the labor force. Local army commanders developed tactics for purposes of riot control and intelligence and surveillance capabilities to monitor suspected party and union militants. The dirty war only extended the Third Corps' authority and widened its responsibilities.

The army's various corps were assigned exclusive authority in distinct geographic regions in the dirty war. The Third Corps' responsibilities ultimately reached far beyond Córdoba and included jurisdiction for the antisubversive campaign over much of the interior, as far south as Mendoza and stretching through the northwest to the Bolivian border.

Such a charge included the province of Tucumán, the site of the country's most important rural-based insurgency. The ruling junta's division of the country into military zones in the antisubversive campaign made zone 3 that this vast region

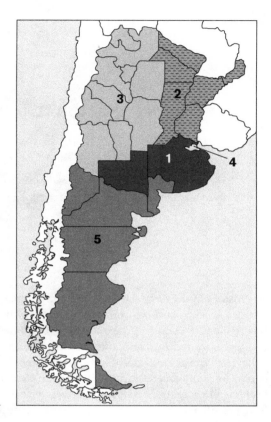

MAP 3. Military zones, 1975–83.

comprised arguably the most difficult assignment of any, given the wide variety of terrain, diverse socioeconomic contexts, the strength of the Left in places like Córdoba and Tucumán, and those provinces' status as epicenters of urban and rural guerrilla activity respectively. The high command of the Third Corps had the final word on the fate of all detainees in its assigned zone.[2] Some seventy-five detention centers, the largest of which by far was La Perla, existed in zone 3, six of which were directly administered by the army, the majority of the rest by local police forces.[3] The military commanders partitioned the various zones into subzones (nineteen in all) with sundry infantry, artillery, and communications brigades and battalions of the Third Corps comprising its resident troops. Subzone 31 comprised the provinces of Córdoba, La Rioja, and Catamarca, which in turn were divided into separate "areas" and then "subareas" (there were 117 throughout the country) assigned to specific military units.[4]

Before Córdoba, the Third Corps waged the dirty war in Tucumán and developed practices there, despite a radically different social and eco-geographical context in that province, later put to use in Córdoba. During the final year and a half of the 1973–76 Peronist government, beginning in 1974, the Third Corps under the command of Menéndez launched a violent, brutal campaign, dubbed Operation Independence, in both the countryside and the provincial capital. In Tucumán, the Ejército Revolucionario del Pueblo (ERP) had undertaken a rural, *foquista*-like insurrection with a nucleus of armed revolutionaries attempting through successful guerrilla tactics to recruit a large, impoverished peasantry in a mountainous, sugar-producing province reminiscent of Cuba's Sierra Maestra. At the same time, an urban guerrilla force whose most important contingent was the Montoneros engaged in the tactics of bank robberies, targeted assassinations, and dramatic, defiant gestures to discredit and weaken the government. Given Tucumán's unique character, the only part of the country where the Left attempted a rural insurgency, the Third Corps adopted some measures there, including an internal passport system and a massive resettlement effort of the *tucumano* peasantry that it would not implement elsewhere. The army's campaign in Tucumán, however, included other tactics such as forced disappearances and a network of clandestine prisons making the province a laboratory for practices that would be extended to the entire country after the March 1976 coup. The antisubversive campaign targeted not only those groups employing violent tactics but also students, union leaders, and intellectuals. Menéndez oversaw Operation Independence during its most critical stage, turning his attention to Córdoba only once the rural guerrilla forces had been decisively defeated, as they had been by late 1975. A training manual—"Lucha Contra los Elementos Subversivos," based largely on the Tucumán experience—provided the tactical lessons that would be employed within months in Córdoba.

This compartmentalization of counterrevolutionary war was one of the many concepts instilled by the French military missions of the late 1950s and early 1960s, what the French termed *quadrillage* in Algeria.[5] Unlike the case of Buenos Aires, the dirty war in Córdoba was largely but not exclusively the monopoly of the army. In landlocked Córdoba there were no naval units involved in state terrorism. The air force played a crucial but subordinate role in surveillance. Its most visible responsibility was its control of the runways at the Fábrica Militar de Aviones, which above all facilitated the movement of prisoners from various points throughout the country, from Tucumán in the north to Rawson on the south, as well as its control of Highway 20, which was the main road leading to the La Perla death camp from the provincial capital. The sprawling Escuela de Aviación Militar y de Suboficiales de la Fuerza Aérea was situated on the highway leading to La Perla, and all movements were subject to its surveillance and searches. In May 1976, in an effort to deploy local military assets more efficiently and share responsibility for the abductions and disappearances, Menéndez assigned the air force, and specifically the Servicio de Inteligencia Aeronáutica (SIA), responsibility for surveillance of the city's factories, thereby giving it a major role in the abduction, arrest, and disappearance of the many working-class victims in Córdoba.[6]

The Third Corps nonetheless held ultimate authority for the state terrorism in Córdoba, and the army's dominance manifested in several ways. The ruling junta's notorious factionalism, the rivalry between the three service branches that led each to colonize different branches of the government bureaucracy—the navy's control of the Ministry of Foreign Affairs was just one example—and assume control of the directorships of the country's myriad public companies had no counterpart in Córdoba. The provincial government remained fully under the army's dominion. With no naval units to compete with and the air force assigned an important but subordinate role, Menéndez asserted command of all branches of the provincial government and of those firms, such as the local electric power company EPEC, not in private hands. He similarly assumed control of the federal penitentiary system in the city as well as the municipal and provincial police forces. In Córdoba, the army was the face of the dictatorship.

The province of Córdoba (designated "area 311") fell under the direct jurisdiction of the commander of the Third Army Corps, Menéndez. Directly responsible to him was the Fourth Infantry Brigade under the command of General Juan Bautista Sasiaíñ, comprising four regiments and battalions charged with the "antisubversive" campaign there.[7] The commanders further divided tasks by groups: G1 (Personnel), G-2 (Intelligence), G-3 (Operations), G-4 (Logistics), and G-5 (Civilian Affairs). G-1 handled matters related to the custody of prisoners, G-5 to prisoner transfers. The G-2 Intelligence group was further divided into sections: the First section with responsibility for the city was divided into discrete subsections authorized to investigate specific sectors (labor unions, student groups, political parties, and others). The Third section under Barreiro was assigned to La Perla.

As was the case elsewhere, considerable decisional autonomy existed at the local level, the military junta providing general instructions on aims and tactics but specific operations and last-minute decisions emanating from Menéndez and his subordinates. This structure had ramifications for and helps explain certain peculiarities of state terrorism in Córdoba. One was the targeting of the country's old guard left-wing party, the Communist Party (PC). The supinely pro-Soviet PC had followed a cautious policy throughout the tumultuous 1960s and 1970s, highly critical of the new Left's embrace of violent tactics and armed struggle and guided above all in its abiding role as custodian of the Soviet Union's interests at the international level. For these reasons and given the increasing importance of trade with the Soviet bloc for Argentina by the time the military assumed power, the junta generally adopted a soft line towards the PC and party members.

Not so in Córdoba. Menéndez made no distinction between the Communists, the ERP, and the Montoneros, regarding them all as part of the same international conspiracy and subversive threat and including them as targets for abduction and murder. Not even a personal intervention by Videla himself to spare the life of Juan Alberto Caffaratti, PC member and member of the executive committee of the Luz y Fuerza union, was enough to dissuade Menéndez from his execution.[8] The local Communist Party's close association with Córdoba's Jewish community, from whom a number of the party leadership arose, also undoubtedly did not favor its situation, despite the party's obliging behavior during the dictatorship.[9] Menéndez's Third Corps proved renegade in other ways. By late 1978, Videla was attempting to relax the repression, fearful of the consequences of greater international isolation and of the internal weakening of authority and the chain of command within the military's ranks, inevitable given the state terrorism's decentralized, fragmented character. Menéndez and local commanders remained recalcitrant, obstinate in their determination to continue the antisubversive campaign. In Córdoba, though in greatly reduced numbers, abductions and disappearances continued through 1978 into 1979. Menéndez even reputedly offered counterrevolutionary training for Latin American officers at the Third Corps' base during the very years the dirty war was being waged.[10]

One factor in the dirty war that has been largely ignored is the role of the conscripts. In 1976, as the dirty war intensified, the age of obligatory military service was lowered from twenty to eighteen. Conscripts were assigned by lottery to the army, air force, or navy and the length of service was one year for the army and air force, two for the navy. Conscripts could substitute service in the armed forces by volunteering to serve in the Gendarmería, Naval Prefecture, or Federal Police. Inducted over the Argentine summer (January–March) and mustered out by the end of the year, the conscripts formed few if any emotional attachments or sense of personal loyalty to their commanders. A wide gulf separated officer from soldier. Conscripted soldiers also better represented the ethnic and class diversity of Argentina. Argentines of all social classes were subjected to obligatory military service, known popularly as the *colimba* (because the soldier performing it would, "*corre, limpia, y barre*" [run, clean, and sweep]). Those of Jewish and Arab descent as well as those from indigenous rural areas, most notably from the northwestern and northeastern provinces, were rare among the officer corps, but were common in the conscripted ranks. Officers in all three branches of the armed forces, in contrast, were overwhelmingly of urban middle-class background, immigrant Spanish or Italian ethnicity, and Roman Catholic in religion. Military families also practiced a high degree of endogamy and residential segregation.

All these factors contributed to the formation of a military caste and isolation not only from civilian society but also from their very troops, a quality reinforced by the Prussian tradition in a German-trained army until World War II and the excessive deference required by soldiers to their superiors.[11] Noncommissioned officers (NCOs) also received different treatment. NCOs lacked access to the

FIGURE 10. Campo de la Ribera detention center.

officer training schools, played virtually no role in broad strategic planning, and were generally drawn from lower socioeconomic groups than the regular officers, adding to the rigid hierarchies at work within the military.[12] One consequence of the character of this military culture was the vulnerability of NCOs and conscripts during the dirty war. To express doubts about the dirty war's methods, to prove uncooperative, not to mention acts of outright insubordination invited more than just punishment. They invited death. Nationally, there are nearly one hundred documented cases of NCOs and conscripts who entered the ranks of the disappeared, and many more suspected victims murdered at the direct orders of their commanding officers.[13] There were several notorious cases in the Third Corps. Unwillingness to participate in the clandestine terrorist state easily thrust NCOs into the category of subversives.

The Third Corps tactics in waging the dirty war in Córdoba predated the March 1976 coup. By late 1975, Menéndez had already assumed direct control of operations in the city. Clandestine abductions, mass arrests, torture, and disappearances appeared quickly. The opening of the first of the detention centers, Campo de la Ribera, marked the intensification of the state terrorist tactics begun under Lacabanne the year before, but now fully in the hands of the army, the private, Peronist dimension of that previous campaign ceding to a more systematic, organized one under the Third Corps' authority. Court testimony in the subsequent human rights

FIGURE 11. Campo de la Ribera detention center, hooks for shackling prisoners.

trials recounted daily arrivals of new prisoners, detainees' shackling to walls, inter-rogation and torture sessions, release for the lucky few, and death for the others.

By late 1977, partly in response to the diplomatic tensions with the Carter administration in the United States on the human rights issue, the junta began to search for procedures to rein in the death squads and camps. In September the junta debated both the creation of a Comisión Asesora to examine the individual cases of all political prisoners and to reestablish the constitutional right of lawful exit from the country, suspended by the junta at the time of the coup.[14] Less than a year later, the junta was establishing rubrics of prisoners according to their degree of involvement in "subversive activities" and prescribing limits on the time of incarceration accordingly.[15] None of this sat well with Menéndez. In September 1979, Menéndez led an abortive uprising against Videla's government, demanding an intensification of the "war against subversion" and the resignation of army commander General Roberto Viola, seen by Menéndez as a "blando" and a partisan of easing the repression. It would lead to Menéndez's forced retirement and imprisonment for ninety days in the Curuzu Cuatiá barracks.

The abortive Menéndez rebellion revealed some essential traits of the dirty war. There was not just one dirty war—there were many, with local contexts and often influencing national dynamics. The personalities of the regional commanders shaped the nature of the antisubversive campaign, but even more importantly local conditions determined the precise practices and methods employed in combatting subversion. The decentralization of the dirty war, represented most graphically in the discrete geographic zones of authority, constituted one of its defining characteristics, markedly different from the experiences of more conventional counterinsurgencies undertaken by the Latin American militaries in Central America or the Andean countries. Partly this responded to the shared responsibility of the various branches of the armed forces in Argentina's dirty war, virtually absent elsewhere in the region where the army alone waged counterinsurgency war against formidable guerrilla movements. Even more determinative were local conditions that influenced the military commanders' broader strategic and tactical considerations. For Menéndez and the Third Corps army commanders, signs of continued subversive behavior, if no longer an indication of guerrilla military capabilities that were always much weaker in Argentina than elsewhere in Latin America, counseled continuing the methods of torture, abductions, and disappearances. The spirit of the Intersindical—the cooperation between unions in different sectors, in the final months of the previous Peronist government—showed new signs of life, not an open resistance by any means but the reappearance of some shop floor activism and clandestine meetings of union militants from different enterprises, and even an important strike in late 1977 by autoworkers in the IKA-Renault plants, leading to the arrest of 17 workers by the army and the firing of 175 others by the company.[16] Such activities could not have gone unnoticed by the military intelligence services. Menéndez's call to continue the dirty war was not simply a product of a contumacious personality, of his status as an incorrigible "hardliner" within the regime, it was also calculated and strategic in nature and fully in accord with what had compelled his campaign in Córdoba from the beginning.

By 1980, the military government's internal factionalism and rivalries nonetheless had led to a state of decomposition. Though there was a compelling logic to continue the dirty war, the one source of cohesion and only real success that the armed forces could claim since assuming power, countervailing pressures including international condemnation and sanctions from the United States counseled an end to the abductions and disappearances. In Córdoba, where General Antonio Domingo Bussi had assumed command of the Third Corps in 1980, a secret memorandum signed by Bussi circulated among the military commanders outlining a plan to establish a mechanism for normalizing the status of prisoners found in various detention centers under Third Corps jurisdiction. Plans especially were being made for a release of political prisoners found in federal penitentiaries.[17] The dismantling of the large detention centers turned death camps such as La Perla accelerated.

The state terrorism unleashed in Córdoba was not only a military matter. It was also a police matter, though the police were thoroughly under the control of Menéndez and the local military commanders. In the early months following the coup, Menéndez had restructured Córdoba's police forces, placing them under the direct command of the Third Corps and fully integrating them into the repressive apparatus. The presence of so many police among the indicted and accused in subsequent human rights trials was not by chance nor did it reflect an independent role for the provincial and municipal police or motorcycle patrol units (Comando Radioeléctrico), completely subordinate to the dictates of Menéndez and the Third Corps. Through its administration of the D-2 detention center, participation in the abductions by sealing off entire city blocks to facilitate raids, and surveillance activities for and supply of intelligence to the military, the police were an integral part of the dirty war. The reach of the police extended even beyond the province. With a shared border with Buenos Aires province, contacts with the provincial police of Buenos Aires province, the Bonaerense, were ongoing. Arrests occurred based on shared intelligence between the country's two largest provincial police forces. Such arrests involved suspected subversives who had fled Córdoba and were believed to be residing in Buenos Aires province. Since the provincial police forces respected jurisdictional boundaries, cooperation generally involved requests for detention, arrest, and extradition.[18] In addition, fairly detailed reports on so-called subversive activities were supplied to the Bonaerense, stressing always the special status of Córdoba as a center of political agitation and subversion.[19]

As with the case of the army's NCOs and conscripts, the victims of the police terror tactics at times included other police officers. A bitter feud between *peronista* and anti-*peronista* police that could be traced back to the 1974 *Navarrazo* culminated during the dictatorship. The downtown station of the provincial police intelligence service, D-2, was second only to La Perla in its importance as a center of detention and interrogation during the dirty war, but at the time of the coup it was already a hub of right-wing, paramilitary activity and had been for nearly two years. The Peronist Right that had supported the police coup against the provincial government then waged a war against the Peronist Left, including within the ranks of the police itself. In order to fully subordinate the police to the Third Corps' overall strategy, suspected police officers, including those simply unwilling to participate in the dirty war, were themselves murdered. The D-2 operated as the clearing house, the crucial first stage in the clandestine state terrorism, where dissent was not an option.[20]

Numbers reveal the methods of the Third Corps in waging its dirty war in Córdoba. In the database of the Diario del Juicio maintained by the local chapter of HIJOS (Hijos e Hijas por la Identidad y la Justicia contra el Olvido y el Silencio) and the national database of the Parque de la Memoria, there are approximately 1,100 documented cases of victims of state terrorism; more than 80 percent are classified as *desaparecidos*. The total number of *desaparecidos* include those from the province as a whole, though the victims were predominantly from the provincial capital. Whatever part of the province they were abducted in, they were generally brought

Córdoba's Victims of State Terrorism, 1973–1983

May 30, 1969–March 23, 1976	207
March 24, 1976–December 31, 1978	828
January 1, 1979–December 1983	48
Date Unknown	20
Total	1,103
Men	808
Women	295
Death by Disappearance	848
Killed	174
Death in Staged Confrontations	81

SOURCE: Databases of Diario del Juicio and the Parque de la Memoria.

to one of the city's detention centers, most to the La Perla death camp. Not all of the 1,100 met their end in detention. The second largest category, *asesinados* (killed), were those who died in real armed confrontations or simply were murdered, with only the occasional body appearing and death certificates filed, a much smaller percentage of the dirty war's victims. Death in *enfrentamientos fraguados* (staged confrontations), the smallest category, refers to the summary execution of prisoners and later staging a scene, as if the executed prisoners died in a gunfight. Overwhelmingly, death by disappearance, which generally meant detention in La Perla before execution, accounts for the greatest number of victims. The figures also include victims who were from Córdoba and abducted or killed elsewhere, but such cases are smaller in number (roughly 20 percent) and the data compiled a faithful reflection of the character of the state terrorism in Córdoba.

The average age of the disappeared, more than 70 percent of those with a recorded age, was between sixteen and thirty years, a sizable number with confirmed activism in left-wing organizations and parties (see appendix 2). The date of disappearance or death reveals that the state terrorism was well underway during the 1973–76 Peronist government, with hundreds of victims already by the time of the March 1976 coup. Unquestionably the greatest numbers occurred during the first two years of the dictatorship. These terrible two years witnessed a steady stream of victims, so great that the local undertakers' union was overwhelmed by the numbers of bodies delivered, sometimes literally thrown at their door steps, and petitioned the military government to reclassify their work along with hazardous occupations such as those in the mining and chemical industries (and therefore entitled to increased wages and vacation time). They alleged the number of bodies unloaded from army trucks and to be buried in unmarked graves to have increased ten- to twentyfold, thereby leading to environmental contamination and more hazardous working conditions.[21] The greatest horrors of the dirty war were concentrated in these two years.

The role of the Third Army Corps during the dirty war formed part of the broader history of the Argentine military in the postwar period. After an early, testy, and fractious alliance between Perón and at least some sectors of the military, the armed forces emerged as Perón and his movement's bitterest adversary. In the decades preceding the dirty war, the army's *Revista Militar* and the publications of the Instituto Geográfico Militar stressed issues of security and defense in more narrow terms than most other Latin American militaries. The Argentine military, and the army specifically, conceived security as essentially a question of military defense and internal order, of "ideological frontiers," of geopolitics and protection of the nation's borders, and a national culture under threat from an internal enemy and a populace corrupted by Peronist populism, easily led astray by demagoguery and international communism. In contrast, Chile's military, perhaps due to the absence of a credible armed rural or urban guerrilla in that country, interpreted the question of security and national defense much more broadly.[22] The link between economic development and national security generally figured more prominently elsewhere in Latin America than in Argentina, and civic action programs often accompanied brutal counterinsurgency tactics in places like Central America and Colombia.

Only in Tucumán did something similar occur. In the rural northwest, the Third Corps embraced nation-building strategies and literacy and antipoverty measures to complement the disappearances and death camps of its murderous dirty war there. There is no trace of such tactics in Córdoba. If Tucumán's poverty and perceived cultural and even racial backwardness animated a twin strategy of repression and economic development, it was Córdoba's very modernity that explained the brutality and pitiless nature of the army Third Corps' dirty war in the city and its environs. As the symbol of Argentina's post-Peronist industrialization programs and integration into the emerging transnational economy, Córdoba occupied a unique place in the dictatorship's obsession with subversion. It threatened a modernizing project prized by an army with longstanding industrialization aspirations and great power delusions. Yet Córdoba's lingering status as an emblem of traditional, creole Argentina, the repository of an idealized national culture, the ecclesiastical center and conservative bastion that had in the previous century resisted the liberal, secular program of the Buenos Aires elites and in more recent times had launched the 1955 rebellion to overthrow Perón, invested the dirty war there with the quality of a crusade against the very modernization in cultural and political terms that industrialization had brought with it. Yet despite its profoundly local concerns and even a certain degree of insularity, the Third Corps, and the country's armed forces generally, had for years been influenced by global forces. These external influences consisted of not simply training and indoctrination but rather an appropriation and reconfiguring of ideas and methods that were also a part of the dirty war's history.

TRANSNATIONAL DYNAMICS

The Cold War and the War against Subversion

The Marxist-Communist International has been operating since five hundred years before Christ.

—GENERAL CRISTINO NICOLAIDES

The history of the army's Third Corps in Córdoba formed part of a larger story, one with national and even transnational dimensions. The Cold War context of the dirty war is perhaps its most notorious characteristic and its human rights abuses and crimes often attributed solely to the National Security Doctrine, American military indoctrination, and overall U.S. geopolitical strategy in the conflict with the socialist bloc.[1] Frequent references to Argentina by the military as a battlefield in a presumed Third World War lent credence to such reductionism. Menéndez himself framed the dirty war in those terms, of Argentina as a decisive battle in this world war.[2] The reality was much more complex. The military's anticommunism and anti-Peronism were longstanding sentiments deeply affected but not determined by U.S. Cold War influences. In the early 1960s, American military training initiatives in Argentina had been modest compared to those in nearby Brazil, with little interest by the Argentine military in counterinsurgency warfare training specifically. Between 1950 and 1979, Argentina ranked ninth in the number of Latin American officers trained by U.S. military missions such as the School of the Americas in the Canal Zone, behind such smaller countries as Bolivia, Nicaragua, and Panama. U.S. army missions complained about their inability to get the Argentine army to accept its mobile training teams for assistance in counterguerrilla training.[3] Though several junta members such as Videla, Roberto Viola, and Leopoldo Galtieri received American training, of the some 60,000 Latin American military personnel who passed through the School of the Americas between 1946 and 1996, only 1 percent were Argentines.[4] In the early months of the Onganía dictatorship, the Argentine military had opposed U.S. efforts to create a more integrated hemispheric defense force, the so-called Permanent Interamerican Defense

Force, at the same time it sought to decrease its dependence on American military equipment and weaponry.[5] Argentina's military leadership would later seek to align itself more closely and cooperate with U.S. hemispheric security policies, but long-standing suspicions and tensions never completely disappeared.

The low level of Argentine participation was due, in part, to the previous French tutelage in counterinsurgency and its theories' early incorporation into Argentine military academies as well as the Argentine military's previous history, confidence in its own institutions and training, as well as some residual anti-American sentiment. There is some disagreement on such figures. Martin Andersen cites a State Department report that places Argentina fourth in the number of Argentine officers receiving U.S. training.[6] These numbers, however, are belied by the more careful scholarship of the abovementioned authors. The dispute also avoids considering the different criteria for what constituted "training." A brief training course at Fort Bragg or Fort Leavenworth likely had little impact on the Argentine officers' worldview or strategic planning. I have found a very low number of officers in the III Corps trained by U.S. mobile teams in counterguerrilla warfare, which could be a peculiarity of that Corps—though, as Heinz and Frühling note, it seems not to be. This apparently was true of the Argentine army generally, unlike the case of the Central American militaries, for example. But in terms of the dirty war itself, aggregate figures of U.S. military aid/training rather than on-the-ground evidence do not prove much one way or another. The country that by far had the greatest U.S. military connection was Brazil, which received the largest share of military aid (almost 40 percent), participated most frequently in joint military exercises, and had the biggest military mission of any of the U.S. embassies in Latin America. Yet twenty years of military rule there produced nothing like the *guerra sucia* in Argentina. So the equation of levels of U.S. support as measured by conventional criteria equals the degree of state terrorism does not hold up; the violence clearly cannot be simply attributed to the U.S. military connection and other things must explain it. Such reasoning overstates the exogenous influences on the *guerra sucia*, simplifies its sources, and underestimates the importance of domestic factors.

A Catholic-nationalist ideology permeated the officer corps and provided the grist for a visceral anticommunism long before the onset of the Cold War and the preeminence of U.S. influence within the Argentine military. After 1945, French counterinsurgency doctrines also competed with those emanating from the Pentagon and had much more influence in how the dirty war was actually conducted, certainly much more than is generally recognized. Perhaps all that U.S. Cold War indoctrination ultimately gave the junta was a sense of fighting a war much bigger than that taking place in Argentina, hence all the hubris of being a battlefield for World War III. Beyond a visceral anticommunism, the U.S. military influence on the precise tactics employed during the dirty war seems slight in comparison to that of the French. Save the abortive campaign by the Ejército Revolucionario del

Pueblo (ERP) in Tucumán, there was no rural insurgency in Argentina. Only there did the army employ conventional counterinsurgency tactics such as the Americans had implemented in Viet Nam, though those too were highly influenced by French theories. In Argentina, the military undertook its counterrevolutionary war in the cities. The precise tactics employed seemed more akin to those of the French in the streets of Algiers than the Americans in jungles and swamps of Southeast Asia.[7] Similarly, a central tenet of the American counterinsurgency strategy, civic action programs, was virtually unheard of in Argentina's dirty war. Only in Tucumán did the Argentine army employ a very modest adaptation of civic action programs. Moreover, American influence in Argentina operated through channels other than the military and the history of Argentine-U.S. relations during the military dictatorship demonstrated complexities and contradictions often unacknowledged or at least underappreciated.

French counterinsurgency theories had been developed and put into practice during the anticolonial struggles in Viet Nam but especially in Algeria. It was the humiliating withdrawal in Viet Nam that had convinced the French military to think more systematically about how to wage counterinsurgency warfare, tactics that the French had implemented in an improvised and ultimately ineffective fashion in Southeast Asia. Former Viet Nam commander Colonel Charles Lacheroy gave a series of influential lectures at Saint Cyr and other French military institutes, expounding the theories of counterrevolutionary war following the failed attempt to subdue their colony in Indochina.[8] Lacheroy's theories of bringing counterinsurgency warfare to the civilian population, focusing on the strategically important leadership and acquiring the intelligence necessary, and breaking an insurgency by any means would be implemented ruthlessly in Algeria. Similarly, a thousand-page report compiled by Viet Nam veteran officers, *Enseignements de la guerre d'Indochine*, detailed the Indochina campaign and the counterinsurgency lessons to be drawn from the defeat. Finally, in 1961 Lt. Colonel Roger Trinquier, veteran of Viet Nam and Algerian commander and head of intelligence there, would publish his *La Guerre moderne*, "the bible for all specialists in counterinsurgency warfare."[9] Trinquier had developed and implemented in Algiers the classic urban counterinsurgency strategy, dividing the city "into sectors, subsectors, blocks and buildings" for purposes of surveillance, abduction, or arrest.[10] All these theories and practices were incorporated formally into French military training and disseminated in France's military academies.

The Algerian war witnessed the broad adoption of counterrevolutionary methods. The French army decentralized its actions, dividing the colony into zones with local commanders granted near-complete operational autonomy.[11] The various police forces were fully incorporated into the repressive apparatus. Broad sweeps coordinated between the army and police led to arrests, detentions, and interrogations with torture.[12] A major objective was to execute the campaign against the insurgents in a clandestine fashion, free from the encumbrances of the law and the justice system. The clandestine detention center was also an innovation of the Algerian war. Confining the prisoners to recondite sites allowed for extreme measures, interrogation under torture but also the forced disappearance of some of those detained. Private death squads of *colons* (French Algerians) closely supervised by the military also operated as part of the counterinsurgency. By one account, some three thousand rebels were disappeared during the infamous Battle of Algiers alone.[13] Throughout it all, the French army feigned any knowledge of the abuses at the same time methods of torture that would become stock in trade of counterinsurgency—submersion in water to the point of suffocation and electric shocks especially—spread throughout the colony. Confronted with a tenacious resistance by the Algerians that included assassinations and acts of terrorism, the French military devised and adopted extreme methods that acquired legitimacy in their eyes and clouded judgment about the morality of such methods, for the simple reason that they were effective. The intelligence gathered under interrogation and torture proved highly useful. The capture and elimination of leaders of the Front de Libération Nationale (FLN) dealt devastating blows to the insurgency. The French army adhered to a formal legality and publicly proclaimed respect for due process, but the reality of the Algerian counterinsurgency was abductions, secret detention centers, torture, and even the disappearances of detainees.[14]

The French experience offered many lessons. One was the general effectiveness of such tactics if ruthlessly implemented. Torture more often than not did in fact provide useful information and provided it quickly before a captured prisoner's comrades learned of the detention and had time to react. The French also taught that interrogation, and the torture that accompanied it, were most effective in the emotionally shattering first hours and days of a prisoner's capture, a practice widely followed during Argentina's dirty war. The specific methods of torture such as submersion in water and electric shocks also demonstrated their utility in forcing the prisoner to talk, and were less likely to leave incriminating marks while also running a low risk of the prisoner dying under torture, save in the rare case of cardiac arrest. Electric shocks, the preferred method of the French army in Algeria, also could be raised or lowered in intensity to provide a carefully calibrated infliction of torment that complemented well the uncertain, changing dynamic of an interrogation.[15] The French even taught the utility of having medical doctors present at torture sessions to monitor the tortured prisoner's health, which allowed taking torture to the limit but avoided a premature death, a practice that would become standard in Argentina's detention centers.[16]

Another lesson was the effectiveness of counterinsurgency as psychological warfare, a way to intimidate the population at large, to instill such a sense of overwhelming dread that sympathy for the insurgents or revolutionaries dried up, an antidote to Mao's famous dictum that guerrillas were swimming like a fish in water among the general population. Torture and terror drained the lake. As would become the practice in Argentina, as many French soldiers as possible would participate in torture in order to diffuse guilt and forge a common stake in the success of counterinsurgency war and its methods.[17] Summary execution of detainees was a final, drastic solution employed by the French military in Algeria, just as it would in Argentina. The *fuyards abattus* (felled fugitives) in Algeria suffered a similar fate to the *subversivos caídos* in Argentina, and the French innovated the practice of the disappearance, with thousands in the Algerian war buried in mass graves or hurled into the sea by helicopters.[18]

French counterinsurgency tactics also meshed with the concept of counterrevolutionary war born of the bipolar postwar world. The Cold War tensions and rivalries present in other anticolonial movements were also found in Algeria.[19] The Algerian Communist Party had allied with the nationalists of the FLN in the anticolonial struggle, complicating the war and inserting it within both French domestic politics and the increasingly acrimonious East-West conflict. With a French Communist Party highly critical of the Algerian war and its methods, the French army saw the communist threat both at home and in the colony. It pursued the counterrevolutionary war with a ferociousness that responded not only to flickering imperial ambitions and national pride but also to the global anticommunist struggle, an understanding of geopolitics that the French military derived not from American military tutelage, which was minimal, but from its own strategic ruminations and national self-interest.

The Algerian war thus became enmeshed in global Cold War politics. The United States early on had refrained from reducing the Algerian war to a Cold War paradigm and understood the predominantly nationalist—not communist—content of the rebellion by the colony's Muslim population.[20] Rather than the Americans, it was the French who insisted on portraying the insurgency there in such terms, though they did so increasingly in a rather cynical fashion to court continued U.S. support, overcoming initial American doubts about the seriousness of the threat for Cold War geopolitics. Despite the U.S. distaste for European colonialism and its general support for decolonization movements in Africa and elsewhere, the slightest hint of communist subterfuge or even mere interest in a country by the communist bloc was enough to prompt American action. The French had preyed on such American fears first in Viet Nam and then did so again in Algeria. Eventually the Algerians would astutely utilize the phantom communist threat to goad the Americans into a posture critical of the continued French war effort and supportive of independence, convincing them that the prolonged war was itself creating the conditions for communist influence in the French colony.[21] The French had greatly overblown the communist presence in what was overwhelmingly an anticolonial insurrection underpinned by nationalism and religion, which eventually worked against their struggle to retain their North African colony. However, Algeria did create a legacy of equating resistance, armed and otherwise and for diverse reasons, with international Marxist subversion.[22]

The first clear example of the influence of the French counterinsurgency strategy in Argentina was in Tucumán where the ERP had initiated a rural guerrilla insurgency during the Peronist government from 1973 to 1976. A number of Argentine officers had served as military observers in Algeria, among them then lieutenant colonel Alcides López Aufranc, a future prominent figure in the military regime. Others, such as General Reynaldo Bignone, commandant of the Campo de Mayo detention center and the last president of the *Proceso*, had studied counterinsurgency in France's military academies. Bolstered by the 1975 decree signed by the Peronist government authorizing the armed forces to "annihilate" the Tucumán insurgency, the army undertook a multifold campaign that included the targeted killing of ERP members according to their importance in the organization, the torture and interrogations of prisoners to acquire intelligence, and disappearances to avoid the cumbersome, and it was believed risky, recourse to the judicial processing of activists.[23] In accordance with French doctrine, the army complemented the rural counterinsurgency by the stationing of some 1,500 troops in the provincial capital and unleashing a simultaneous urban campaign directed against supporters and even mere sympathizers of the guerrillas fighting in the *monte*.[24] Following the 1976 coup, these tactics were expanded to the country as a whole, especially to the urban areas where the dirty war was largely waged, and the number of disappeared increased exponentially.[25]

Globally, counterinsurgency strategies and tactics had a genealogy that stretched back to the early years of the postwar period. The U.S. Army had published a translation of the Nazis' 1944 manual *Fighting the Guerrilla Bands* and subsequently produced a special series of pamphlets based on the Germans' tactics in fighting against partisans in occupied Europe.[26] Yet it was only with the onset of the Cold War and communist insurgencies in the late 1940s employing guerrilla tactics in Greece, the Philippines, and elsewhere that counterinsurgency came to play a prominent role in U.S. military strategic thinking. The army introduced counterinsurgency for the first time in its officer training courses in 1948 in Fort Leavenworth.[27] After a lull in interest in the 1950s when nuclear war strategies and a largely conventional war waged in Korea dominated military thinking, counterinsurgency doctrine experienced a new urgency with the Cuban Revolution. The success of Fidel Castro's guerrilla campaign against the dictatorship of Fulgencio Batista revealed the ability of guerrilla tactics to overcome overwhelming odds, especially in the former colonial world where the Cold War was increasingly being waged. The subsequent radical turn of the Cuban Revolution, culminating in an alliance with the Soviet Union and the Cuban missile crisis, demonstrated the potential consequences of successful guerrilla tactics in the global Cold War. In

October 1960 the National Security Council ordered the Defense Department to develop a new doctrine for counterinsurgency, a charge subsequently entrusted to the army.[28]

It was at this point that the French experience in Algeria began to influence counterinsurgency doctrine, in the United States as well as other countries, including Argentina. Former officers of the Organisation de l'Armée Secrète (OAS) developed theories on counterinsurgency based on their experience in Algeria's anticolonial war. The French concept of the *guerre revolutionnaire et frontière idéologique*, thereby melding the idea of revolution and a global communist threat into a single doctrine and devising specific tactics to combat it—including the use of torture and psychological warfare—the tactics of even a self-proclaimed *sale guerre* (dirty war), struck a chord with U.S. concerns about Third World insurgencies following the Cuban example.[29] For Latin America, the increased emphasis on counterinsurgency, even in the midst of Kennedy's Alliance for Progress, became apparent as the 1960s progressed.[30] In 1961, the Soviet Union's publicly declared support for so-called wars of national liberation, coming as it did in the days of the Cuban crisis, confirmed the Kennedy administration's new concern for irregular warfare. Latin America emerged as a testing ground for counterinsurgency tactics. Carefully studying Che Guevara's influential manual *On Guerrilla Warfare*, the army also examined recent counterinsurgency operations for guidance. The French experience in Algeria continued to be a lodestar, though France's failed strategy in Viet Nam conversely offered for the U.S. military a model of how not to wage counterinsurgent war.[31] The army's doctrinal statement, the 1963 manual *Counterguerrilla Operations*, followed French thinking with the division of operations into discrete geographic areas and the emphasis on gathering intelligence, though it gave a greater emphasis to population removal, a tactic it would later apply in its "strategic hamlet" policy in Viet Nam.[32] American counterinsurgency did follow the French tradition, as one scholar of its evolution has noted, in yet another way: the idea that the ends justify the means. This could include the arguments of a later defense analyst that even something so apparently odious as a death squad was a legitimate response to terrorism, noting the specific case of Argentina where mass murder, including of innocent family members, had been a sound strategy in combating a revolutionary challenge.[33]

The implications of this interest in counterinsurgency for Latin America and Argentina specifically operated on a number of different levels. There were the direct interventions by the U.S. military and adoption of these tactics in the Dominican Republic in 1965. In Central America, U.S. military advisors were sent to train, and in some cases directly participate in, counterinsurgency operations there in the 1970s and 1980s. For the vast majority of Latin American countries, training and indoctrination at U.S. sites in the Canal Zone and American military bases were the channels of influence. U.S. doctrine was most effectively implemented in those countries with large rural insurgencies, such as El Salvador, Colombia, and Guatemala. In the more urban countries such as Argentina, American methods proved less applicable. Though Cold War indoctrination occurred among the officer corps of these countries, U.S. military influence on precise tactics to combat the Left gave way to the riot control, surveillance, and interrogation methods provided by the CIA and the Office of Public Safety responsible for police training and administered by the Agency for International Development.[34] It is very difficult to make the argument for a direct influence by the U.S. military on the conduct of the dirty war beyond a broad anticommunist indoctrination of some of the officer corps.[35]

How and where precisely then did the U.S. influence appear in the conduct of the dirty war? The Cold War, and specifically the American indoctrination in the East-West bipolar world, though its influence has been exaggerated, nonetheless formed part of the Argentine military's culture and was an essential component of the dirty war. Between 1960 and 1975 some three thousand to four thousand officers studied in American military schools and academies. Though Argentina trailed far behind many countries in the region in terms of absolute numbers indoctrinated, the American influence on some level is undeniable. Among the results was the growth in the influence and prestige of the military's intelligence services and techniques of surveillance, kidnapping, torture, and assassination, though it must be emphasized that these too had an established precedent with the French influence and the tactics of the OAS with their focus on "guerre d'action psychologique."[36] The Psychological Warfare Center at Fort Bragg did continue to transmit French counterinsurgency teachings in the late 1960s and early 1970s at a time when the French military missions' presence declined in Argentina. Yet the French teachings had already been incorporated into the curriculum of the Escuela de Guerra and other officer training programs. Rather than passive recipients of U.S. training in counterinsurgency, the Argentines appear to have already become well versed in the practice of the death squad, indeed recognized as experts by the United States as is well documented in the role played by Argentine military advisers in Central America in the 1980s.[37]

The U.S. role thus seems to have operated more at the level of ideology than specific tactics and overall strategy. Here the U.S. influence was profound. The famous "National Security Doctrine" was itself merely a reconfiguring of the French counterinsurgency theories into a single doctrine with a strictly anticommunist, Cold War focus, adapting the French anticolonial experience to the global confrontation between East and West. The doctrine's guiding idea of the "internal subversive" had long been present in French strategic thinking. Yet the U.S. reconfiguration did give it a more singularly Cold War global dimension, stressing the international character of revolutionary war. In broad strategic terms, this meant emphasizing military responsibility for domestic security. In practical terms it meant foregoing military assistance in the form of state-of-the-art military hardware, often much to the displeasure of some of the military hierarchy, and more emphasis on intelligence gathering, surveillance, and riot control. Included now were also the Latin American police forces whose modernization became a priority and training was administered through the recently established Agency for International Development (AID). National security was essentially to be farmed out to the respective nation-states and their security forces, both military and police. Their guarantee of domestic tranquility was understood as an essential part of the Cold War's waging. Blurring the line between national defense and internal security also perforce sanctioned an increased political role for the Latin American militaries in matters not directly related to defense, such as public administration and the economy.

The transmission of these ideas worked through both national and transnational channels. Nationally, the Colegio Militar offered training courses for officers and the doctrine was disseminated there and in the Escuela Superior de Guerra (ESG) and other officer training academies and programs.[38] The origins of the French influence in counterinsurgency long antedated the dirty war. The curriculum reform undertaken in the ESG beginning around 1957 influenced a generation of officers. The driving force in the dissemination of new theories of counterrevolutionary war there was Col. Carlos Jorge Rosas. As both a professor and vice-director of the ESG, Rosas oversaw a complete overhaul of the army's doctrines. The arrival of a French advisory mission in 1957 had a particular influence on the Argentine army's strategic thinking. The French conception of counterrevolutionary proved more eclectic than that of the Americans would ever be, taking more into account its psychological dimensions in contrast to the American approach that stressed the military and technical aspects of counterinsurgency, and even those conceptualized in very conventional terms.[39] The Argentines would stress even more than the French the nonmilitary aspects of counterinsurgency. The French missions ended around 1962, at which point the U.S. influence became preponderant through officers' training courses, military aid, and participation in hemispheric defense organizations and, to a much lesser extent, joint military exercises. Nonetheless, by that point French theories had been fully incorporated into the ESG curriculum and enjoyed the preeminent prestige among a generation of Argentine officers.[40]

The Argentine army never utilized the American term *counterinsurgency*, preferring alternately *counterrevolutionary war* or *war against subversion*, both employed by the French army and disseminated by the French military missions in Argentina.[41] The idea imbedded in both terms was obviously that of an assault on fundamental values, even on some intrinsic national essence, something beyond an antidote to a particular way of waging war. In this formulation, international communism pursued revolution through subversion and subversion worked on multiple levels: ideological, cultural, as well as military. It also implicated the civilian population, who both harbored and bred the armed revolutionary, as guilty of subversion, thereby blurring or even erasing the distinction between combatant and the rest of society. From these assumptions emerged the obsession with intelligence gathering, which provided not only information of a strictly military nature but also the social networks that harbored and fomented subversive ideas. Such ambitions made the established military intelligence services inadequate and caused the military to greatly expand its intelligence training and create greater numbers of specialized intelligence units while also broadening their responsibilities beyond surveillance and information gathering to intimidation and psychological warfare.[42] The articles that henceforth populated the *Revista de la Escuela Superior de Guerra* and the counterrevolutionary doctrine's most important theoretical statement, Col. Osiris Guillermo Villegas's *Guerra Revolucionaria Comunista* (1962) left no doubt about the impact left by the French on the Argentine military and the army specifically.[43]

Though the French influence on the precise counterrevolutionary strategy and tactics adopted was preponderant, there is no denying that the incubus of the ensemble of ideas, assumptions, and even mere prejudices bundled together in the National Security Doctrine (an elaboration, it must be stressed, of the French ideas in a sharper Cold War key) was the U.S. military. Fort Bragg, Fort Benning, Fort Gordon, Fort Leavenworth, the Inter-American Defense College, and Fort Gulick, popularly known as the School of the Americas in the Canal Zone, divided responsibilities for training in psychological and counterguerrilla warfare, intelligence, propaganda, and other tactical specializations. Permeating all these training missions was the overarching ideological assumptions of the international communist threat, internal subversion, and the legitimacy of irregular warfare to combat them. The manuals prepared jointly by the Pentagon and the CIA included the staples of dirty war tactics: nighttime raids, police cordoning of neighborhoods, and harsh interrogation techniques. At the School of the Americas, the content of U.S. indoctrination and training had the effect, intended or not, of instilling in the Latin American officer corps a broad definition of "subversive" to include all dissidents and a justification of the harshest means at the military's disposal to combat all who threatened national security.[44] Yet examining closely the tactics employed in the years preceding and following the 1976 coup, what stands out is the similarity to the French doctrine. The very decision immediately following the coup to abjure the Chilean precedent of public, mass arrests and executions in favor a secret campaign of clandestine repression, abductions, secret interrogations, and disappearances demonstrated the impact of the French teachings. The U.S. influence on the dirty war was significant, but far from determinative. From its origins through the dirty war's ending, the French legacy weighed far more.

A singular focus on exogenous influences moreover misses the Argentine armed forces' own original strategic thinking and the dominant domestic influences, rooted in Argentine history and the military's institutional culture, that made the dirty war possible. Even the French influence was not borrowed wholesale, spurning, for example, the French model of establishing special forces, commandos within the army to undertake the abductions, and relying instead of a combination of military and civilian so-called *grupos de tarea*. The Argentines adapted French, and to a lesser extent, American strategies to local conditions. They criticized both the French and especially American counterinsurgency strategies for their preoccupation with military strategies at the expense of counterrevolutionary war's political, social, psychological, and cultural dimensions. French and American theories were moreover somewhat tainted by their ultimate defeat in both Algeria and Viet Nam.[45] As a result, the Argentine military developed and eventually implemented its own reconfigured strategy of counterinsurgency, concentrating almost exclusively on intelligence gathering and targeted assassination, mainly by disappearance.

The army's 1969 manual, "Operations against Internal Subversion," and a similar manual by the navy in 1975 are just two of the better-known examples of writings in military journals and internal documents that circulated in the years preceding the dictatorship. Both distilled the methods of counterrevolutionary war and their application to the Argentine context. By nearly all accounts, the strategy for the dirty war had been worked out years before the March 1976 coup, with a final text elaborated by General Cesáreo Cardozo, director of the Escuela Superior de Guerra.[46] Rather than interpreting their dirty war as strictly part of an East-West conflict, the military was more influenced by an immediate guerrilla threat, correctly believed by them to be largely free of foreign direction, as well as its deep anti-Peronist sentiments.[47] The ideological roots of the state terrorism have thus been simplified, exaggerating their Cold War underpinnings while neglecting their strictly Argentine origins. The influence of "ultramontane Catholic nationalists" is one domestic influence ignored by all but a handful of scholars.[48] Though only one faction among the officer corps, the Catholic nationalists nonetheless exercised an influence far beyond their numbers. The role of religion and specifically of an integralist Catholicism sets apart Argentina's experience with military dictatorship from other Latin American countries in the 1960s and 1970s. Here again, in terms of foreign influences, the French were paramount: the writings of French theologians such as Jean Ousset, Jean Madiran, and Michel Crouzet and the reviews *Verbe* and *Cité Catholique* that railed against Marxism, modernism, even democracy were read and influential, including those of French Catholic priests who had participated directly in Algerian war.[49] French priests fresh from the Algerian war nurtured the Ciudad Católica Argentina (CCA), a sister organization of the Cité Catholique, which disseminated an "intransigent Catholicism" and an intense anticommunism to military officers in the Escuela Superior de Guerra and Colegio Militar through its publication, *Verbo*.[50]

Yet even the vital French contribution only added force, precise techniques, and perhaps a bit of Gallic polish to an already established military culture. Federico Finchelstein has traced the ideological origins of the dirty war to what he terms a "Christian fascist" tradition potent in the interwar period, especially within the ranks of the military.[51] The writings of Argentina's own Catholic Far Right intellectuals had penetrated military schools and academies since the 1920s, and their antiliberal, antimodernist, as well as anti-Marxist ideas formed the foundation of much of the Argentine military's worldview. Instead they offered a vision of a corporatist society rooted in a medieval Catholic ethos, deeply nostalgic not only for the past, but for the distant past.[52] After World War II, theologians such as Jordán Bruno Genta, Leonardo Castellani, and the Jesuit Julio Meinvielle influenced several generation of Argentine military officers as much if not more than the ideas imbibed through U.S. training at places like the School of the Americas or Fort Bragg. Genta in particular had an influence on officers in Córdoba where he had taught courses in the early 1960s. A Christian order and national community under threat by cultural elites such as university professors and students, an ensemble of fears and obsessions leavened by a visceral anti-Peronism—these sentiments rather than economic restructuring or even East-West Cold War considerations animated much of Argentina's state terrorism.[53]

Armed with such concepts, the Catholic Church loomed as an essential ally, "la cruz y la espada" so often exalted in nationalist discourse and now aligned in a titanic endeavor as part of a global struggle that the Cold War merely exposed in its terrific magnitude. An ultramontane Catholicism had created a vision of mortal threats to the nation from diverse sources, now wedded to a global power struggle between East and West. In the course of the 1960s, the Church's internal conflicts stemming from Vatican II, the growth of the Third World Priests' movement, and the embrace of a militant, even revolutionary interpretation of Catholicism by the Left, distilled in the highly influential publication *Criterio*, galvanized Church support not only for the dictatorship but for its brutal methods. Juan Carlos Onganía was a figure closely associated with the integralist, nationalist, Catholic current in the armed forces, and his dictatorship represented the final merging of such sentiments with the Cold War bipolar dynamic. The 1976–83 dictatorship openly spoke of its mission as "protector of the Catholic nation," deepening the already close ties between the Church and the military and making unlikely any opposition to the military's tactics and its human rights violations, indeed emerging, with the notable exception of a handful of dissident bishops, as a shameless apologist for the regime.[54] No better example of this religious ethos was Menéndez himself, a devout and "antisecular" Catholic who viewed with abhorrence the values of the modern world, excoriated the influence of the Third World Priests movement and wished to see Argentina embrace an *integralista* Catholicism, with religion and state as one.[55] In Córdoba, given its history as an ecclesiastical center and the Church's social and cultural influence, the tensions within Catholicism were perhaps their most acute as anywhere in the country. When the new military authorities there placed a crucifix in the public university's Salón de Grados, it was more than a telling metaphor; it was s purposeful statement about the primordial role religion should play in both the university and society at large in a Catholic nation.[56]

The *guerra sucia* was also a product of the military's own internal history, beyond training, indoctrination, and ideology. The internal factionalism between *azules* and *colorados* in the army during the 1960s had left deep institutional cleavages. The *azules'* purge of the viscerally anti-Peronist *colorados*, a faction opposed to democracy and in favor of direct military rule, had bequeathed resentments over forced retirements and frustrated promotions that would surface in the 1970s and influence the military's behavior. Leading figures of the post-1976 dictatorship such as future presidents Jorge Rafael Videla and Roberto Viola and essential architects of state terrorism such as Carlos Guillermo Suárez Mason were former *colorados* who survived the purge but, as events would demonstrate, retained much of the original *colorado* ideology.[57] Now in control of the army, they implemented a violent counterrevolutionary war against a population they had long been suspicious of and even hostile to, unfettered now by the democratic scruples of the *azules*.

The vast majority of victims in Argentina's dirty war, in Córdoba as elsewhere, were union activists and members of leftist organizations or individuals believed to be sympathetic to them. The violence was not indiscriminate but carefully targeted. There were some innocent victims with no such ties, the unlucky individual caught in the wrong place at the wrong time, the unfortunate *desaparecido* abducted in a case of mistaken identity or whose name appeared in a Montonero's address book, even the factory manager with no such political sympathies, kidnapped and presumably murdered because of threatening to expose government corruption in a business deal.[58] But these were the tragic exceptions.

Rather than seeing the military as a mere executor of class interests, perhaps a not altogether inaccurate characterization of its praetorian politics between 1955 and 1973, its actions during the dirty war were rooted in very particular institutional obsessions. Its history, internal dynamics, and military culture explain state terrorism better than the explanations as an agent of capitalist restructuring so favored in much of the social science literature on the military.[59] Save in the deregulation of the financial sector, the military government did not faithfully execute neoliberal restructuring. Its control of the defense-related industries in the military industrial complex *fabricaciones militares* and nationalist factions within the armed forces worked against wholesale privatization of the public sector and call into question structuralist explanations for the dictatorship.[60] In Latin America generally, lacking a credible external threat, the military saw internal subversion as the regional expression of international communist aggression. Yet in Argentina especially the concerns went beyond leftist militants and sympathizers to include the peculiar subversive influences that Marxism was seen to represent—on the family, on religion, on order and the integrity of the nation.

Subversion conceived in these terms represented not so much an aggression as an infiltration, a virus infecting the national organism, one contrary to national traditions and therefore an immediate threat to the country's armed forces, seen as both a repository and protector of those traditions. The Marxist subversive threat was one of values and some kind of immutable national essence. A "war" against it was therefore relentless, without clear temporal limits, and to the death, with no thought of compromise, no "détente" or coexistence possible, much as it was not for the Left it combated. Total war therefore also meant total annihilation. In the Southern Cone, far from the centers of direct Cold War conflict in the Caribbean basin, such a broad if somewhat diffuse understanding of communist subversion was particularly potent and helps explain the similarities in the so-called dirty wars of the period in the region and the nature of counterrevolution there, with its abductions, torture, and disappearances.[61] In Argentina, such concerns built on a previous history of loathing and repression of revolutionary groups, dating all the way back to the repression unleashed against anarchists early in the twentieth century and stretching in a violent arc to the dirty war against New Left groups in the 1970s.

Its terrible "war" of annihilation against subversion won, the military government confronted in subsequent years an erosion of its power, international isolation, and growing domestic criticism, albeit largely confined initially to a small but vocal human rights movement. The 1982 Falklands-Malvinas war, this one a conventional war it was not prepared to wage, merely hastened its exit from power. Yet even with its greatly weakened state and acrimonious internal feuds and finger pointing following the disastrous war with the British, the military imagined a transition to democracy staged largely on its own terms. The so-called Delta Document, a disingenuous apologia for its campaign against what it now labeled "terrorism" and a brazen denial of its methods of torture and disappearances, also preached a national "reconciliation" intended to exempt the armed forces from future investigation and prosecution.[62] Plans to disseminate the document and launch a publicity campaign justifying the military government's actions reveal the degree to which the country's former military rulers were on the defensive and concerned about future repercussions in a restored democracy.[63] But old habits died hard. In the final months of its tattered rule, the junta viewed the capture and death of a reputed Montonero, Raúl Clemente Yager, in a confrontation in Córdoba as a fortuitous opportunity to exploit for propaganda purposes, with

Yager supposedly in possession of documents revealing the continued existence of the subversive menace.[64] Whatever the veracity of the military's rendering of the event, the moment for waging war against subversion had passed; what awaited the military for the next thirty years was a demand for accountability and justice for its methods during the dirty war.

6

FIVE TRIALS

Public Reckonings of a Violent Past

We are the first country in the history of the world to judge its victorious soldiers who struggled and prevailed for the safety of its fellow citizens.
—GENERAL LUCIANO BENJAMÍN MENÉNDEZ

The fall of the dictatorship in 1983 brought with it a period of national introspection and demands for justice for the crimes committed. Considerable moral ambiguity, even contradictions, surrounded the process of indicting and bringing to trial the former junta members who had presided over the state terrorism. The crimes of the previous decade were restricted to those of the dictatorship. Little mention was made of the violent tactics of the Left including the assassination of trade union leaders, business executives, as well as military and police officers that had preceded and contributed to the lawless, sinister response of the security forces. Nor did the trials ultimately extend beyond the military leadership into the lower ranks, the actual perpetrators of most of the acts of torture and other crimes associated with the abductions and disappearances. Thanks to the two amnesty laws of the Alfonsín government, one establishing a statute of limitations on indictments (Full Stop Law) and another exempting those simply following orders (Dutiful Obedience Law) from prosecution, justice stayed within carefully prescribed limits. Yet the trials were an enormous achievement, an unprecedented attempt to hold the military accountable for its actions, for crimes that surpassed anything Argentina had ever known before from any of its military governments. Unlike the case of their French mentors whose crimes in Algeria had been exonerated in a broad amnesty, the Argentine military's crimes would not go unpunished.[1] The final outcome of the trial with guilty verdicts for most of the accused and long prison sentences imposed, marked a decisive moment in the history of human rights and accountability for crimes against humanity (*crímenes de lesa humanidad*), not only in Argentina but in the entire world.[2]

The subsequent trajectory of justice and accountability was more checkered. The amnesty laws, in great measure coerced by an insubordinate, seditious military unwilling to accept responsibility for its actions but very willing to destabilize and even overthrow a democratically elected government, did represent a step backwards for the rule of law in Argentina. An even more detrimental pardon by Alfonsín's successor to the presidency, Carlos Menem, of the junta members already tried and serving prison sentences as well as those under indictment all but bestowed legitimacy for what the military now vindicated alternately as the "war against subversion" and the "dirty war." The Menem pardons, the product of some one hundred executive decrees during the ten years of Menem's presidency, led to a decade in which the human rights issue as state policy was virtually moribund. As with the Alfonsín amnesty laws, only those accused of the abduction and trafficking of children and babies and of the illicit appropriation of private property were excluded from the pardons. A 2001 federal court decision during the brief *Alianza* government (1999–2001) declaring unconstitutional the Full Stop and Dutiful Obedience laws remained a dead letter in the face of an executive power intent on burying the human rights issue.

With the ascension of Nestor Kirchner to the presidency in 2003 the issue of the crimes of the former military government came again to the forefront of Argentine politics and reappeared in the public's conscience. The decision to repeal Alfonsín's amnesty laws and resume trials, extending them beyond the military leadership to the lower ranks, the police, and civilian accomplices, rode on a wave of renewed indignation and demands for justice, stoked both by human rights groups and the new government. Even prior to Kirchner's ascension to power, Argentine courts had begun dismantling the amnesty laws and pardons of the Alfonsín and Menem years. Relying on the use of his country's universal jurisdiction statute, Spanish judge Baltasar Garzón requested extradition and tried naval officer Alfredo Scilingo for crimes against Spanish nationals. Argentine courts in 2001 subsequently overturned the Full Stop and Dutiful Obedience Laws, and in 2004 the Supreme Court ruled that a 1994 amendment to the country's constitution held that the country's international treaties on human rights superseded national law on crimes against humanity.[3]

These rulings and the subsequent actions of the Kirchner government opened the floodgates to litigation. By July 2010, 435 criminal proceedings resulting from human rights violations during the dictatorship had begun and 1,234 persons had been declared suspects subject to pretrial investigations. Of these, 419 persons were actually charged.[4] Five years later, the number of trials stood at 500 with 600 convictions and 1,000 others indicted. HIJOS (Hijos e Hijas por la Identidad y la Justicia contra el Olvido y el Silencio), first established in La Plata in 1995 with chapters to soon emerge throughout the country, initially composed of the children of the victims of the state terrorism but eventually including former political prisoners and exiles and even common citizens, became a driving force in the process of recovering the memory of those years and demanding new indictments. At the same time, the Kirchner government supported the establishment of archives, monuments, and museums, converting both the navy's ESMA and La Perla, two of the death camps, into public sites devoted to displaying the horrors of the state terrorism and memorializing its victims.

Procedurally, the new trials were markedly different from those of the Alfonsín era. After stonewalling by the military courts and their refusal to hold their brothers in arms accountable for egregious crimes, Alfonsín passed the indictments and lawsuits to the federal court system and appointed two federal prosecutors to make the case against the military. Argentina was thus not to repeat the recent experience of Greece with the efficacious justice carried out by the military itself following that country's dictatorship. Argentina entered unchartered waters under Alfonsín, which perhaps helps explain the limits imposed on the human rights question, including the passage of the two amnesty laws. In the Kirchner trials, far more extensive in their scope, indictments and trials took place at the provincial level through the federal appeals courts, a remarkable decentralization of the judicial process but one that led to a somewhat improvised and even arbitrary quality to the proceedings, particularly in the first years of the renewed trials. Common procedural steps were not agreed upon, not even common criteria of what constituted torture, and the trials' outcomes were uneven, with a wide variance in the integrity and effectiveness of the judicial process depending on extraneous factors such as the influence of the local human rights movement and the strength of the local military presence.[5]

The Kirchner trials, stretching over more than a decade, allowed new evidence to be discovered and introduced as well as the gradual establishment of some common procedural norms through the Ministerio Público Fiscal (Office of Public Prosecutions), though local conditions continued to influence mightily the trials and their outcomes. Beginning in 2010, oral hearings with witnesses emerged as the common procedure in trials throughout the country with the litigants represented in both individual and class action suits. HIJOS continued to be the most active in sponsoring such lawsuits, both as a plaintiff and in providing lawyers who are members of the organization to represent individual victims.[6] The number of defendants increased exponentially, no longer limited to the military commanders but moving down the ranks to include those who had direct involvement in the human rights crimes and including police and civilian collaborators. Other differences from the Alfonsín-era trials was the voluminous, graphic testimony of the victims, the trials of the 1980s having concentrated on what happened to the fate of the *desaparecidos* rather than the sufferings of survivors and families of victims of state terrorism. The Kirchner-era trials also openly acknowledged, indeed extolled, the political identities of the victims, kept hidden during the Alfonsín trials under the cloud of the

CONADEP (Comisión Nacional sobre la Desaparición de Personas) truth commission's "dos demonios" (two devils or twin evils) thesis, which held the military dictatorship and the Left equally responsible for the human rights abuses but with the government and prosecuting attorneys reluctant to sully the memory of those murdered by the regime and provide grounds for the defense.[7] Only the trials and convictions of a small number of the former Montonero leadership—Mario Firmenich, Roberto Perdía, and Fernando Vaca Narvaja—brought into the open and in the judicial realm the political affiliations of that sector of the Left included as part of the *dos demonios* thesis during the Alfonsín presidency.

As in the 1980s, the human rights issue contained many contradictions. Both the Kirchner government and human rights organizations proved indifferent or at least reluctant to undertake a broader and necessary debate about the causes of the state terrorism, leaving it reduced in many ways to a simple morality play of sadistic torturers and innocent victims. There were certainly plenty of both, but the crimes of the dictatorship responded to a cluster of complex institutional, national, and transnational influences that begged for a rigorous explanation worthy of the scale of the tragedy. In what has been described as the "Holocaustization" of state terrorism, the Kirchner government's very loose if deliberate use of the word *genocide* to describe the military's crimes added dramatic rhetorical flourish to a history of abuse, murder, and mayhem but obfuscated the real nature of state terrorism and a deeper understanding of its causes. Though not their intended purpose, the new wave of trials did nonetheless provide details on which to begin to offer an explanation, at least as they relate to the state terrorism of these years if not the political violence generally of the period.

The Kirchner trials did not match the high drama of those of the junta in the Alfonsín years and certainly attracted much less international attention, but in their scope, both geographic and institutional, they were unique and far reaching. During the Alfonsín administration, with judicial appointees held over from the former dictatorship, Cordoba's courts brazenly had ruled to dismiss all charges against Menéndez. Local military justice had also contributed to Menéndez's freedom from prosecution, exonerating his actions during the dictatorship. At one point the commander in charge of the local military tribunal, Colonel Timoteo Gordillo, claimed *desaparecidos* named in the CONADEP report were actually exiles living in Mexico, as revealed by a list of 129 Argentine victims compiled by the Argentine embassy after the 1985 Mexico City earthquake, a claim vehemently denied by Alfonsín's government.[8] An attempt to indict him in 1998 by the local Federal Appeals Court, the so-called Verdad Histórica lawsuit, ended stillborn in January 2003 when a local judge overturned previous rulings of "unconstitutionality" of the amnesty laws and pardons. Menéndez thus walked a free man for two decades.

The new charges brought against him therefore had added significance, given a previous long period of immunity from prosecution. Judicial proceedings against

Menéndez commenced in Tucumán and Mendoza, both part of the Third Corps' vast zone of operations. In Córdoba, five separate trials subsequently took place, each with Menéndez as a central figure, under the recently elected Kirchner government. The local chapter of HIJOS provided the impetus for the litigation as they sought out local lawyers such as Claudio Orosz and Kirchner's future secretary of human rights, Martin Fresneda, who were willing to represent them in a lawsuit against Menéndez and other perpetrators.[9] The first trial, dubbed "Menéndez I," took place between May and July 2008 and led to sentences of life imprisonment for Menéndez and seven other defendants accused of human rights abuses during the dictatorship. The second suit, an eight-week trial called "Menéndez II," brought by another group of victims in 2009 against six former military and police officers, again led to a sentence of life imprisonment for Menéndez.[10]

The following year, the third and most important of these trials up until that point, dubbed "UP1," saw not only Menéndez on trial but former president and junta member, Gen. Jorge Rafael Videla, along with twenty-nine other accused, both military and police officials, making it the largest human rights trial to date to take place in Argentina. UP1 involved the execution of thirty-one political prisoners in the federal penitentiary (Unidad Penitenciaria Número Uno) located in the city's San Martín neighborhood. UP1 had come under the direct control of the army on April 2, 1976, for a period of eight months, the period when all thirty-one political prisoners were murdered. Videla's culpability in the UP1 suit stemmed from the fact that as president the political prisoners were under his direct authority and he was responsible for their fate. Political prisoners in the country's federal prison system were held separately and treated somewhat differently than were common criminals and indeed than those political captives held in detention centers such as La Perla. Some minimal visitation rights, for example, were granted to prisoners classified as "special detainees" in the federal prisons, rights unknown to those held secretly in the detention centers.[11] The treatment otherwise was equally brutal, until the dictatorship began recognizing the legal status of prisoners in the federal penitentiary system as the worst phase of the state terrorism was coming to an end. The UP1 executions occurred in the months immediately following the March 1976 coup at various moments between April and October 1976 and later falsely justified as the result of failed escape attempts by the prisoners. With the amnesty laws repealed in 2003, the case against Videla, Menéndez, and other police and prison personnel defendants began to be assembled, and a suit was filed in March 2010. A separate case involving the imprisonment and torture in the federal penitentiary of former police officers accused of subversive activities, the so-called Gontero Case, would be combined with the other in a common lawsuit.[12]

The trials began with the controversial indictment of the twenty-nine former military and police officers to be tried together with Videla and Menéndez. Such a decision was partially due to judicial expediency, the prospect of prolonged trials

FIGURE 12. Federal penitentiary Unidad Penitenciaria Número Uno (UP1).

FIGURE 13. UP1 front entry.

for each of the accused individuals beyond the means of the already overburdened court system in Córdoba. Yet it also conveniently served as a symbol, an open repudiation of the logic of the now repealed Dutiful Obedience law, holding equally responsible commanders and subordinates for the crimes of the dirty war. By including accused police officers and not confining the trial to the military, it was also intended to emphasize the complicity of the security forces beyond the military's ranks and even to open a debate, barely begun, about the broader institutional and even societal role in the repression. For Menéndez, this was his third trial, having been convicted in 2009 and condemned to life imprisonment for kidnappings, torture, and murder of prisoners in the D-2 detention center. The previous year in Córdoba, the same sentence had followed a conviction for crimes committed there, the so-called Menéndez I or Brandalisis trial, named for Humberto Horacio Brandalisis and three fellow members of the Partido Revolucionario de los Trabajadores (PRT) kidnapped and murdered in 1977, which began in May 2008 and ended in July of that same year with a conviction and the first of his life sentences. In both cases, Menéndez's defense consisted of rejecting the jurisdiction of the civilian courts and demands that the defendant be tried by a military tribunal.[13]

The Videla-Menéndez or UP1 trial began in July 2010. For Videla, this was the first and only time he would be tried in Córdoba. The trial would last some six months, hear the testimony of some 120 witnesses, and lead to convictions for the majority of the accused including life sentences for both Videla and again for Menéndez and fifteen other defendants. The defense lawyers early in the trial presented an ingenious and, for the court, uncomfortable defense: the claim that the federal courts during the dictatorship had sanctioned the activities of a number of the defendants that the prosecution charged as criminals. By shifting responsibility to the craven court system, the defense not only transferred blame; it also sought to discredit the entire judicial process by exposing the institution's complicity in the state terrorism.[14] The defense failed to work, but it did cast a light on the failings of the court system during the dictatorship and raised the issue of a broader societal complicity in the state terrorism.

The UP1 trial concerned the execution of some thirty-one political prisoners over a period of several months between April and October 1976. Imprisonment in the federal penitentiary and therefore a formal legal status eventually provided some degree of protection, but not so in the early months of the dictatorship. The execution of the UP1 prisoners originally was to form part of the case for crimes against humanity in the 1985 trials of the ruling juntas, but, for reasons never explained, was left out. The trial of some six months' duration had a few dramatic moments, such as the appearance of Spanish judge Baltasar Garzón who attended one day of the proceedings, encountering heckling there from the military families present at the hearings and a collective withdrawal of the defendants from the courtroom in protest.[15] Mostly, though, the trial comprised lengthy testimonies of victims and their families of similar accounts of terror and torture, later repeated by the plaintiffs' attorneys in their formal allegations, which gained a certain dreadful monotony as days, weeks, and months passed. Throughout the trial the accused maintained a stony silence, occasionally interrupted by obscene gestures and insults hurled at witnesses and their families. Menéndez and Videla offered spirited albeit brief defenses of their actions at the trial's conclusion, but these were the only deviations from the defendants' pact of silence.[16]

Most significant was the intervention of Menéndez in the next trial. In the fourth trial Menéndez, for the only time in the judicial proceedings, sat alone as the defendant. This particular trial involved the arrest and murder, at Menéndez's orders, in June 1976 of three university students who were also activists in the Juventud Universitaria Peronista (JUP). Responsibility for the arrest and executions fell to the Comando Radioélectrico, the motorized division of the Córdoba police, whose members were tried and found guilty in a separate criminal trial in 2012.[17] The new trial, dubbed Menéndez IV, was on a much smaller scale than the preceding three human rights trials in Córdoba, involving only Menéndez and a single plaintiff, the brother of one of the murdered students. Perhaps for that very reason it provided Menéndez the opportunity to speak at length and articulate most clearly his defense of his conduct in Córdoba's dirty war (see appendix 3). Before sentencing, Menéndez exercised his right to speak. His words distilled both his rationale for the dirty war and his duplicity in its defense. Menéndez framed his defiant justification for his actions, including an abortive rebellion against Videla, as a defense of democracy and personal freedoms, including outlandish and false claims that all, or almost all, political prisoners had been tried in the federal court system. Menéndez's spirited and indeed truculent defense was to little avail. The trial brought him yet another life sentence.[18]

In December 2012 had already begun the fifth, longest, and most complicated of the human rights trials in Córdoba and in Argentina, one that addressed the egregious crimes committed at the La Perla and Campo de la Ribera detention centers and in which Menéndez again was among the accused. With 45 defendants, 417 plaintiffs (including 162 survivors of the two detention centers), 900 witnesses, and a vast number of individual charges against the accused, the trial would last almost four years and represented an unprecedented expense and administrative effort. Eighteen of the defendants were former military personnel, eighteen others onetime police officers, along with several civilian collaborators who had worked for the intelligence services. As the trial progressed, new defendants and plaintiffs were added. A year and a half into the trial, the number of defendants had risen to fifty-two and the plaintiffs to almost seven hundred.[19] The most common charges were those of the unlawful deprivation of liberty, the infliction of aggravated torments, and homicide.[20] The trial had at its center the actions

FIGURE 14. Defendant Luciano Benjamín Menéndez, Menéndez IV trial.

of the Operaciones de Inteligencia (OP3) of the Third Army Corps' Destacamento de Inteligencia 141. The OP3 operated first out of the Campo de la Ribera, and then after the March 1976 coup moved its operations to La Perla. Procedurally, the decision to combine so many defendants, numerous victims, and crimes in a so-called *megacausa* (a class action lawsuit against multiple defendants) was unique in Argentina's human rights trials. The rationale for such a massive judicial process was to avoid both an almost endless process of litigation and to subject witnesses to providing emotionally traumatic testimony multiple times.

Four years of proceedings, interrupted at various moments for procedural reasons, put the leading figures of Córdoba's state terrorism on trial together for the first time. In addition to Menéndez, the defendants included Jorge Exequiel Acosta, Guillermo Ernesto Barreiro, and Héctor Pedro Vergez from the army; Miguel Angel (Gato) Gómez of the police; and a handful of civilians from the intelligence services such as Ricardo Lardone. The initial, prolonged phase of the trial was monopolized by the prosecution, a procession of witnesses testifying, each with harrowing tales of abduction, torture, and murder over a period of some three years, a drawn-out process that dulled the emotional impact found in some of the previous trials. The trials did have some dramatic highpoints, such as when a fellow unindicted military officer who testified for the plaintiffs denied the state of "war" at the time of disappearances and death camps, eliciting an angry response from Menéndez in the courtroom.[21] Mostly though, the trial consisted of a long succession of witnesses and PowerPoint presentations by the prosecuting attorneys elaborating the individual biographies and the dire fate of the state terrorism's victims.

When it came to the defense's turn, the accused relied almost solely on a single argument: a state of war in the country and the status of the victims as combatants. Such a defense might have seemed self-defeating and could come back to haunt them, subjecting the defendants later to international tribunals and the Geneva Convention for having committed war crimes. The calculus, one can surmise, was that the advanced age of the defendants and procedural delays would prevent that from ever happening. The immediate and real threat was conviction by Argentine courts and lengthy prison sentences. The sudden and unexpected death of the leading defense attorney, Osvaldo Viola, in late November 2015 threw the trial into a tailspin. Viola had served as a stalwart and spirited defense lawyer in previous trials, and his presence lent the proceedings legitimacy, deflecting military criticisms of being merely show trials. The court-appointed attorneys to replace him continued the line of defense that Viola and others had chartered in previous trials, emphasizing the supposed state of war then existing in the country at the time and the status of the victims as combatants. Such a defense proved shaky on many grounds, including the inconvenient fact that the vast majority of the disappeared were not members of guerrilla organizations but students, workers, and political activists. The trials of the 1980s had already rejected the "superior orders" defense for acts that were manifestly illegal such as rape, robbery, and the killing of noncombatants in custody.[22] Defense attorneys had few available arguments to counteract the years of graphic testimony verifying that such criminal acts were routine hallmarks of state terrorism.

As was true in the trials from the 1980s, the prosecution's case was hampered by the absence of any incriminating written evidence on the part of the military commanders for the crimes perpetrated. Even orders for the murder of a detainee were obliquely expressed as a "transfer," the generals apparently aware of the legal protection afforded by a new lexicon.[23] In the absence of any paper trail, the La Perla trial and the four that preceded it thus came to rely on almost exclusively on a preponderance of oral testimony, so overwhelming in its sheer volume and horrific in its details that it stood as an indictment and proof of guilt.

Not everyone viewed the human rights trials positively. Some called for, in the name of an equitable justice, that former Montoneros and *erpistas* found among the ranks of the accusers to stand trial as well for crimes committed, including kidnapping and assassinations of business executives, union leaders, as well as military officers. Dissenting voices on trial proceedings generally included leading intellectuals such as Luis Alberto Romero, perhaps the country's most renowned historian, who lambasted the trials for violating judicial norms and even condemning innocent

FIGURE 15. Defendants, La Perla–Campo de la Ribera trial.

individuals in an indiscriminate "roundup" that served no other purpose than *revanchismo* and *kirchnerista* political theater. Romero supported the trials in principle but criticized rumored procedural irregularities and the Kirchners' political opportunism, for ignoring the previous progress of the rival UCR's (Unión Cívica Radical) Alfonsín on human rights and weaving a fictitious narrative that portrayed Nestor and Cristina Kirchner as longtime human rights activists.[24] At least in the case of Córdoba, criticisms of procedural irregularities seem unfounded. The defendants were indicted on specific charges; the presiding judges, led by highly respected judge Jaime Díaz Gavier, scrupulously followed correct judicial proceedings; defendants had competent defenses; and there were even acquittals.

Another criticism by Romero had more merit: the lengthy trials in Córdoba failed to undertake complete justice for all crimes committed and also to live up to their promise as a record for posterity and potential source for historians, weakening their ability to fully account for Argentina's descent into violence. The pact of silence by the indicted military and police, the ones in the best position to cast some light on the terrorist state in Córdoba—punctuated only by occasional outbursts such as that of Menéndez in the Menéndez IV trial—stripped the years of trials of their potential as a historical record. The excruciating, detailed testimony of survivors and family members stretching over an nine-year period, for all its pathos and cathartic value for the witnesses and family members, acquired a repetitive, almost numbing quality. Necessary to hold accountable the military government for its terrible crimes, the trials ultimately were vitiated by the unwillingness of those indicted to testify, demonstrating the same brazen contempt for human rights and democracy that they had practiced to terrible effect during the years of the dirty war. Moreover, by confining the indicted defendants strictly to the perpetrators of state terrorism and not including acts of homicide and other crimes perpetrated by private groups and individuals, the trials proved to be highly partisan and limited in their pursuit of exemplary justice and in reasserting the rule of law in a country where both had been debased and hollowed out by multiple actors.

Despite such limitations, the La Perla–Campo de la Ribera trial especially was an enormous achievement for human rights in Argentina. By the time of the sentencing, eleven of the original defendants, all now old men in their seventies and eighties, had already died, depriving the plaintiffs the satisfaction of a complete accountability and full justice. For the remaining defendants, half held in prison and half under house arrest, the verdict came on August 25, 2016. In an atmosphere of frayed nerves, rancor, and intense emotions of all kinds, twenty-eight of the defendants, including Menéndez, were given life sentences while another ten were given reduced sentences between two and a half and twenty years, virtual life sentences for them as well given the advanced age of all the accused. There were five acquittals. Two of the commanders who once reigned with pitiless terror in the La Perla death camp, Ernesto Barreiro and Héctor Pedro Vergez, received their first life sentences. The verdicts were read to a packed courthouse and broadcast to the thousands waiting outside on a large screen, the nearly four years of the trial ending with massive popular support and emotion but also with a pervasive sense that an era had come to an end in Córdoba's pursuit of justice for the crimes committed.

7

___

REMEMBERING

Memories of Violence and Terror

Silence is health.

—GOVERNMENT BILLBOARD SIGN (BUENOS AIRES, 1974)

Histories of Latin American dictatorship, state terrorism, and human rights violations in the postwar era have largely been ethnographic: memory studies of societal trauma as conveyed through oral testimonies of victims and family members.
This literature has both enriched our understanding and limited it. Oral history
has conveyed the scale of human tragedy, but also the slips in recollection and both
the manipulation and constructive purpose of memory as newly established
democracies grappled with the twin and not always compatible pursuits of carrying out justice for crimes committed and rebuilding democratic practices.[1] What
they have tended to miss are the historian's overriding concerns for causation,
societal as opposed to solely individual experiences, and change over time. To
ignore the personal testimonies of those who lived the terror of these years at its
most intimate and excruciating would be an act of intellectual arrogance, not to
mention callous insensitivity to other human beings' suffering. But to rely solely
on such testimonies, to be content only with personal narratives even of the most
compelling kind, avoids the enormously daunting but not impossible task of
explaining the violence and terror of those years.

The oral histories of the state terrorism in Argentina, of the military's dirty war,
are so vast in number and variegated that they daunt the historian's purpose of
discerning patterns and commonalities from the particular. They span the thousands of testimonies in the CONADEP (Comisión Nacional sobre la Desaparición
de Personas) truth commission report, to the vast repository of testimonies in the
Memoria Abierta project, to a lengthy published collection of testimonies by survivors of the La Perla death camp, to a smaller but more focused collection of oral
histories in Córdoba's Archivo Provincial de la Memoria, to an even more reduced

number of circumscribed interviews personally conducted by the author. As the vast literature on memory has rightly concluded, though memory seems the most private and personal of things, it is actually a publicly contested terrain whose appropriation has deep and broad societal and political consequences. Different narratives compete to claim the past, and the outcome of that competition determines the range of future possibilities any society will face. This is especially true of societies where memory engages terrible, tragic events: a natural disaster, a war, a genocide. In Argentina, human rights organizations have succeeded most in establishing that narrative. Others have contributed as well. Raúl Alfonsín's 1983 electoral campaign, the CONADEP truth commission report, the subsequent trial of the junta, and the resurrection of the junta's crimes by the Kirchners in the first decade of the new century all played their part in constructing a narrative, an emotionally powerful, even ethical and functional narrative, though one also simplistic historically, stripped of any complexities and contradictions. That narrative has decidedly shaped social memory and the testimonies of those most directly affected by the violence of those years.

Anthropology is predictably the discipline that has most engaged the question of memory and violence. One anthropologist who has studied the specific case of Argentina has warned of the dangers of "ethnographic seduction" in which interlocutors manipulate the anthropologist through narrative strategies and even empathy, thereby distorting memory and undermining fieldwork.[2] Other anthropologists express no such doubts and offer distinct paradigms to explain Argentina's experience with state terrorism, all of which in one way or another are concerned with "problematizing the political, social, and psychological meanings" of violence.[3] This same anthropologist proposes subliminal, psychological motivations for the terror, even a "paranoid ethos"; the military's wildly exaggerated fears of infiltration from international Marxism, Zionism, and others intent on Argentina's corruption and subordination. Different psychological wellsprings also explain the behavior and memories of the victims of the terror, including denial and a truncated mourning process resulting from the disappearances and "the absence of a corpse to ritually mourn."[4] Other anthropologists, more modestly, seek simply to convey meaning using the familiar linguistic and ethnographic tools of cultural anthropology. All form part of their discipline's relatively recent interest in issues of war, violence, and genocide. Such fieldwork strives to understand the cultural framing of violence, how those who perpetrate it and especially those who suffer it understand that violence's meaning in their lives as lived in the past, in the moment, and projected into the future.[5]

Historians, especially oral historians, have grappled with such subjects for some time. In the Latin American case, the military dictatorships, civil wars, and human rights abuses of the region's revolutionary decades from the 1960s through the 1980s have produced a rich corpus of literature. Chile's experience with a dictatorship contemporary with Argentina's, that of Augusto Pinochet's regime, has provided the most insightful, subtle studies of memory. In addition to Steve Stern's cited volumes, both Chilean and foreign historians place memory, traumatic memory, at the forefront of Chile's recent history, history writing, and its use in reconciliation and democratization.[6]

There exist various attempts to collect, organize, and interpret memories of the dirty war. A vast oral history project, Memoria Abierta (Open Memory), sponsored by various human rights organizations has collected hundreds of testimonies of former political prisoners and family members of the disappeared, all victims in one way of another of the state terrorism. For Córdoba, the Archivo Provincial de la Memoria has undertaken a smaller project that provides a rich social narrative on the history of the period regionally. It too has confined itself to the victims of the dirty war. Memory for victims, those who suffered from it first hand and family members who lost loved ones, inevitably revolves around questions of trauma.

Studies on Córdoba's specific experience with state terrorism remain rare. One of the few forays into local memory, *Vivencias frente al límite*, is a compendium of testimonies around such themes as abductions, mourning, and exhumations. Memory in Argentina's dirty war has also had a pronounced familial content, almost a monopoly of those most affected by the state terrorism rather than a societal good and cause for self-examination and criticism.[7] Survivors and family members offer vivid memories of loss, of youthful idealism turned to blind terror, of truncated grief, of a lingering sadness and anger. For all the pathos conveyed in such testimonies, there is nonetheless an absence of historical context: memory often seems uprooted from its political and cultural moorings, serves a useful role as therapy, of individual catharsis, but is frequently historically flat. It is so through no fault of the editors, who handle the interviews deftly, much less through the moving, vivid memories of those interviewed, but simply because memory, though able to communicate the trauma of history, is insufficient, standing alone, to convey its complexities.[8] There is no shortage of oral histories of the state terrorism of the dictatorship. Indeed, thanks to the *Nunca más* truth commission report alone, we have thousands of them. They provide a wealth of detail on the military's crimes but are less satisfactory in providing an explanation for them. Select ones do, however, provide insights absent in the archival record.

For Córdoba, the most comprehensive attempt to reconstruct if not interpret memory is a thick collection of testimonies by the survivors of the La Perla death camp.[9] The testimonies brim with details about the abductions, the torments suffered, the cherished memories of lost loved ones and comrades. The volume forms part of an ongoing struggle over the legacy of Argentina's violent decade, in Córdoba's case complicated by a Peronist governor during the Kirchner years, José Manuel de la Sota, and much of a local Peronist political class hostile to an emerging narrative of the *guerra sucia*. Córdoba's Peronist politicians have faced the uncomfortable truth of the 1973–76 Peronist government's complicity in the first stages of the state terrorism, often directed at Peronist militants from the movement's own left wing. Córdoba's Peronists have bristled at the charges of human rights organizations dominated by activists drawn from sundry leftist parties and groups. Even *kirchnerismo*, though technically Peronist, was seen as comprising leadership drawn from the very leftist sectors of Peronism persecuted first by the 1973–76 Peronist government and then by the military dictatorship that followed. Controversy surrounding the human rights trials in Cordoba stood as only one expression of escalating tensions between local Peronists and *kirchnerismo*'s human rights policies.

The La Perla volume offers much that refines and even corrects established notions of the horrors of the death camp. Ana "la Turca" Mohaded, an activist in the small Marxist organization, Poder Obrero, recounts the practice, apparently unique to Córdoba, of rotating transfers from the local detention centers, prisons, and death camp: Christmas of 1976 was spent in a prison cell in Campo de La Ribera and New Year's in a cell in the penitentiary in the San Martín neighborhood (UP1). From there began a long journey through Córdoba's jails and clandestine centers; from the UP1 to the Police Department of Information (D2), back to the UP1 and then to the Perla Chica (Malagüeño), back to the D-2 again, and from there to the Campo de La Ribera (in the second half of 1978 on the occasion of the inspection of international human rights organizations), transferred subsequently to the UP1 and later to the Buen Pastor (Good Shepherd) women's prison, and from there to the Villa Devoto penitentiary in Buenos Aires. Each move brought with it the *capucha* (hood), beatings, and an "invitation" from the guards to attempt to escape for purposes of executing her in a staged escape.[10]

Some former prisoners astutely noted the perceived peculiarities of Córdoba's experience with state terrorism. Patricia Astelarra cogently observed that

> the concentration camps did not appear in a void, nor were they aberrations isolated from the genocidal social practices in their totality. In diverse ways, Argentina operated as a concentration camp, the essence of state terrorism. In Córdoba the repression was ferocious and the power of the assassin-in-chief of the Third Corps and his troops remained intact for a long time. Social movements and human rights organizations, except Familiares de Desaparecidos y Detenidos por Razones Políticas, emerged and became consolidated in Buenos Aires before they did in Córdoba, and that deserves study. Very early on Córdoba had mobilized over the abhorrent crimes of the Comando Libertadores de América, there were strikes, protests, but after the coup everything went silent, an inability to recover from a repression of such magnitude. Society's condemnation marched slowly, as did the judicial process.[11]

Former prisoners relate the physical abuse and torture suffered in graphic detail, also conveying the often arbitrary, terrifying absurdity of the torture session. In one particularly horrendous testimony, Cecilia Suzzara recalls her torment in a second round of torture:

> They removed the blindfold, they wanted me to see them. They continued with the electric shocks, combining the *picana* with lashes to my stomach with a thick leather belt. Fortunately for me, the interrogation was incoherent, the torturers interspersing long tirades on their political philosophy and their duty as "enlightened soldiers of western and Christian civilization" who were combating evil, the evil represented obviously by my very person. That session lasted various hours. I think they got tired again. They left me lying in the big hall, in the *cuadra*, on a straw mattress, with my body numb. I could hear murmuring, steps, distant screams. . . . The worst was yet to come. I was about to meet the cruelest torturer in La Perla: "Texas," staff sergeant Elpidio Tejeda. Soon I understood that all the preceding had been a mere prelude. The punishment with the rod, with the club, was the most atrocious that one could imagine, its effect intensified by the terrifying setting that Texas created with his shouting. The physical torment began upon being dragged to an office with hands tied in front. They removed the blindfold in order for me to see their violent expressions, this seemed part of the technique. Then Texas, with sunglasses of the kind with mirrors for lenses, began to beat me. He did it in a precise way, rhythmically, with a small, dark wooden club, about fifty centimeters in length. He shouted and said that he had to come to get results, that the fooling around and wasted time were over. With each blow, a shout. This time there was no speech or political justification, only a blow and a question, then another blow and a question. Since I did not have my feet tied, I tried to dodge the blows, running around the room, limping because I did have my leg in a cast, but it was impossible. He was surrounded by his colleagues who laughed, celebrating his actions. When I would bump into them and fall to floor, they would quickly throw me back into the center of the room, like a beast in a cage. I began to faint, while the rhythm of the interrogation continued unabated. I finally fell and could not get up. Several of them held me up so I could be beaten further until I lost consciousness. I later learned that they took me back and threw me again on the straw mattress in the *cuadra*, I could not eat or move for various days. My body was one big bruise.[12]

In addition to physical torture, La Perla was a site of intense emotional trauma. Susan Sastre recalls:

> Psychological terror was everywhere because you heard the truck arriving and you immediately began thinking that this time it could be your turn. I never managed to figure out where the trucks would take the captives. No one knew, we would only hear it. There were periods in which a truck would come every day, and at other times two or three days would go by and you would begin to calm down, but then the truck would arrive and the torment would begin again. The truck's noise would put you in a situation of extreme emotional stress, you knew someone's moment had come or that it could be your own. Some prisoners did not know that the "move" meant death, they were told that they were being taken to another camp to recover, so they would learn to think differently and return to society. Others were told they

were going to the San Martín Penitentiary or to the Buen Pastor women's prison. During the *traslados*, a ghostly silence reigned; when called, the comrades walked with dignity to their death, without faltering. Various hours would pass by before our voices could be heard again.[13]

Gustavo Contepomi commented on the *traslados*: "One heard comments about the pit [*pozo*] but it was never said where it was. It was obvious that it was located not far from La Perla, undoubtedly was on military property. The truck would make the *traslados*, would return to the concentration camp, half an hour later, as if giving notice of a mission completed."[14]

Graciela Geuna's testimonies to the CONADEP and international tribunals have been the most cited of any former prisoner on La Perla. Among her insights were those regarding the internal organization of the camp:

> There is a point of fundamental importance since it reveals the existing relationship between the legal system of the Armed Forces and the clandestine concentration camp La Perla: every day at the end of the day a list was assembled of the disappeared prisoners who were found that day in La Perla. To that list was added in order the day of the abduction, the new prisoners, not mentioned were the *traslados* of that day. This list had the following heading: "List of Detainees in the University." The University was La Perla. Below the name of each prisoner found that day in La Perla was put, along with the prisoner's nickname, if he or she had one, party affiliation, real or imagined, and prisoner number, mine was 252. These lists were made in triplicate: the first remained in La Perla, the second was taken each evening, at the end of the day, to the Destacamento de Inteligencia, and the third to the headquarters of the Third Army Corps. This was made clear to me through a personal experience. Just a few days after being kidnapped an army officer came to speak with me. He wanted to know what branch of my family I had come from since some of my relatives, according to him, had been friends of his. He told me that his name was Raúl Fierro and that he had seen my name on the lists of the Third Army Corps. That was the first sign that I had that I was in some official place of the Third Corps. While family members would go and make inquiries at the Corps headquarters, and those receiving them would feign to consult and then say they knew nothing, in reality they had daily lists of all those kidnapped and executed.[15]

The sectarianism of the Left, particularly pronounced in Córdoba' given the Left's size and diversity there, reappeared in La Perla, despite the torments all the prisoners were subject to. PRT (Partido Revolucionario de los Trabajadores) member Carlos Vadillo relates:

> There were even people from the Partido Comunista Revolucionario who would sleep by day and be up at night. They would spend all their time discussing imperialism and the relationship between Videla and Moscow because of the wheat trade. It is incredible to realize that each individual had a different perspective on the world and acted accordingly. For example, we survivors of the PRT, we would fight over

the newspaper to see the soccer scores. And whenever we would do that, the PCR [Partido Comunista Revolucionario] members would approach us and tell us that soccer was nonsense that distracted us and it was necessary that we continue to debate the political reality even while in jail. We told them to go to hell.[16]

Survivor testimonies also revealed three discrete stages in La Perla's two-year history as a detention and torture center and death camp. The first, encompassing an entire year beginning with the March 1976 coup, witnessed the greatest number of abductions and increasingly large executions. The second from roughly April to June 1977 was a period of smaller numbers of executions, selective ones in groups of three with a new contingent of the Gendarmería posted as guards and a shake-up in the camp commanders. The final period of some ten months' duration revealed a notable decline in abductions, torture sessions, and executions and greater freedom of movement and relaxed restrictions. By the third stage, Menén-dez, apparently confident that the "subversives" had been defeated in the ten prov-inces under the Third Corps' jurisdiction but also in direct response to orders from Videla, had begun a process of legalizing the status of certain prisoners ("blanque-ando" in the prisoner parlance) and sending them to Campo de la Ribera or, more frequently, the penitentiary in the San Martín neighborhood of the city. By Sep-tember 1978 there were no more prisoners in La Perla and the camp had been reconverted to strictly military purposes. The junta vetoed Menéndez's plan that any prisoners remaining in Córdoba's other detention centers would be tried by military tribunals with the power to impose the death penalty. By late 1978 most of the killing had come to an end in Córdoba, though isolated incidents of abduction, torture, and murder continued to occur until the end of the dictatorship.

Former La Perla prisoner Mirta Iriondo commented on the peculiarities of Córdoba's experience with the human rights trials: "In Córdoba there are always unique complications in everything. . . . It is a special province, different from the others. I am always struck by the special consideration given to the survivors of ESMA, something that does not happen in Córdoba, nor in Paraná where I live. To that we can add the judicial system delayed many years before one could offer testimony, which led many survivors to decide not to relive the past and to get on with their lives."[17]

Others, such as former prisoner Andrés Eduardo Remondegui have com-mented on the stigma attached to being one of the handful of the camp's survivors:

I continued with my life and moved away from the human rights environment because, sincerely, I am bothered by this funny look one gets, it hurts and wounds me. This busi-ness that "they must have done something" to survive, this thing of turning upside down the "they must have done something" that people said to justify the repression . . . it is not right that we survivors have a tough time showing our face without others pointing at us. These underhanded accusations, in the end, the only thing they contrib-ute to is to keep alive the doctrine that the military wielded as a justification.[18]

In contrast to the victims of state terrorism, the voices of its perpetrators have remained silent and only fragments exist from official pronouncements and the handful of interviews granted by former military commanders immediately after the restoration of democracy in 1983. Court testimony from the 1985 trials of the junta leaders provides an imperfect but also the richest source of insights on their rationalizations for the violence and unyielding defense of their actions.[19] Subsequent human rights trials have proven valuable for reconstructing the memories of former political prisoners and family members of the victims of the violence, but less so for the hundreds of indicted military and police officers, counseled by their attorneys not to testify and to sit stoically in the defendants' dock, an attempt to strip the proceedings of legitimacy through a kind of silent, sullen protest. The guilty verdicts and prison sentences handed down in the 1985 trials undoubtedly had convinced defense lawyers and defendants alike of the risks involved in even minimal cooperation and the recognition of judicial authority.

In the Córdoba trials, only the final statements of the accused offer us their voices, though almost in unison they comprise a categorical and vehement denial of all charges and a denunciation of the proceedings as politically motivated and violating all judicial norms. Videla's final statement in the UP1 trial was representative of the tone and rationale of the military's memories of the state terrorism. After a long peroration reviewing the state of "war" existing in these years, emphasizing the full support of the Peronist government in a campaign against the subversive threat, Videla asserted the judicial proceedings underway were proof of the continued state of war, albeit no longer one of armed conflict, but ideological and political in nature, to vilify and punish the victors of a previous stage in said war and to proclaim indignantly his status as "political prisoner." Videla's memories of the 1970s, in which he now rejected the characterization of a "dirty war" but rather claimed it as a "civil war" (*guerra interna*), were absent of innocent victims, disappearances, and crimes, and offered a sanitized version of the state terrorism, functional to his defense but wildly inaccurate historically.[20] Menéndez's declarations during the Menéndez IV trial were similarly a compilation of half truths and outright falsehoods, all professed in a key of victimhood and persecution (see appendix 3).

Remembering the dirty war in Córdoba has involved much more than individual, private recollections; it has encompassed an institutional memory fomented and fashioned by government policy. In the case of the La Perla death camp, on March 24, 2009, the date of the coup's thirty-third anniversary, the camp was opened as a public museum, formally called Espacio de la Memoria y la Promoción de los Derechos Humanos (Remembrance and Human Rights Center). Two years previously President Nestor Kirchner had announced from the camp's grounds that the site henceforth ceased to be military property and would be turned over to a special commission. This was not the first attempt to reclaim memory on the site

FIGURE 16. Façade of the former D-2 detention center that now houses the Archivo Provincial de la Memoria.

of the former death camp. In 1980, the military itself had premiered there a traveling museum, the Museo Móvil de la Lucha contra la Subversión (Traveling Museum of the Struggle against Subversion), to celebrate its victory in the place of some of its most egregious crimes.[21]

Kirchner's inauguration of the La Perla museum followed the establishment years prior of an archive in the buildings of the former D-2 detention center, the Archivo Provincial de la Memoria (APM), which functioned as a museum and memory site. Unlike the well-known cases of Paraguay's so-called Archivo del Terror or Guatemala's Archivo Histórico de la Policía Nacional, Córdoba's archive did not emerge on the foundation of a happenstance discovery of a trove of documents neglected and then abandoned by the repressive apparatus of a fallen dictatorship. Information about the dirty war was fragmentary and dispersed; the detailed files on detainees so often referred to by former La Perla prisoners did not surface, save some stray *legajos* located in various government agencies, most likely forwarded to them as prisoners were moved from one detention center to another. Such dossiers were unusual discoveries. Upon the explicit orders of the expiring dictatorship under General Reynaldo Bignone, the military and police authorities had destroyed such records of incriminating evidence.

Political circumstances made the APM possible. The Kirchner government's promotion of human rights and recovery of the memory of the dirty war was

FIGURE 17. Archivo Provincial de la Memoria with names of the disappeared engraved on its walls.

driven by both genuine ethical principles and strategic political calculations, linking such policies to the broader repudiation of the neoliberal *menemista* decade of the 1990s on which *kirchnerismo*'s political legitimacy resided. Such a dramatic reversal of policy from the blanket pardon granted by Menem emboldened the federal government to repeal not only the Menem pardons but also the Ley de Obediencia Debida and Ley de Punto Final from the Alfonsín years, thereby allowing the indictments and trials of human rights violations. Linked to such efforts, the Kirchner government established memorials (*sitios de memoria*) at various sites throughout the country. In Córdoba, a 2006 law passed by the provincial legislature (Ley Provincial de la Memoria No. 9.286) established the APM and created a supervisory board composed of representatives of human rights organizations and members of Córdoba's executive, legislative, and judicial branches. The law gave the APM broad responsibilities for educating the public on state terrorism and to serve as a repository of information of the most diverse kind on the dirty war. The archive's fortunes nonetheless remained somewhat precarious. The APM depended on provincial funds, guaranteed by law. The 2011 reelection for governor of the Peronist José Manuel de la Sota, an individual with greater affinities for the right-wing sectors of Peronism than *kirchnerismo*, especially strained the archive's relations with the provincial government.

Building a repository of documentary material was a laborious, slow process made possible by legislation empowering the APM to subpoena government bureaucracies to produce documentation from the period of military rule deemed within its authorized purview. The APM provided invaluable support for family members seeking information on missing family members, most seeking closure on their personal, private grief and others searching for the documentation needed to receive the indemnity payments made possible by previous governments for surviving family members of those unlawfully abducted and disappeared during the dirty war, now under *kirchnerinsmo* expanded beyond the *desaparecidos* to include those fallen in combat with the military and security forces.[22] The archive's most crucial role was in support of the judicial process as a source of information and evidence for the prosecuting attorneys in the various human rights trials. Though technically independent of the judicial process, in reality it functioned in a supportive capacity for those trials, and indeed the 2006 law's very provisions sanctioned a role in the "search for justice" as did subsequent agreements with the federal court system.[23]

The APM's value to researchers proved more problematic. With so much of the material classified or subject to privacy laws, open access to its collection—as in the case of the other major repository of documentation on the dirty war, the Archivo de la Dirección de Inteligencia de la Policía de la Provincia de Buenos Aires (DIPBA) in La Plata—was forbidden. Research thus involves ad hoc requests for specific material, to be approved or denied, and in the case of the La Plata archive, an actual formal written request to the Federal Appeals Court in La Plata to authorize consultation. Fruitful research, though laborious, thus is possible in both archives, but also faces formidable obstacles. The APM, for example, filmed each hearing of every trial since the proceedings began in 2008, but these remain classified until after final sentences are pronounced and enter the public domain, a process that takes years, making personal observation the only option to tap into the trials' rich corpus of testimony.

Memory as constructed in sites such as the former D-2 police commissary and now APM, and the La Perla and Campo de La Ribera detention centers, offers a narrative on the dirty war that is both compelling emotionally and imperfect historically. The sites are meant to memorialize the victims but also, in their displays and very setting, offer a representation of history, just as the former concentration camps in Europe do the Holocaust.[24] The dictatorship's egregious crimes, the stark brutality of the torturers, and the sufferings inflicted on its victims are graphic and necessary reminders of the period. All the sites offer guided tours to schoolchildren and tourists of displays of former prison cells, instruments of torture, photographic collections, and sundry other aspects found in their permanent collections. Their premises are also used to sponsor both academic conferences and gatherings for contemporary human rights activism. The APM even offers an extensive and useful

FIGURE 18. Entrance to the La Perla death camp turned memory site and museum.

publication series on such diverse themes as the detention centers and the human rights trials, some of them liberally cited in this book. Memory here becomes a societal good, preventing any forgetting of the crimes committed and insisting on continued vigilance to the abuse of state power. The rendering of history is none- theless incomplete, perhaps unavoidably so given the APM's origins and purpose, which was precisely to preserve the memory of an indisputable national tragedy and make use of such a memory to protect human rights in the future. Causation and history as a process of manifold influences are understandably not their con- cerns. Yet representations do influence perceptions of that history.

Perhaps the most notable example of the institutional effort at memory con- struction in Córdoba has not been public but rather a private initiative, the activities of the local chapter of HIJOS (Hijos e Hijas por la Identidad y la Justicia contra el Olvido y el Silencio). The HIJOS website, "Diario del Juicio" (www.eldiariodeljuicio .com.ar), remains the most complete electronic record of all the human rights issues surrounding Córdoba's experience with state terrorism, including live web camera coverage of all the trials, though by law such filmed proceedings cannot be archived and made immediately accessible to researchers. These children of the victims of state terrorism undertook a task over the course of years, from the very beginning of the human rights trials, to assemble a record not only of the trials but also multiple voices through videotaped interviews, photographic collections, and sundry links on human rights issues. Collectively it comprises an enormously valuable record of the dictatorship's crimes, though also an incomplete one. Memory, with all its anguish in this case, provides a complement to history but not a replacement for it. Memory has best served in Argentina the cause of human rights, in the present and the future.

The South African experience offers an interesting comparison with Argentina. After the gradual dismantling of apartheid in the early 1990s, the South African government embarked on a prolonged effort to memorialize the struggle against racial segregation and racial violence. It did so through the creation of "memory sites," which included Robben Colony, the former penal colony near Cape Town where Nelson Mandela spent eighteen years in prison. In Johannesburg, Mandela's former home in Soweto and the Apartheid Museum near the downtown became major memorials. Outside the city, Liliesleaf, the former underground headquarters of the African National Congress (ANC), is a museum with video and audio recordings documenting the antiapartheid struggle. As with Argentina's memorials, such memory sites have become tourist attractions, especially for foreign tourists. Unlike in Argentina or Guatemala, South African memory construction did not accompany a process of litigation for past human rights abuses and its memory sites are confined to museum status removed from current human rights issues. The comparison highlights the enormous efforts in Córdoba and Argentina to link memory with ongoing human rights struggle.[25] Brazil offers an even more extreme case. In Brazil it would take seventeen years from the fall of the military government to establish a government truth commission to investigate its crimes while a 1979 amnesty law passed by that same government failed to spark popular opposition and undermined the possibilities for trials of the kind undertaken in Argentina.[26] In a process described as "institutionalized forgetting," Brazil approached the human rights question in a manner starkly different from that of Argentina, and indeed no other Latin American country confronted the issue with the resolve and scope as did Argentina.[27] Even in periods of official indifference, as in the *menemista* 1990s, human rights groups and much of larger society as well continued to demand justice on such crimes as the black market in the babies of former political prisoners. The legacy of the dictatorship weighed heavily: forgetting was not an option for many.

Among the controversies raised by remembering the dirty war is the actual numbers of its victims. Most scholars of the state terrorism now roundly reject the figure of 30,000 *desaparecidos*. Such an inflated figure provided, and still provides, the operative number for many human rights organization, most notably the Mothers of the Plaza de Mayo, as it did for the Kirchner governments between 2003 and 2015. The origins of that figure remain a matter of dispute. Some claim

Eduardo Duhalde, the author of an influential study on the state terrorism and later Nestor Kirchner's secretary of human rights, first proposed the figure while in exile during the dictatorship in order to draw attention from European governments and the international human rights movements in support of claims of "genocide" already being blandished during the dictatorship. Others point to the Mothers of the Plaza de Mayo, in particular to its incendiary leader, Hebe Bonafini, as the author. Whatever the source, measuring the disappeared remains controversial.[28]

For Córdoba, the Diario del Juicio and Parque de la Memoria databases have documented roughly 1,100 victims, which includes both the disappeared and those killed in confrontations with the security forces, and not only those killed or disappeared in Córdoba but those from Córdoba killed or disappeared in other parts of the country (see appendix 2). Taking the official CONADEP figures of roughly 9,000 (comprising only the disappeared) the figures of a bit more than 800 *desaparecidos* would amount to a little less than 10 percent of the total number of the disappeared. CONADEP's lowball figure elicits angry reactions from human rights organizations such as HIJOS that continue to wield the 30,000 "genocidal" number as the accurate estimation of the disappeared and dead of the dirty war. Perhaps the most reliable source, the forensic anthropology group of the EAAF, estimates an even lower total number of *desaparecidos* than the CONADEP report, between 6,500 and 7,000, of whom some 900 account for Córdoba's share. Its calculations are based on the number of cases recorded by the CONADEP commission, drawn largely from family members who provided testimony and documentation to the commission, and the smaller number of witnesses who independent of CONADEP provided credible cases of disappeared individuals to various human rights organizations but were included in CONADEP's final estimates, with the total numbers modified by the EAAF's own forensic investigations.[29] The most thorough and up-to-date database for all victims in the country, disappeared and not, is that of the Parque de la Memoria, which lists a total of 8,800 victims, disappeared and killed.

Such figures, terrible as they are, weaken even further claims of "genocide" in Argentina. The crimes committed by the dictatorship did not meet the original 1948 United Nations Convention definition of genocide, which did not include political groups and required the specific intent to exterminate. Claims of genocide similarly are not echoed in the social science literature. Argentina does not figure in any of the major scholarly works on the subject.[30] Neither the numbers of victims nor the intent qualify it as a genocide properly understood. Argentina's dirty war lacked the character of many modern genocides from Nazi Germany to the Khmer Rouge and what Eric Weitz has described as a "utopian high modernist" impulse to build a future (however terrible) society; it was reactive and rather sought the restoration of an idealized past. The distinction was not the political nature of the murders. Stalinist genocide moved the definition beyond the original

UN parameters of race, ethnicity, and religion to include ideological and political groups, and indeed political genocide was included in Raphaël Lemkin's original definition of genocide. It was instead the scale and intent that distinguish Argentina's experience with state terrorism from modern genocides. In Argentina, state terrorism can best be understood as something akin to a targeted political mass murder rather than an outright genocide. David Pion-Berlin and Pilar Calveiro among others have suggested the term *politicide* as a possible alternative, though that neologism still does not address satisfactorily the relatively small numbers murdered in Argentina's dirty war. Ultimately, the dispute may reside in a historian's definition of genocide versus a lawyer's definition.[31]

The issue of genocide, however, is not strictly semantic. Such a characterization of the period raised the societal stakes in the search for any national reconciliation by aggravating enormously the military's egregious crimes and expanding guilt and accountability to other sectors of society.[32] Bitter and ultimately irreconcilable memories of the 1970s as a period of civil war, or of a dirty war, of state terrorism or of genocide, provided no common ground for national reconciliation. The Kirchner government took the position that such reconciliation could only be achieved through accountability. The repeal of the amnesty laws and the pardons, and the resumption of the human rights trials expressed this sentiment. The discourse on genocide had even wider implications as the judiciary, members of the press, and the business community were all potential defendants in the genocidal crimes against humanity.[33] Accountability served justice. It hardly furthered reconciliation, though the South African case demonstrates that choosing reconciliation over justice may prove an ephemeral choice, simply postponing unresolved tensions and lasting legacies of human right abuses, which, if left unpunished, threaten a recently restored democracy and civil liberties. South Africa's Truth and Reconciliation Commission documented human rights violations, but unlike in the Argentine case its findings did not serve as the basis for future litigation and was paired with a broad amnesty, deepening divisions in the country.[34] Reconciliation in a context of crimes against humanity and egregious human rights abuses may not only ultimately be incompatible with justice and accountability for crimes committed, but it also may even weaken the reconciliation it seeks to advance.[35]

So what to do with memory? The Kirchners' human rights policy had another effect, an unintended one perhaps, which was to provide a single narrative, an "imposed memory" propagated and sanctioned by state power, of the dictatorship and the entire historical context in which it emerged.[36] Beatriz Sarlo has brilliantly analyzed the halting steps in *kirchnerismo*'s struggle to consolidate legitimacy and enhance governance through public discourse and ritual that suited the fragile moment and societal fragmentation that existed upon Nestor Kirchner's assumption of the presidency in 2003. Perhaps nowhere was this better seen than in his embrace of the human rights issue and its organizations, ones he had virtually no contact with before while governor of Santa Cruz province, and offering a bold interpretation of the dictatorship and the violence of the 1970s. Kirchner's visit to the ESMA detention center and its inauguration as a memory site on March 24, 2004, the twenty-eighth anniversary of the 1976 coup, was the defining moment in his claiming of that tragic history, of the state terrorism as Holocaust and genocide and his government the first since the reestablishment of democracy to demand full accountability and justice. Absent was any recognition of Alfonsín's efforts on the human rights question (the trial of the juntas, the CONADEP report). Absent too was any recognition of the state terrorism that had begun during the 1973–76 Peronist government, much less an invitation for society to engage in self-criticism and recover a memory of the violence not confined to that perpetrated by its military rulers.[37]

Oral testimony in recent years has tended to replicate the official narrative of the period. It has provided an exemplary, urgent record of the suffering and human costs to its victims but also to family, friends, an entire society. It serves its greatest "historical" purpose there, as testimony and tribute. No one can deny its value and moral worth in these terms. Yet it is also necessary to recognize how an "imposed memory" has impoverished historical analysis, limited the parameters of the debate, and weakened the pursuit of a deeper understanding of the circumstances and events surrounding Argentina's greatest national tragedy. Memory as fashioned under the Kirchners tells us a great deal about recent political dynamics, a struggle over remembering to further and vindicate a political project not limited to the human rights issue. Its silences and even deliberate omissions, however, make more difficult understanding the full dimension of that past.

8

ASSIGNING BLAME

Who Was Responsible for the Dirty War?

There are none who are unaware, there are only accomplices.
—GENERAL IBÉRICO SAINT JEAN

The human rights trials and public construction of memory took place within the context of a broader social mobilization in Córdoba on the previous history of violence and state terrorism. Long before the trials began, in the midst of the dictatorship, Córdoba had produced a human rights movement with its own characteristics, the local expression of what had emerged as arguably the most important human rights movement in the world at the time. In early 1976, months before the coup, family members of those who had disappeared during the expiring Peronist government had already founded the Comisión de Familiares de Desaparecidos de Córdoba. Unlike the well-known case of Buenos Aires and the Mothers of the Plaza de Mayo, the first years of the activities of this group crossed gender and generational lines, as would subsequent organizations (and as eventually would the Mothers themselves) demanding information on the whereabouts of the detained and disappeared and later justice and punishment for the perpetrators of the state terrorism. Local chapters of national organizations such as the Asamblea Permanente de Derechos Humanos were subsequently established, and by the early 1980s silent marches around the Plaza San Martín, the civic heart of Córdoba, took place on a regular basis, merely the public expression of a human rights movement that antedated the coup with a notable participation of the family members of the disappeared.[1]

After the fall of the military dictatorship, much of the initiative on the human rights issue passed to the city's university and youth population, some in political organizations such as the Peronist Familiares de Presos y Desaparecidos Peronistas but most in nonpartisan organizations, of which the most important would be

FIGURE 19. Human rights groups marching around the Plaza San Martín.

the local chapter of the organization HIJOS. Composed initially of the children and grandchildren of the disappeared, it expanded to include others and in Córdoba gathered especially young people of university age concerned with the human rights issue. The local chapter of HIJOS would be a major advocate for the repeal of the Alfonsín-Menem amnesty laws and a litigant in the trials against those accused of human rights abuses under the military dictatorship begun under the Kirchner governments.[2]

With the restoration of democracy in 1983, there began a long, arduous, still unfulfilled process of coming to terms with the dirty war in arenas outside the human rights movement. The first foray into such a reckoning came as a result of government initiative. The truth commission findings, the famous CONADEP (Comisión Nacional sobre la Desaparición de Personas) report, not only provided evidence for the prosecution of the junta in the trials; the report was both a rich corpus of information for historians and a revealing document about the particular conjuncture in which it was elaborated. A factual compendium through testimony of the military government's egregious crimes, the truth commission report neither explored the political affiliations and activities of the victims nor offered an explanation for the state terrorism. Written in a liberal key vindicating democracy and the rule of law, it also conformed to the contemporary standards of international human rights organizations that prioritized intrinsic rights to be protected in any circumstance and for any individual. The only social relations mentioned for any of the disappeared were as family members, their individual identities confined to names, age, gender, and occupation.[3] Such an approach, as Emilio Crenzel

FIGURE 20. Members of Córdoba's chapter of HIJOS with banners of the *desaparecidos*.

has noted, though it recognized the humanity of the disappeared "omitted in the analysis the responsibility of the political class and civil society before and after the coup and failed to historicize the causes of political violence."[4] It perpetuated the myth of both a guiltless civil society and the *desaparecidos* as removed from any political involvement, mere bystanders and "innocent victims" of a state terrorism run amok, a narrative fashioned first by family members and human rights organizations in the campaign against the dictatorship but then appropriated by the prodemocracy forces and especially Alfonsín's government. The narrative provided an "emblematic memory" functional to both rebuilding democracy and furthering the cause of human rights and accountability but deracinated from history.[5] The fiction continued with an even greater intensity, this time laden with an imperious sectarianism, with the new emphasis on human rights and the resumption of the human rights trials under the Kirchners. An organization such as HIJOS, a fierce critic of CONADEP's "dos demonios" (the two demons or twin evils) thesis, recognized and indeed vindicated the political militancy of the disappeared but refrained from any critical perspective at least publicly on that militancy and ultimately returned to the "innocent victims" narrative of the truth commission report and the new *kirchnerista* human rights policy, a policy that converted the *desaparecidos* into an almost sacred state of martyrs and their tragic deaths into a modern political martyrdom.[6] Within the HIJOS organization, intense debate and dissent did exist on questions of the Left's armed struggle tactics and other political and moral dilemmas as the children of the disappeared grapple with the actions of their parents and its consequences.[7] The public positions of HIJOS, however, only very rarely have revealed such tensions, its members wary of ceding any moral authority to those indicted and sentenced for the crimes of the dictatorship.

Much of the narrative on the dirty war does not hold up to historical scrutiny. As Marina Franco has demonstrated, upon Perón's return to the presidency, policies as reflected in legislation and the public discourse of the government and the political class generally as well as the press harped constantly on the "subversive" threat, making possible not only the death squads and the right-wing terror campaign against the Left during the Peronist government but also emboldening and legitimizing the military's direct assumption of responsibility for carrying out the dirty war.[8] Societal complicity of the country's "silent majority" was not far behind.[9] The emotionally powerful testimonies of the CONADEP report were similarly uprooted from history. The truth commission charged with investigating the dictatorship's crimes avoided the thorny subject, which it rightly feared might be used by the military to defend its actions, of political militancy and involvement in "subversive" organizations of many of the disappeared. Testimonies of survivors were devoid of any references to any prior activities that might have compromised the status of "innocent victim": even mere political activism was absent in CONADEP's recorded testimonies.[10] The very temporal limits of the report, documenting human rights abuses only under the military government, served the Alfonsín government's political objectives of democratic consolidation by exempting from scrutiny the last Peronist government, when state terrorism had first appeared, and thereby from any association of guilt, both of the governing party and those of the opposition that supported the government's antisubversive logic. The report also served the objectives of the country's human rights organizations, including Córdoba's, heavily represented by family members of the disappeared and state terrorism's victims generally, to seek justice and hold those accountable for their crimes, but in the process avoided any examination of a broader societal responsibility for the violence, much less those of disappeared loved ones.

The CONADEP report, for all its value in other ways, thus corrupted history, providing a sanitized and simple if functional narrative of state terrorism as a confrontation between democracy and dictatorship, uprooting the crimes of the previous decade from any of their historical, political, and cultural foundations.[11] Historian Greg Grandin has criticized CONADEP and other truth commission reports in Latin America for "presenting an interpretation of history as parable rather than politics, denied the conditions that brought them into being." But in its stead he offers a parable of his own, of state terrorism as a simple "reactive campaign against social-democratic nationalist projects . . . as an essential element in the consolidation of a new neoliberal order." In Argentina, the causes of the violence, and culpability for it, cannot be reduced so effortlessly to a formula of

FIGURE 21. Campo de la Ribera, photos of the disappeared.

neoliberalism and reaction. History demands, so far lacking a voice, a deeper, more nuanced explanation, not merely reconfiguring simplistically the equation of guilt from that offered by the CONADEP truth commission.[12]

Perhaps the rawest and most polemical attempt to account for Argentina's decade of violence is the extended essay of former Montoner Héctor Ricardo Leis. Leis departs from the voluminous exculpatory memoirs and first-person accounts of former leftist militants with a self-lacerating confession of his errors in political judgment and even moral failures. He distinguishes first between the actions of the rural guerrillas, a revolutionary violence engaged in revolutionary war, and the actions of groups operating in the urban setting like his own Montoneros, whose actions he describes as "terrorism." Leis criticizes the politics of memory under the Kirchners, including that on public display, the former detention centers turned political shrines, for debasing the history, assigning those who perished there as simple victims, converted into mere students or office workers, while denying their revolutionary militancy.[13] His definition of "terrorism" certainly is highly problematic: deadly, homicidal acts that he reduces to partisan violence, downplaying terrorism's deliberate targeting of innocents for purposes of delegitimizing a regime, demoralizing a society, or simply making a statement. Leis's spacious definition makes virtually any individual act of political violence leading to death an act of terrorism and almost seems to justify, intentionally or not, the dictatorship's brutal methods and crimes. His essay nonetheless does have the virtue of demanding a full reckoning of the violence and a rigorous historical analysis of its causes and consequences, including acknowledging the responsibility of all its perpetrators and their legal liability under the rule of law. With the Kirchners, the generation of the 1970s appropriated "human rights" as its sole preserve, but the revolutionary Left hardly concerned itself with that cause, or despite Grandin's assertion "social democracy," during that tragic decade as it sought a radical transformation of Argentine society. The disregard for human life by at least certain sectors of that Left, though not terrorism properly speaking, left a trail of assassinations of business executives, trade union leaders, and others that made possible the dictatorship's dirty war and crimes.

In Córdoba, a solitary exception to this muteness was a controversial letter to the editor by philosopher Oscar del Barco and a subsequent polemic with poet and former Montonero leader Juan Gelman, in the political and cultural review *La Intemperie*. Del Barco, a former staunch member of the Communist Party and, unlike many of those in that venerable and stalwart if somewhat doctrinaire voice of the Argentine Left, was himself once sympathetic to its many new leftist offspring in the 1960s and 1970s. Del Barco wrote in 2004 an emotional mea culpa, published separately throughout the country as an essay titled "No matarás" (Thou Shall Not Kill). In his apologia, del Barco recognized his own guilt for supporting the violent tactics, expressed remorse for the deaths that resulted, and urged a broader societal soul searching for the tragedy of the country's recent history. The plea fell on deaf ears. Little of del Barco's self-criticism filtered into the mainstream of Argentina's revitalized human rights movement in the Kirchner era or the country's intellectual life. His missive was met with more hostility than sympathy. A few were more discriminating, and books such as Emilio Crenzel's *La historia política del Nunca Más* and Hugo Vezzetti's *Pasado y presente: Guerra, dictadura y sociedad en la Argentina* demonstrated like del Barco an admirable critical rigor and independence of thought. These were the notable exceptions.[14]

Myths, misperceptions, and societal amnesia abound. One of the most widespread images in contemporary Argentina remains the direct complicity of the United States. The official narrative of the state terrorism, on prominent display in the memory sites such as La Perla and the Campo de la Ribera, has become that it was pure and simply a product of the Cold War, the National Security Doctrine, and American tutelage of the Argentine military in the School of the Americas and other training facilities for the Latin American officer corps. Human rights groups in Córdoba often directly attributed the state terrorism to American indoctrination and the Plan Condor, an arrangement between the Southern Cone military governments and their intelligence services to combat communist influence in the region, supported and at least partially financed by the United States.[15] American influence in these terms and on many levels is undeniable. Everywhere in Latin

America, Argentina included, the most important institutional channel for advancing U.S. interests in the postwar period was the military. So-called foreign aid to the region was predominantly military aid. In the years prior to the 1976 coup, Argentina ranked second only to Brazil in arms purchases, procurements that came overwhelmingly from U.S. suppliers.[16] The American embassies catered to business interests and to defense contractors in particular, and the military sections of the embassies had resources and an influence that towered above those such as the political and cultural officers. Joint military exercises by naval units cemented relationships between the militaries of both countries, as did membership in hemispheric security programs such as the Inter-American Defense Board. Cold War indoctrination of the officer corps, though less widespread than in the case of a number of other Latin American militaries, certainly happened and had serious consequences.

Yet none of this by itself offers an adequate explanation for state terrorism in Argentina. Other Latin American countries experienced similar and even more pronounced influences and yet no military regime, save the genocidal, ethnic-cleansing one in Guatemala, was guilty of crimes on the scale even remotely approaching that of Argentina. In Brazil, twenty years of military rule with military leaders who had much closer relations to the United States, both institutional and personal, than their Argentine counterparts did not produce anything resembling the dirty war. Brazil's unofficial truth commission report (*Brasil: Nunca mais*), compiling two decades of military rule and human rights violations there with 125 disappeared, would have barely qualified as a single bad day in the Argentina of the *desaparecidos* and death camps.[17]

The narrative also ignores the important shift that took place under the Carter administration, the new emphasis on human rights in U.S. foreign policy that perhaps had its most transcendent application in Argentina during the period of military rule. Kissinger's blessing for the coup and his silence on the human rights abuses during the final months of his tenure as secretary of state have been widely commented on in Argentina. All but forgotten were the much greater efforts over the course of several years by the Carter administration to redirect the country's foreign policy and sanction foreign governments guilty of human rights abuses, especially Argentina. Carter named former civil rights worker Patricia Derian as the new assistant secretary of state for human rights, and Derian set the U.S. embassy in Buenos Aires on a collision course with the military junta. The U.S. Congress vetoed loans from the Export-Import Bank and blocked several others from additional multilateral lending agencies. The 1978 Humphrey-Kennedy amendment to the Foreign Assistance Act banned certain military aid to Argentina, important above all for the arms embargo and difficulties this implied for the Argentine military to acquire not only new weaponry but especially also vital spare parts and to fund training. Such legislative measures, combined with Derian's personal meetings in visits to Argentina with human rights groups such as the Permanent Assembly for Human Rights and the Mothers of the Plaza de Mayo and the efforts of the embassy in Buenos Aires to provide a place where family members and friends of the disappeared could come to report the abductions, played an important role, if not in reducing the killings, at least in energizing the human rights issue and providing some degree of U.S. protection for those Argentines seeking information on the *desaparecidos*.[18] Early in the Kirchner era, in 2006, Derian's role was officially recognized with the new president awarding her the Order of San Martín. The acknowledgement proved to be short lived, eclipsed by a new official history that asserted a direct American role in the state terrorism. Memory sites such as La Perla and Campo de la Ribera showcased U.S. involvement through the Condor Plan in its displays and guided tours.

Though the Carter human rights policy was only moderately successful as abductions and disappearances continued unabated in 1977 and 1978, it simply flies in the face of the historical record that the U.S. government supported in any meaningful way the junta during the darkest days of the *guerra sucia*. Prior to Carter, Kissinger, the Pentagon, and the CIA unquestionably had played an instrumental role in establishing the Condor Plan, which allowed the Southern Cone military dictatorships to share intelligence across borders and extradite, abduct, and murder their own nationals resident in neighboring countries. The most authoritative study of the Condor Plan insists that the United States remained deeply involved in that operation despite Carter's attempt to "tame" covert operations in Latin America generally. CIA and Pentagon involvement may have continued at some level, apparently defying executive authority.[19] The assertion, however, relies on a few random documents and more importantly ignores the simple fact that, at least in Córdoba, the kind of detailed intelligence needed by the Third Corps to wage the antisubversive terror campaign there was beyond the broad surveillance powers of the Condor Plan, an operation after all intended primarily to track the movement and apprehend suspected leftist militants in neighboring countries. The victims of state terrorism in Córdoba do include foreign nationals, mainly Paraguayan and Bolivian university students studying there. The Condor Plan may have provided information on such individuals, but the most important intelligence was gathered locally. Waging the dirty war in Córdoba required an intimate knowledge of the local scene, the individuals and organizations that they belonged to as well as family members and friends, workplaces, and residences. Such detailed knowledge came from the local intelligence services, especially the Destacamento de Inteligencia 141, not the Condor Plan.

If the U.S. influence on the dirty war mattered, it was not as an orchestrator of state terrorism but in very precise ways. Kissinger's failure to criticize the regime in the early months of Argentina's dirty war was unquestionably a shameful relinquishing of moral authority at a time when a vigorous U.S. response might have made some difference and saved some lives. Its real import on the coup itself has probably been exaggerated. By this point the Frank Church Senate subcommittee hearings on the U.S. destabilization campaign in Chile had taken place. Kissinger's role in the overthrow of Allende's government was public knowledge and his influence on U.S. foreign policy, especially as it related to Latin America, greatly diminished. More importantly, the Argentine military planned the coup separate from U.S. direction and certainly was not waiting for the Americans to sanction it. Argentina was not Chile.

Nonetheless, declassified State Department papers demonstrated incontrovertibly that the U.S. government with Kissinger as its representative failed to express misgivings about the regime's brutal methods in the crucial early months of the dictatorship. One event in particular, the official visit from Argentina's foreign minister César Augusto Guzzetti to Washington in October 1976, convinced the junta that the U.S. government understood and even approved of its actions. The U.S. ambassador to Argentina at the time, Robert Hill, who had for several months been sending alarming cables back to Washington about reported widespread human rights violations, expressed dismay after a meeting with Guzzetti and what the ambassador perceived as the "euphoria" of the foreign minister with his reception in Washington, and pessimism that, with the failure of the U.S. government to express concern over the human rights issue, the embassy would have any leverage on the issue in its future dealings with the junta.[20] The U.S. government had clearly failed to adopt a vigorous, principled response to the flagrant and by now notorious crimes that the regime had already committed, forfeiting both its moral responsibility and any real chance to change the junta's policies.

Yet the failure of the Carter administration, despite such a response, to rein in the killings calls into question the limits of U.S. influence on the junta. Argentina's military leaders certainly sought good relations with the United States and feared reprisals in the form of suspended military and economic aid, but the institutional pressures to undertake the dirty war weighed far more heavily than the implications for relations with Washington. The loss of access to state-of-the-art military technology provided by the United States may have concerned them, but with the kind of terroristic strategies practiced by the regime, what could only most generously be described as low-intensity warfare, such military hardware mattered little if at all. Clandestine disappearances, torture, and summary executions required organization, planning, and an absence of any moral compunction, but little else. The most sophisticated piece of technology employed in the dirty war was the electric prod, long a staple in this livestock-based economy. Only in Tucumán, with its brief guerrilla rural insurgency, did surveillance equipment, napalm, and attack helicopters have any use and were employed by the military to combat the Left. The army never complained of shortages in essential equipment in its Operación Independencia campaign that handily suppressed the Tucumán insurrection. The U.S.

spreading of the Cold War ethos and ideas such as the internal subversive, domestic security, and a global confrontation with communism were much more important, though in many ways they only added gravitas and superpower imprimatur to some firmly established attitudes and obsessions within the military, which had been viscerally anticommunist since the time of the 1919 *semana trágica* and deeply suspicious of the populace and popular movements since the rise of Peronism in the 1940s. In many ways, U.S. Cold War indoctrination was preaching to the choir, telling the military things they already knew, indeed fervently believed.

Societal actors other than the military were implicated in state terrorism during the dirty war. The complicity of the Catholic Church is a well-known case.[21] Much of the Church hierarchy defended the regime publicly, and in some cases its clergy even persuaded the military personnel involved in the worst human rights abuses of the Christian nature of their campaign against the subversive threat.[22] Even more were guilty of the kind of moral failings, lack of courage, and betrayal of their priestly oaths seen in the case of Córdoba's Cardinal Raúl Primatesta. The Church, supported by the state as specified in the country's constitution, benefitted from an expanded range of economic benefits including tax exemptions, pensions, and real estate, presumably in exchange for the Church's support for the regime, or at least its silence.[23] While the Catholic Church in other Latin American countries offered comfort and protection to the victims of the military dictatorships then widespread in the region and even became the focal point of opposition to those regimes, the Church in Argentina acted as apologist and occasional collaborator for its military rulers.

Attention recently has turned also to the business interests and their collaboration with the dictatorship. In a number of cases this apparently involved a direct participation in the dirty war's tactics of abduction, torture, and murder.[24] Though the dictatorship and its violence cannot be reduced to a crude and simple formula of a project to impose "neoliberalism," there is little doubt that certain sectors of the country's capitalist classes supported policies intending to restructure the country's economic architecture and especially weaken labor as a political actor and at the point of production, and tolerated if not participated outright in the military's state terrorism as it affected their labor forces and union representatives.

The military's subsequent proclamation of the state of "war" and the provocations of the Left must be taken seriously in any rigorous historical analysis of the period. Estimates on the numbers killed by the guerrilla organizations in the decade range between 500 to 800 victims of the armed Left. Paul Lewis offers the most precision, with a total of 523 military and police victims, 54 businessmen, 24 trade union leaders, 21 politicians and government officials, 6 family members of the military, and 5 civilians killed accidentally, for a total of 633, just a bit below the Amnesty International estimate of around 700 casualties.[25] These assassinations were overwhelmingly perpetrated by the Peronist Left, especially the Montoneros.

The most careful study of the ERP's (Ejército Revolucionario del Pueblo) killings gives the total number of victims between 1972 and 1977 as 62, with the largest number coming from the ranks of the security forces (36 military and police) followed by business executives (17, not randomly targeted but those accused of exploitation of workers and/or violence against them).[26] Political assassination formed part of the Left's tactics, though on a scale in no way comparable to the state terrorism of the dictatorship. Violent tactics, moreover, did not occur in a void and were a product of long periods of military rule, political proscription, and repressive policies of all kinds. But all life is sacred and human rights belong to everyone, even one's enemies. Other options existed and the *Cordobazo*, the source of such much of the Left's revolutionaries reveries, rather than demonstrating the revolutionary disposition of the working class showed the strength of the country's people and institutions, including the trade unions, to contest the power of its military rulers, a profoundly democratic protest, not the product of a revolutionary vanguard.

The historical conditions and broad societal complicity notwithstanding, responsibility for the dirty war lies overwhelmingly with those who perpetrated it: the military, police, and civilians who planned and executed its terrible crimes. The state and the security forces had a legitimate right to respond to the violence of the Left, that minority sector of the Left that embraced such tactics, through lawful remedies that recognized due process and civil liberties. Instead they chose acts of wanton cruelty that spilled over into ones of depravity and sadism on a massive scale. The response was totally disproportionate to the threats, a state terrorism that cost the lives of many, the vast majority with no connection to armed struggle or acts of violence and of those perhaps guilty of crimes but who never faced a judge, never had their day in court, whose very imprisonment was almost never legally acknowledged and whose rights and dignity as human beings were brazenly, arrogantly, routinely violated. The great flaw of CONADEP's theory of "dos demonios" was not the assumption that the Montoneros and other groups disregard for human life constituted a crime, which it often did, but that these acts were moral equivalents, which they were not. The Left's violence was on a much smaller scale, less premeditated, and responded more to a military logic, however misguided, than did the dictatorship's state terrorism with its egregious crimes of massive and unlawful abductions, torture, and disappearances. Moreover, the vast majority of those disappeared were not members of guerrilla organizations. They were workers, students, Catholic laymen, and neighborhood activists, overwhelmingly young and defenseless. The ongoing trials and the testimony of survivors and family members bore witness to the scale of the crimes that took place and the responsibility of those who committed them. Blame for the dirty war sits squarely on their shoulders.

EPILOGUE

The victory of the Center-Right alliance that supported candidate Mauricio Macri in the November 2015 presidential runoff elections ushered in a new era in the human rights movement in Argentina. The welter of bills crafted and passed by the *kirchnerista* legislative majority in the weeks between the election and the December 10, 2015, inauguration of the new president included a little-noticed law creating a bicameral committee to investigate those business accomplices of the dictatorship who had thrived under military rule and cooperated with the activities of the security forces whose murderous tactics fell disproportionately hard on labor activists and the working class generally. Opposed for diverse reasons by the Unión Cívica Radical, dissident Peronists not aligned with *kirchnerismo*, as well as Macri's own party, the Propuesta Republicana, the new law was nonetheless passed by the *kirchnerista* majority and represented a stage apparently already underway: expanding the issue of culpability and crimes against humanity to social actors beyond the military, the police, and the intelligence services. Human rights activists had already begun to address the same question with an investigation and an extensive, well-documented report partially funded by the Secretaría de Derechos Humanos, published just days after Macri's election. The report offered evidence not only of economic benefits obtained by certain firms under the dictatorship but also of outright participation in the state terrorist apparatus, providing lists of union activists and personal information, including their addresses, thereby facilitating their abductions and later disappearances.[1]

Macri's victory was nonetheless ominous for the human rights movement. Never sympathetic to what had become broad-based social movement, dismissing its activists as "the human rights con artists" (*los curros de los derechos humanos*), upon assuming office he pledged to let the justice system carry forward with its proceedings but would not commit his government to support of human rights as had occurred under the Kirchners. Such a policy effectively meant the eclipse of human rights as a government priority and assigning its fate to the judiciary, a branch of government in Argentina never known for its political courage or independence and habitually taking its cues from executive power. Future lawsuits were likely to languish in procedural delays and because of political opposition certain to fragment between loyal *kirchneristas* and more traditional Peronist sectors, the latter much less committed to the human rights cause than *kirchnerismo*. The abovementioned law proved to be a dead letter, with the indictments of business executives stalled, apparently headed toward abeyance if not oblivion.

In Córdoba, the final verdicts handed down in the La Perla–Campo de la Ribera trial, the fifth and greatest of the human rights trials to take place there, seemed to end an era. The Archivo Provincial de la Memoria and the detention centers turned into memory sites continued to function but with declining financial support from both the federal and provincial governments. Human rights concerns generally appeared to have entered a period of dormancy as the country struggled with an austerity program and rising levels of unemployment, the commodities boom of the Kirchner era increasingly a fading memory. Córdoba's strong support for Macri in the recent election, a province that his electoral alliance of the Center-Right, Cambiemos, won overwhelmingly, was perhaps the most startling sign of a change in the political temper there and an indication of the populace's shift in priorities, one that portends a waning in the remarkable activity on the human rights issue in Córdoba of the previous decade.

The continued vigor of the human rights movement in Argentina, all its flaws, tendentiousness, and current challenges notwithstanding, nonetheless augurs for a revival of demands for "memory, truth, and justice" at some point in the future. Human rights organizations such as the Centro de Estudios Legales y Sociales continue to press for accountability and legal remedies for the dictatorship's crimes through litigations. The Abuelas de Plaza de Mayo remain steadfast, undaunted in the pursuit of reuniting the children of the disappeared with their rightful families. Hijos e Hijas por la Identidad y la Justicia contra el Olvido y el Silencio perseveres with a broad strategy to keep alive the memory of the period and its victims while supporting the actions of other human rights organizations and demanding a commitment from government authorities on these issues. The mood of the population at large will remain fickle, enthusiasm ebbing and flowing in response to recurrent crises in a country that has yet to recover its economic dynamism and social progress lost over the course of the last half century. Popular support for human rights issues will depend on the country's ability to make progress on these other concerns as well as government willingness to pursue them.

WORKING-CLASS VICTIMS
IN LA PERLA–CAMPO DE LA RIBERA LAWSUIT

Name	Age	Union Affiliation	Political Affiliation	Date of Disappearance
Carlos Julian Allende	24	SMATA	JG/PRT	12-15-1975
Angel Santiago Baudracco	29	Municipal Workers	ASA	01-08-1976
Horacio Luis Blinder	20	UOM	OCPO	08-09-1975
Juan Alberto Caffaratti	29	Luz y Fuerza	PC	01-15-1976
Patricio Federico Calloway	31	SMATA	JP	11-01-1976
Hugo Francisco Casas	25	UOCRA	Unknown	08-19-1976
Eduardo Castello Soto	28	SITRAM	PRT	04-02-1976
Humberto Cordero	38	UOCRA	PC	09-24-1976
Carlos Hugo Correa	46	FOECT	PRT	10-22-1976
Carlos Alberto Coy	25	Transit Workers	Unknown	06-30-1976
Marcelo José Di Fernando	27	SMATA	Unknown	08-27-1975
Tomás Di Toffino	37	Luz y Fuerza	Unknown	11-30-1976
Oscar José Dominici	28	Sancor	Unknown	07-01-1976
Ana María Espejo	34	UEPC	PRT	06-07-1976
Dina Silvia Ferrari	26	FOECT	Montoneros	11-08-1976
Mario Luis Finger	25	Caucho	OCPO	04-02-1976
Pedro Cipriano Finger	24	SMATA	OCPO	01-27-1976
Pedro Ventura Flores	28	Perkins	Unknown	03-09-1976
Alfredo Fornasari	28	Unknown	Montoneros	09-05-1976
Jorge Horacio Gallo	31	Public Employees	Montoneros	06-24-1976
Juan Carlos Galván	23	Sancor	PRT	06-15-1976
Navor Gómez	50	AB	JTP	03-19-1976
Horacio Francisco Heredia	31	Public Employees	Unknown	08-01-1976
Justino Honores	37	UOCRA	OCPO	11-03-1976

(continued)

Name	Age	Union Affiliation	Political Affiliation	Date of Disappearance
Pedro Antonio Juárez	28	SANCOR	Unknown	06-15-1976
Oscar Ventura Liwacki	36	Comercio	Unknown	05-12-1976
Luis Alberto López	31	SITRAM	Unknown	01-08-1976
Adolfo Ricardo Luján	28	Perkins	Unknown	03-09-1976
Graciela del Valle Maorenzic Ramos	27	Comercio	PRT	03-21-1975
Luis Alberto Márquez	28	SMATA	PCR	01-10-1974
Juan Jacobo Mogliner	33	SMATA	PCML	12-05-1977
Luis Carlos Mónaco	30	Prensa	PRT	01-11-1978
Héctor Guillermo Oberlín	31	Municipal Workers	ASA/FAP	01-08-1976
Hugo Ochoa	41	Public Employees	JP	11-12-1975
Pedro Jorge Ontivero	29	SMATA	Unknown	09-29-1976
Daniel Orozco	21	Unknown	JG	03-26-1976
Daniel Ortega	36	SITRAC	Unknown	07-28-1978
Pascual Ortega	34	SITRAC	Unknown	07-28-1978
Pablo Ortman	36	SANCOR	PRT	07-10-1976
Mario Oviedo	31	SITRAM	Unknown	06-24-1976
Néstor Paez	38	UOCRA	Unknown	05-12-1976
Nora Peretti de Gallardo	31	Labor lawyer	FIP	05-12-1976
Eduardo Requena	37	CTERA	Unknown	07-23-1976
Jorge Reynoso	34	Public Employees	Unknown	12-01-1976
Jorge Rodríguez	25	SMATA	JTP	12-15-1975
Carlos Roth	27	UOM	Montoneros	01-19-1976
Reynaldo Saénz	24	Caucho	Unknown	07-14-1976
René Salamanca	35	SMATA	PCR	03-24-1976
Perla Schneider	22	Unknown	PCML	12-06-1977
Reineri O. Segura	41	SMATA	Unknown	07-20-1976
María del Carmen Sosa de Piotti	32	UEPC	Montoneros	01-09-1976
Raúl José Suffi	30	SITRAM	Unknown	07-28-1978
Marcelo R. Tello	25	Madera	Unknown	03-09-1976
Carlos A. Velázquez	25	UOM	Unknown	06-09-1976
Julio César Yáñez	26	SMATA	JP/Montoneros	09-28-1976

SOURCES: "Dossier del Juicio"; Archivo Provincial de la Memoria (Córdoba). Database on deaths and disappearances; Parque de la Memoria http://parquedelamemoria.org.ar/ "Registro de Víctimas"

Union Affiliations

AB	Bank Workers Union
Caucho	Rubber Workers Union
CTERA	National Teachers Union
FOECT	Postal Workers Union
Luz y Fuerza	Light and Power Workers Union
Madera	Carpenters Union
Perkins	Perkins company union
Sancor	Sancor company union
SITRAC	Fiat company union
SITRAM	Fiat company union
SMATA	Autoworkers Union
UEPC	Córdoba Teachers Union
UOCRA	Construction Workers Union
UOM	Steel Workers Union

Political Affiliations

ASA	Acción Sindical Argentina
FAP	Fuerzas Armadas Peronistas
FIP	Frente de Izquierda Popular
JG	Juventud Guevarista
JP	Juventud Peronista
JTP	Juventud Trabajadora Peronista
OCPO	Organización Comunista Poder Obrero
PC	Partido Comunista
PCML	Partido Comunista Marxista Leninista
PCR	Partido Comunista Revolucionario
PRT	Partido Revolucionario de los Trabajadores

CÓRDOBA'S VICTIMS OF STATE TERRORISM, 1973–1983 (1,103 TOTAL)

Name	Age	Known Political Affiliation*
Ana Catalina Abad	25	OCPO
Roberto Omar Aballay	19	
Mirta Noemí Abdón	29	
Ricardo Elías Abdón	35	PRT/ERP
Victoria Abdonur	40	
Angel Luis Abraham	19	
Marcelo Hugo Abregu	30	PC/PJ
Eduardo Héctor Acosta	22	
Nestor Albino Acosta	20	PRT
Raúl Acosta		
Victor Hugo Acosta	27	
Marta Graciela Acuña	26	
Julio Agnelli	25	
Nillo Agnoli	27	PRT
Bella Josefina Aguilar	30	
Guillermo Aníbal Aguilar	22	
José Luis Aguilar	21	OCPO
Nestor Rafael Aguilar	24	
Adrián Oscar Aguirre	24	
Fernando Félix Agüero	30	FR 17
Orlando Ruben Agüero	21	OCPO
Tomás Rodolfo Agüero	22	PRT
Ana María Ahumada		PRT/ERP

*Acronyms are defined on last page of this appendix.

(continued)

(continued)

Name	Age	Known Political Affiliation*
José Oscar Akselrad	20	
Marta Susana Alaniz	28	ERP
Ricardo Fermín Albareda	36	PRT/ERP
Hernán Albisu	27	Montoneros
Elvira Nolasca Albornoz	23	
Pedro Armando Albornoz	25	
Cristobal Solano Aldana	20	JUP
Delfina Alderete	18	
Fernando Horacio Alderete	19	
Juana Agostina Alendro	19	
Rita Ales	32	PCML
Jorge Horacio Alessandro		
Carlos Allende	24	JG
Carlos Alberto Almada	21	OCPO
Elvio Alberto Almada	21	PRT
Manuel Almada		
Severino Alonso		
Carlos Felipe Altamira	28	
Estela Mary Altamirano	31	OCPO
Lucio Bernardo Altamirano	19	
Alejandro Alvarez	29	
Antonio Francisco Alvarez	28	
Carlos Eduardo Alvarez	27	PRT
Horacio José Alvarez	25	OCPO
Conrado Oscar Alzogaray	38	Montoneros
José Santiago Amato	22	
José Antonio Andrada	42	
Ernesto Andreotti	25	
Enrique Angelelli	53	
Daniel Martin Angerosa	25	
Humberto Orlando Annone	33	JUP
Daniel Victor Antokoletz	39	OCPO
Oscar Roque Antonini	33	
Amado Vicente Aostri	27	
Ricardo Américo Apertile	20	
Aldo Enrique Apfelbaum	45	
José Antonio Apontes	24	PRT/ERP
Luis Horacio Arana	24	
Eduardo César Araujo	26	
Hector Antonio Araujo	33	Montoneros
Rosario Gudeles Aredes	31	PRT
Justino Oscar Argañaraz	38	
María de las Mercedes Argañaraz	33	PRT/ERP
Isauro César Argüello	23	Montoneros
Ramón Oscar Arguello		
Florentino Arias	42	
Miguel Angel Arias	19	

Andrés Lucio Ariza	35	
Analia Alicia Arriola	29	
Juana María del Valle Arzani	26	OCPO
Antonio Daniel Asef	42	
Roberto Elías Asef	29	
Norma Isabel Asís	22	
Amanda Lidia Assadourian	29	PRT/ERP
Rosa Estela Assadourian	32	PRT/ERP
Emilio Carlos Assales	29	Montoneros
María Inés Margarita Assales	24	
Zulma Rosario Ataydes	23	PRT
Arturo Angel Avellaneda	27	JP/Montoneros
Juana Del Carmen Avendaño	27	PRT/ERP
Benjamín Gabriel Avila	28	
Carlos Erlindo Avila	41	
Fernando Alfredo Avila	20	
Reinaldo Alberto Avila	22	PRT/ERP
Susana Cristina Avila	31	
Paula Aybal	39	
Daniel Eduardo Bacchetti	21	JG
Carlos José Badric		
César Augusto Baldini	21	
Carlos Alberto Ballarino	20	PRT
Irene Josefina Ballester	27	
Pablo Alberto Balustra	32	JTP/Montoneros
Alfredo Guillermo Barbano	31	
Elena Cristina Barberis	23	PRT/ERP
Esther María Barberis	19	PRT/ERP
Miguel Angel Barberis	21	PRT
Juan Manuel Barboza	29	PCML
Julio Elias Barcat	22	
Carlos José Bardejo		
Hugo Valentin Baretta	27	Montoneros
Daniel Oscar Barjacoba	23	
María Del Carmen Barreda		
Miguel Angel Barreda	25	PRT/ERP
Guillermo Carlos Barrientos	24	
Daniel Barrionuevo		
Edy Barrionuevo		
Liliana Sofia Barrios	20	PRT/ERP
Washington Javier Barrios	22	PRT/ERP
Eduardo Daniel Bartoli	29	PRT
Guillermo Enrique Bartoli	25	
Angel Santiago Baudracco	29	ASA
Raúl Augusto Bauducco	28	PRT/ERP
Juan Carlos Bazan	33	PRT
Miguel Angel Bazan	24	PRT
Alberto Bello	26	JUP
Norma Argentina Benavidez	21	

(continued)

(continued)

Name	Age	Known Political Affiliation*
Zulema Edith Bendersky	23	PRT
Elvira Orfila Benitez	25	
Osvaldo Pablo Benitez	24	Montoneros
Juan Carlos Berastegui	30	
Carlos Antonio Bergometti		
José Pablo Bernard	26	VC/PCML
Carlos Guillermo Berti	22	
Guillermo Bertini Campana		
Marta Alicia Bertola	34	
Susana Beatriz Bertola	30	
Silvia Raquel Bertolino	22	OCPO
Horacio Amadeo Bertolotti	41	
Manuel Antonio Bertrán	25	
Dalila Matilde Bessio	26	Montoneros
Silvia Ester Bianchi	23	Montoneros
Enrique Antonio Bianco		PRT
Hector Aquiles Bianco	39	
Eduardo José Bicocca	24	
Silvia Susana Blanc	26	
Roberto Blanco	36	
Armando Blaser Bastos	25	
Sonia Alicia Blesa	33	
Horacio Luis Blinder	20	OCPO
Pastor Omar Bobbio	21	
Victor Pablo Boichenko	30	
Luis Oscar Bonfanti	36	
Nelly Yolanda Borda	28	
Oscar Alberto Borobia	26	
José Luis Boscarol	29	PRT
Alberto Santiago Bournichon		
Luis Alfredo Bracamonte	30	
Raúl Aristobulo Bracco	24	Montoneros
Humberto Horacio Brandalisis	27	PRT
Gabriel Braunstein	53	PC
Jorge Bernabe Bravo	19	
Mirta Graciela Britos	27	
José Antonio Brizuela	27	
José Nicolás Brizuela	50	PC
Oscar Omar Brizuela		
Julia Angelica Brocca	29	
Raúl Carlos Brogin	36	JTP/Montoneros
Raúl Leonel Bru	24	
Eduardo Budini	19	
Eduardo Oscar Bulacio	26	PRT/ERP
Daniel Leonardo Burgos	30	
Isabel Mercedes Burgos	23	PRT

Name	Age	Affiliation
Delia Estela Burns	28	
Guillermo Tomás Burns	27	
Ramiro Sergio Bustillo	27	PC
Edelmiro Cruz Bustos	25	
Graciela Noemí Bustos		
Jorge Dante Bustos	21	
María Aurora Bustos	43	
Miguel Angel Bustos	29	Montoneros
Carlos Horacio Buzzetti		
Wenceslao Eduardo Caballero	26	Montoneros
Mario Oscar Cabral	26	
Jorge Eliseo Cáceres	21	
Juan José Cadepón		
Humberto Miguel Cafani	23	
Juan Alberto Caffaratti	29	PC
Carlos Antonio Cafferata	34	
José Roberto Calderón	29	
Patricio Federico Calloway	31	JP
Aldo Jesus Camaño	19	PRT
Armando Arnulfo Camargo	36	
Carmela Juana Camargo		
Jorge Fortunato Camilion	34	OCPO
Orlando Campana		
Manuel José Campos	35	PRT
Ramón José Campos	38	
Horacio Canelo	29	
Luis Canfaila	23	PRT
Juan Antonio Cannizzo	21	
Alberto Canovas	26	
Ramón Aldo Cantero	39	PC
Ana Silvia Canziani	26	
Lelio Antonio Canziani	31	
Carlos Mateo Capella	29	OCPO
Carlos Alberto Capuano	51	
Gabriela María Carabelli	35	PRT/ERP
Hilda Yolanda Cardozo	26	FR17
Raúl Osvaldo Cardozo	27	
Daniel Hugo Carignano	27	PRT
Adriana María Carranza	18	
Cecilia María Carranza	18	
Alejandro Gustavo Carrara	22	Montoneros
Enrique Oscar Carreño	25	OCPO
María De Las Mercedes Carriquiriborde	27	PCML
Miguel Andres Casal	22	OCPO
José Alberto Segundo Casale	22	
Carlos Aníbal Casas	20	
Emilio Alvaro Casas	27	
Hugo Francisco Casas	25	

(continued)

(continued)

Name	Age	Known Political Affiliation*
Ruben Oscar Casas	26	
Elizabeth Cassanovas	20	PRT
Raúl Antonio Cassol	28	
Bruno Carlos Castagna	28	
Daniel Octavio Castellano	19	
Raul Alberto Castellano	19	
Eduardo Guillermo Castello	28	PRT
Miguel Angel Castiglioni	27	PRT
Mauricia Zulima Castillo	39	
Ramón Roque Castillo	26	
Hugo Alberto Castro	25	FAL
Juan Carlos Catnich	27	JTP/Montoneros
? Cavanagh		
Jorge Omar Cazorla	22	
Carlos Raúl Ceballos	23	
Miguel Angel Ceballos	37	PRT
Raúl Oscar Ceballos	23	
Jorge Oscar Cebrero		
José Ricardo Cepeda		
Juan José Chabrol	17	PRT
Oscar Domingo Chabrol	19	PRT
Ana María Ramona Chapeta	32	
Mónica Roxana Chertkoff	18	PRT/ERP
Victor Hugo Ramón Chiavarini	22	OCPO/PRT
Ignacio Manuel Cisneros	29	
Beatriz Citani		
Oscar Ernesto Cocca	22	PRT
Manuel Enrique Cohn	39	
David Coldman	51	PC
Marina Coldman	18	PC
Ernesto Collura		
Liliana Teresa Colombetti	24	PRT/ERP
Patricia Colombetti	19	PRT/ERP
Daniel Antonio Colón	25	PRT/ERP
Elsa Gladys Comba	44	
Sergio Héctor Comba	22	
Juan Carlos Conocchiari	23	Montoneros
Luis Alberto Conti	29	
Alicia Contreras	20	
Humberto Cordero	38	PC
César Gerónimo Córdoba	29	JP/Montoneros
Juan Victor Córdoba	22	
Carlos Hugo Correa	46	PRT
Gustavo Adolfo Correa	26	PRT
Jorge Cortez	38	PRT/ERP
Cristina Noemí Costanzo	25	JP

Carlos Alberto Coy	25	
Roque Benito Crespin	25	
Roberto Luis Cristina	37	VC
Victor Miguel Valentin Crosetto	24	OCPO
Carlos Cayetano Cruspeire	22	JP/Montoneros
Francisco Cuello	31	PRT/ERP
Hermengildo Alfonso Cuenca		PRT
Berta Cuesta	30	PRT/ERP
Jorge Eduardo Cupertino	22	
Alfredo Alberto Curutchet	33	
Alicia Raquel D'Ambra	21	PRT/ERP
Carlos Alberto D'Ambra	23	PRT
José Alberto D'Angelis	22	
Alfredo Gustavo D'Angelo	22	
Alberto Oscar D'Elia	34	
Alicia María D'Emilio	24	Montoneros
Antonio Dadurian	42	
Gregorio Dadurian	46	
Yolanda Mabel Damora	20	PRT
Osvaldo De Benedetti	30	PRT/ERP
Gustavo Adolfo De Breuil	23	JP/Montoneros
Nestor Enrique De Breuil	28	
Alicia Ester De Cicco	23	
José Esteban De Grandis		
Carlos Enrique De la Fuente	40	JUP
María Del Carmen Del Bosco	21	JG
Oscar Vicente Delgado	25	Montoneros
Ernesto Ramón Dellafiore	24	
María Cristina Demarchi	20	
María Rosa Depetris	39	
Jorge Carlos Depiante	25	
Graciela Josefa Devallis	20	
Marcelo José Di Fernando	27	
Juan Carlos Di Lorenzo	29	
Carlos Hipólito Di Paolo		
Tomás Di Toffino	37	
Adriana María Díaz	23	FAL
Florencio Esteban Díaz	45	Montoneros
Jorge Luis Díaz	28	
Juan Antonio Díaz	29	PRT
Miguel Angel Díaz	23	
Susana Elena Díaz	21	PRT/ERP
Victor Carlos Díaz	35	PRT
Rubén Dieguez		
Jorge Manuel Diez	26	JUP/Montoneros
Luis Vicente Dimattia	24	FJC
Graciela María De Los Milagros Doldan	34	
Mirta Del Valle Domina	22	

(continued)

(continued)

Name	Age	Known Political Affiliation*
Carlos Edmundo Domínguez	20	
Domingo Dominici		
Oscar José Dominici	28	
Hugo Eduardo Donemberg	21	PRT
José Alfredo Duarte	26	
Ramón Duarte	55	
Raúl Ignacio Duarte	51	
Eduardo Agustín Duclos	26	
Jorge Luis Duretto	23	
Amalia Stella Echegoyen	23	
Rodolfo Echinque	42	
Lucas Egras		
Jesus Gabriel Ehdad		
Raúl Nicolás Elias	32	
Elvira Ellacuria	61	
Fred Mario Ernst	33	Montoneros
Miguel Angel Esborraz	22	
Carlos Alfredo Escobar	27	
Marcelo Enrique Escobar	22	
Alberto Eusebio Esma	23	
María Zulema Espeche	58	
Rodolfo Lucio Espeche	27	
Ana María Espejo	34	PRT
Adriana María Esper		
Gerardo Espindola	32	
Luis Alberto Fabbri	29	OCPO
Alberto Samuel Falicoff	35	PRT/ERP
Herminia Falik	21	PRT/ERP
Raúl Edgardo Fanchi	21	
Nestor Manuel Fantini		
Raúl Bernardo Fantino	24	Montoneros
Victor Orlando Farfan	19	
Antonio Julio Farris	56	
Elena Feldman	18	OCPO
Ester Silvia del Rios Felipe	27	PRT/ERP
Enrique Horacio Fernández	27	JP
Hector Raúl Fernández	54	
José Honorio Fernández	21	JUP
Raúl Eduardo Fernández	22	
Vicente Fernández	60	
Dina Silvia Ferrari	26	Montoneros
Fernando Alberto Ferreira	22	
Ysidoro Ferreiro	24	PRT
Silvia Cristina Ferrer	26	PRT
José Miguel Ferrero	22	
Adrian Daniel Ferreyra	19	

Adrian José Ferreyra	22	PRT
Ana María Ferreyra	25	PRT
Diego Alejandro Ferreyra	22	
Jorge Luis Ferreyra	30	
José Carlos Ferreyra	28	PRT/ERP
Marcos Eduardo Ferreyra	25	Montoneros
María Prosperina Ferreyra	26	
Alberto Ferreyra Patrocinio		
Carlos Alberto Fessia	28	OCPO
Diana Beatriz Fidelman	23	Montoneros
Hugo Enrique Figueroa	24	JP/Montoneros
Osvaldo Figueroa		
Mario Luis Finger	25	OCPO
Pedro Cipriano Finger	24	OCPO
Guillermo Finoglio	24	OCPO
María De Las Mercedes Fleitas	25	Montoneros
Paulo Emiliano Flores	38	
Pedro Ventura Flores	28	
Fernando Hector Florez	24	
Gloria Nelida Fonseca	35	PST
Enrique Osmar Fontana	21	
Nidia Cristina Fontanellas	31	OCPO
Alfredo Fornasari	28	Montoneros
María Del Carmen Franchi	17	
Ricardo Alfredo Franchi	24	PRT
Carlos Alberto Franco	24	
Marta Ines Franzosi		Montoneros
Florencio Ramón Frias	37	
Raúl Haraldo Fuentes	41	
José Cistián Funes	23	Montoneros
Carlos Gustavo Gagliardo	24	
Antonio Galan		
Conrado Mario Galdame	25	
Carlos Alberto Galeazzi	24	
Ramona Cristina Galindez	26	
José Manuel Gallardo	32	
Rodolfo Gustavo Gallardo	33	
Roberto Ismael Gallegos	31	
Jorge Horacio Gallo	31	Montoenros
Juan Carlos Galván	23	PRT
Secundino Galván	19	
Ricardo Gamarro		
Roberto Gandeni		
Elbira Garaicoechea	58	
Alberto Armando Garbiglia	23	PRT
Angel Horacio García	29	Montoneros
Carlos Roque García	32	
Hugo Alberto García	27	

(continued)

(continued)

Name	Age	Known Political Affiliation*
Jorge Oscar García	26	Montoneros
José Alberto García	24	PRT
Pablo Alberto García	19	
Rodolfo García	25	
José Ramón García Becameil		
Gustavo Hugo García Calderón	24	PRT/ERP
Alejandro Daniel Gargaro	18	
Alfredo Gargaro	20	
Teresa Garzón	40	
Nelo Antonio Gasparini	25	
Luis Bernardo Gattavara	22	
María Irene Gavalda	27	PCML
Liliana Tersa Gel	21	JUP
Adriana Ruth Gelbspan	17	JG
Jorge Alberto Germain	22	
Hector Hugo Ghisolfi	44	
Rafael Gustavo Gigena	27	PRT/ERP
Alberto César Giménez		
Félix Roque Giménez	24	PRT
César Antonio Giordano	20	
Alberto Horacio Giusti	31	
Carlos Oscar Godoy	25	
Rosa Cristina Godoy	23	Montoneros
Rodolfo Goldin	26	OCPO
Rubén Manuel Goldman	24	PC
Alejandro Héctor Gómez	20	PRT
Enrique Horacio Gómez	39	
Hector Raúl Gómez	30	
José Guillermo Gómez	28	PRT
Lila Rosa Gómez	20	JUP
María De Las Mercedes Gómez	26	PRT
María Elena Gómez	35	PRT/ERP
Navor Gómez	50	JTP
Ramón Antonio Gómez	31	
Tomás Eduardo Gómez	21	
Alberto Rubén González	31	
Aldo Roque González	32	
Antonio Manuel González	31	
Estrella González	27	PRT-ERP
Horacio Mario González	27	Montoneros
María Graciela González	29	Montoneros
Marta Juana González	26	Montoneros
Nelson González	37	
Pedro Antonio González	18	
Ruth González	24	PRT-ERP
Sergio González	21	

Victor Francisco González	28	
Victor Hugo González		
Raúl González Iturbe		
José González Olmos	31	
Juan Carlos González Velarde	32	
Rodolfo Cesar Gordillo	23	FJC
José Luis Goyochea	30	
Mario Roberto Graieb	20	
Leticia Gramajo	24	
Rafael Angel Grimaldi	34	
Carlos Grossi		
Martha Angelica Guerrero	31	
Pedro Esteban Guerrero		
Ana María Gueuverian	21	JUP
Luis Alberto Guevara	33	
Carlos Francisco Guidet	32	PCML
Oscar Roger Mario Guidot	34	PRT
Enrique Daniel Guillen	25	PC
Leonardo Gulle	18	
Amelia Isabel Gutiérrez	19	
Carlos Gutiérrez		
José Heriberto Gutiérrez	33	PRT
Manuel Gutiérrez	33	
Marcela Josefina Guzmán	29	ERP
Adriana Isabel Haidar	28	Montoneros
Mirta Malena Haidar	34	
Ricardo Rene Haidar	38	Montoneros
Ricardo Ruben Haro	20	
Federico Juan Harriague	31	
Helena María Harriague	24	Montoneros
Jorge Rodolfo Harriague	27	
Susana Paulina Hauche	24	
Mario Alberto Haymal	20	
Ana María Del Valle Heinz	30	
Alicia Ester Heredia	24	
Horacio Francisco Heredia	31	
Eduardo Alberto Hernández	21	JUP/Montoneros
Claudio Daniel Herrera	19	JG
Julio Pio Herrera	66	
Juan Del Valle Hidalgo	18	
Manuel Hiel		
Alicia María Hobbs	21	
Justino Honores	37	OCPO
Susana Noemi Huarte	21	PRT/ERP
Hugo Oscar Hubert	34	JP/Montoneros
María Theresa Huerta	28	
Claudia Elisabeth Hunziker	21	
Diego Raúl Hunziker	18	

(continued)

(continued)

Name	Age	Known Political Affiliation*
Hector Ernesto Hunziker	24	
Miguel Ibarbe	26	
Dardo Omar Ibarra		
Roberto Illanes	21	FIP
Bernardo Inguerman	44	
Amelia Nelida Insaurralde	57	PC
María Eugenia Irazuzta	28	VC
Victor Hugo Iribarren	33	JP
Oscar Daniel Iturgay	21	JP
Zulima Araceli Izurieta	22	Montoneros
Angel Gustavo Jaeggi	25	
Alejandra Jaimovich	17	JG
Sergio Abdo Jaul		
Eduardo Juan Jensen	29	
Alejandro Ernesto Jerez	22	PRT/ERP
José Luis Jiménez	23	POT
Letizia María Jordan	29	Montoneros
Ada Alicia Juaneda	28	Montoneros
Lucinda Delfina Juárez	28	
Máximo José Juárez	21	
Osvaldo Hugo Juárez		
Pedro Juárez	28	
Hugo Alberto Junco	39	JTP/Montomeros
Luis Pablo Jurmussi	26	Montoneros
Hugo Alberto Kogan	21	PC
Emma Raquel Konig	20	PRT
Sara Kosoy	40	
Rosa Dora Maureeen Kreiker	30	Montoneros
Ana María Kumec	25	
Irma Leonor Laciar	50	JTP/Montoneros
Jorge Lafure		
Alberto Carlos Lago	29	
Carlos Enrique Lajas	23	
María Raquel Laluf	24	OCPO
Adriana Landaburu	24	JUP/Montoneros
Elsa Alicia Landaburu	26	
Leonor Rosario Landaburu	25	Montoneros
Barbara Lanuscou	3	
Matilde Lanuscou		
Roberto Francisco Lanuscou	27	FAR/Montoneros
Roberto Francisco Lanuscou	5	
Matilde Lanusocu Miranda		
Juan José Laso	21	JP
María Luisa Latorre	21	
Eduardo Felipe Laus	24	JUP
Claudio Jorge Lazo		

Heriberto Del Carmen Leal	25	MIR
Luis Enrique Leal	25	JP
Juan Carlos Ledesma	21	
Marta Susana Ledesma	28	PRT
Luis Roque Leiva	21	
María Dalia Leiva	28	PRT/ERP
Norma Beatriz Leiva	35	PRT
Silvia Del Valle Leiva	18	
Nestor Gilberto Lellin	27	PC
Jacobo Lerner	67	
Adriana Amalia Lesgart	31	
María Amelia Lesgart	24	
Rogelio Aníbal Lesgart	31	
Roberto Lujan Lesta	31	PC
Raúl Carlos Levin		
Ricardo Marcelo Levin	21	PRT
Ana María Liendo	25	PRT/ERP
Oscar Andres Liñeira	20	
Adolfo Cesar Liscovich	29	
Oscar Ventura Liwacki	36	
Marta Teresita Lizarraga	27	Montoneros
Sebastian María Llorens	28	ERP
Cesar Hugo Loker	41	
Alfredo Horacio López	18	JG
Arcangel Gabriel López	23	
Carlos Alberto López	25	
Felix Roberto López	24	OCPO
Francisco Lino López	26	
Hugo Osvaldo López	27	PRT
Jorge Gustavo López	21	PRT
José Eudor Del Pilar López	41	
Luis Alberto López	31	
Ruben Oscar López	27	
Clara Josefina Lorenzo	27	Montoneros
Victor Alberto Lorenzo	28	JP
Alberto Isodoro Losada	22	
Ernesto Ronaldo Lowe	29	
Victor Lowe	27	OCPO
José María Loyola	25	PC
Elisa Dionisia Loza	40	
Pascual Delfin Ludueña	29	
Adolfo Ricardo Lujan	28	
Jesus María Lujan	32	Montoneros
Gustavo Armando Luna	27	JP
Ignacio Jesus Luna	26	
Juan Carlos Luna	26	
Manuel Nicasio Luna		
Susana Elena Luna	21	

(continued)

(continued)

Name	Age	Known Political Affiliation*
Esther Del Rosario Luque	33	
María Isabel Luque	21	
María Teresa Luque	23	
Marta Del Pilar Luque	31	
Adrian Renato Machado	31	
Emma Norma Machado		
Alcira Enriqueta Machi	35	Montoneros
Mabel Veronica Maero	23	OCPO
Walter Ramon Magallanes	21	
Nancy Estela Magliano	28	
Leon Alberto Magran		
Guillermo Maidana		
Ramón Alberto Maidana	33	
Jorge Eduardo Malberti	26	JUP
Miguel Angel Maldonando	29	
Roberto Maldonado	26	
Julio Maluto		
Olga Yolanda Mamani	24	PRT
Luis Abel Manasero	33	
Ernesto Manchi		
Hermes Juan Bautista Manera	32	
Eduardo Luis Manghesi	24	CURS/OCPO
Jorge Alberto Manzanelli	24	Palabra Obrera
Juan Carlos Manzanelli	33	
Graciela Del Valle Maorenzic	27	PRT
Liliana Alicia Marchetti	26	Montoneros
Angel Dante Marchi	26	
Victor Hugo Marciale	21	JP/Montoneros
Luis Alberto Marconetto	24	OCPO
Jorge Horacio Marmol	30	PRT/ERP
Arturo Gustavo Marotta	21	
Jorge Gabriel Márquez	30	JP
Luis Alberto Márquez	28	PCR
Luis Ernesto Márquez	23	
María Cristina Márquez	21	
Alberto Federico Márquez Mariño	31	
Alfredo Horacio Martellotto	28	
Orlando Alonso Martin	22	PRT
Roberto Martinelli	23	
Enrique Gabriel Martínez	23	PRT/ERP
Graciela Herminia Martínez		
Hector Hugo Martínez	20	
Hugo Alberto Martínez	18	
José Agustin Martínez	23	Montoneros
Martha Irene Martínez	28	
Jorge Eduardo Martini	28	

Ilda Esther Martino	27	
José Luis Marzo	20	
María Susana Mauro	32	
Carlos Eduardo Mayo	30	Montoneros
Carlos Gustavo Mazuelos	30	
María Cristina Mazzuchelli	25	
Norma Hilda Melani	27	
Graciela Aida Meléndez	27	
Máximo Mena		
Jorge Raúl Mende	30	Montoneros
Jorge Omar Mendez	24	JUP
Raquel Rina Menna	27	PRT/ERP
Osvaldo Raúl Messagli	19	PRT
Rubén Fernando Messiez	44	PC
María Magdalena Miainer	27	Montoneros
Luis Fermin Miani	37	Montoneros
Hector Micillo		
Lidio Antonio Miguez	35	
Raúl Enrique Milito	26	Montoneros
César Antonio Minué	21	
Haydee Lucia Miralles	32	
Amelia Barbara Miranda	26	FAR/Montoneros
Juan Jacobo Mogilner	33	PCML
Buenaventura Molina	54	
Donaldo David Molina	25	
Jorge Carlos Molina	32	PRT/ERP
Juan Antonio Molina		
Lucia Esther Molina	21	
Olga del Carmen Molina	28	
Raúl Mateo Molina	25	PCR
Eduardo Tomás Molinete	28	FAR/Montoneros
Guillermo Marcelo Möller	27	
Luis Carlos Monaco	30	PRT
Norma Gladys Monardi	19	
Susana María Monasterio	25	
María Cristina Mongiano	25	PB
Alejandro Jorge Monjeau	21	JUP/Montoneros
Federico Angel Monjeau		
Roberto Luis Montali	21	OCPO
Juan Carlos Montañez	53	
Beatriz Montejo		
Miguel Angel Montero	28	
Mirta Liliana Montero	20	
Roald Montes	28	FAR
Carlos Eusebio Montoya	33	JP
Juan Alberto Montoya	34	
Enrique Luis Mopty	19	
Noemí María Mopty	26	PRT

(continued)

(continued)

Name	Age	Known Political Affiliation*
Ernesto Martin Mora	26	
Alejandro Manuel Morales	27	
Miguel Angel Moran	16	
Cristina Del Valle Morandini	23	JUP/Montoneros
Nestor Luis Morandini	22	JUP
José Luis Morel	27	Montoneros
Ana Vilma Moreno	22	
Nelida Noemi Moreno	32	
Miguel Angel Moresi	30	
Pedro Francisco Moresi	27	
Ester Moretti	37	
Miguel Angel Morini	22	
Lita Mosiscle		
Ruben Hugo Motta	25	
José René Moukarzel	26	PRT/ERP
Aristóbulo Daniel Moyano	32	
José Daniel Moyano	21	
María Del Carmen Moyano	22	Montoneros
Miguel Angel Mozé		
María Ines Muchiutti	27	
María Luz Mújica	24	
José Luis Muñoz		
Osvaldo Muñoz	45	
Ana María Murguiondo	21	Montoneros
Jorge Raúl Nadra	20	JUP/Montoneros
Caram Nahum	50	
Claudio Norberto Nardini	34	
Elba Rosa Navarro	31	OCPO
Juan Carlos Navarro	25	PC
José Luis Nicola	25	OCPO
Adriana Silvia Nieto	20	
Mario Alberto Nivoli	28	
Rosa Eugenia Novillo	25	PRT/ERP
Alberto José Nuñez	21	
María Del Carmen Nuñez	32	Montoneros
María Elena Nuñez	29	
Victor Hugo Nuñez	20	
Elsa Monica O'Kelly	18	
Horacio Victor O'Kelly	19	
Hector Guillermo Oberlin	31	FAP
Rosa Elena Ocampo	24	
Candido Victor Ochoa	32	
Fernando Alfredo Ochoa	29	
Hugo Estanislao Ochoa	41	JP
Pablo Eduardo Ochoa	27	
José Manuel Ochuza	31	

María Josefa Oddonetto		
Aldo Oscar Ojeda	24	
Luis Rodolfo Ojeda	29	
Omar Alejandro Olachea	26	
Carlos Delfín Oliva	20	JUP/Montoneros
Hilda Ines Olivier	21	JP/Montoneros
Gustavo Gabriel Olmedo	19	
José Horacio Olmedo	23	OCPO
Silvia Martin Olmedo	23	
José Enrique Olmos	23	
Miguel Angel Olmos	20	
Chris Ana Olson	30	
Carlos Ernesto Ontivero	29	
Pedro Jorge Ontivero	29	
Elber Mario Hugo Oria	40	
Alberto Marcelo Oro	28	
Daniel Francisco Orozco	21	JG/PRT/ERP
Daniel Santos Ortega	36	
Pascual Hector Ortega	34	
Maria Cristina Ortiz	25	PCR
Vilma Ethel Ortiz	21	OCPO
Pablo Daniel Ortman	36	PRT
José Antonio Orueta	29	
José Osatinsky	15	
Marcos Osatinsky	41	FAR/Montoneros
Mario Andrés Osatinsky	18	
Lucio Oscar Otegui		
Carlos Otta	39	PC
Hugo Ricardo Oviedo	20	
Mario Domingo Oviedo	31	
José Antonio Oyarzabal	22	JUP
Humberto Pache	29	
Carlos Benito Pacheco		
Hugo Hernán Pacheco	23	
Victor Hugo Paciaroni	24	PCML/VC
Adolfo Hugo Paez	46	
Liliana Felisa Paez		PRT/ERP
Nestor Carmides Paez	38	
Hector Francisco Palacio	30	
Hilda Floria Palacios	26	
Rubén Amadeo Palazzesi	32	FAP
Santiago Pampillón		
Silvia Papan de Remey		
María Leonor Pappaterra	28	Montoneros
Silvia Mónica Parodi	20	JG/PRT/ERP
Guillermo Osvaldo Paryszewski	31	PRT
Cesar Tomás Passamonte	20	
Aida Alicia Pastarini	24	

(continued)

(continued)

Name	Age	Known Political Affiliation*
Victor Hugo Patat	23	
Hector Mario Patiño	29	Montoneros
Omar Nelson Patiño	35	PRT/ERP
Carlos Ernesto Patrignani	29	PCML/VC
Osvaldo Hector Paulin	23	PRT/ERP
Martha Cecilia Paulone	26	PRT/ERP
Hugo Alberto Pavon	20	PRT
Pablo Eugenio Payer	20	
Patricia Marta Pedroche	22	
Juan Carlos Pellegrini	30	JP
Aldo Cirilo Pellico	37	
Nelida Orlanda Pelossi	43	
Miguel Angel Peña		
Esteban Peralta	19	
Justo José Peralta	45	
Silvia Peralta	23	
Berta Perassi	24	
Juan Carlos Perchante	27	Montoneros
Nora Graciela Peretti	31	FIP
Carlos Alberto Pereyra	29	
Guillermo Pereyra		
Gustavo Alberto Pereyra		PRT
José Antonio Pérez	33	
José Carlos Perucca	26	
Alberto Oscar Pesarini	20	
Osvaldo Pesce		
Cecilia Alicia Pessina		
Victor Miguel Piazza	35	
María Luisa Piedra	21	PRT
Horacio Miguel Pietragalla	27	
Ana María Piffaretti	32	
Nicolas Mario Pilipchuk	36	
Lucía Pino		PRT
Jorge Luis Piotti	28	Montoneros
Daniel Pitrelli		
Estela Pitrelli		
Carlos Alberto Pizarro	31	
Felipe Rodolfo Pizarro	17	
Juan Carlos Pizarro	23	
Julio César Pizarro	15	
Carlos Simon Poblete	32	JP/Montoneros
Horacio Norberto Poggio	35	
Hugo Alberto Pogliotti	24	
Vicente Polombo		
Rodolfo Alberto Ponce	21	PRT
Ernesto Edelmiro Ponza	23	

Miguel Angel Porta	28	
José Andres Portillo	24	
Mario Eugenio Pottigiani		
Antonio Luciano Pregoni	37	
Salvador Privitera	33	Montoneros
Monica Protti	24	PC
Elba Rosario Pucheta	38	PRT/ERP
Guillermo Abel Pucheta	30	PRT/ERP
José Angel Pucheta	31	PRT/ERP
Graciela Gladys Pujol	23	OCPO
Mario Alberto Purino		
Norberto Puyol	34	ERP
Alicia Mabel Queiro	22	ERP
Carlos Alberto Quieto	32	
Alfredo Ramón Quinteros	32	
Carlos Fabian Quiroga	18	PRT
Pedro Antonio Quiroga	26	Montoneros
María Haydee Rabuñal	26	FAL
Norma Raquel Raggio	24	JP
Mario Hugo Ramello	19	
Antonio Cesar Ramírez	20	Montoneros
Hector Eduardo Ramírez	41	
Julio Cesar Ramírez	32	Montoneros
Mercedes Del Valle Ramírez	22	
Ramón Antonio Ramírez	23	
Oscar Julio Ramos	37	
Osvaldo Raúl Ravasi		
Constantino Razzetti	58	
Viviana Beatriz Real	26	
Eduardo Luis Reale	23	
Antonio Reartes		
Victor Mario Reartes	23	
Emilia Patricia Reñanco	18	
Eduardo Lucio Renedo	25	
Eduardo Raúl Requena	37	
Liliana Beatriz Retegui	22	JUP
Eduardo Daniel Reyes	49	
Manuel Federico Reyes		
Oscar Omar Reyes	45	PC
Francisco Irineo Reyna	21	
María Adela Reyna	29	Montoneros
Jorge Alfredo Reynoso	34	
Vicente Manuel Ribero	40	
Gerardo Ramón Ricardone	28	
Mirta Susana Ricciardi	22	
Luis Anselmo Ricciardino	20	
Elias Humberto Rios		
Rosalino Rios	20	PC

(continued)

(continued)

Name	Age	Known Political Affiliation*
María Del Valle Riso	22	
Fernando Enrique Risso	24	
Jorge Eduardo Risso		
Silvia Juana Rivadera	34	
Inocencio Primitivo Rivarola	57	
Liliana Gladys Riveros	24	
José Elio Robles		
Ramón Humberto Robles	45	
Daniel Rodríguez	31	
Daniel Hector Arturo Rodríguez		
David Rodríguez	21	
Gustavo Adrian Rodríguez	20	Montoneros
Jorge Oscar Rodríguez	25	JTP
José Rodríguez		
Luis Cristobal Rodríguez	25	PRT/ERP
Marcelo Daniel Rodríguez	24	JUP/Montoneros
María José Rodríguez		
Miguel Agustin Rodríguez	30	
Miguel Angel Rodríguez	29	
Pablo Tomás Rodríguez	35	PRT/ERP
Sebastian Raúl Rodríguez	21	
Fernando Sergio Rojas	22	
Claudio Luis Román	16	Montoneros
Daniel Oscar Romanutti	23	
Agustin Guillermo Romero	34	
Cristobal Rodolfo Romero	24	
Jorge Ernesto Romero	24	
Raúl Romero		OCPO
Daniel Alberto Roque	35	
Juan Julio Roque	36	Montoneros
Francisco Rosales	38	
Luis Enrique Rosales	28	
Pablo Javier Rosales	19	
Marta Del Carmen Rossetti	27	PRT/ERP
Erik Rossmann		
Carlos Guillermo Roth	27	Montoneros
Oscar Ruarte	27	PRT/ERP
Jorge Reynaldo Ruartes	24	
Teodoro José Ruedi	35	OCPO
Ricardo Armando Ruffa	23	
Manuel Alberto Ruzo	22	
Alfredo Saavedra	24	
Julio Ramón Sachi	31	
Reynaldo Lázaro Saénz	24	
Ricardo Manuel Saénz	33	
Ricardo Enrique Saibene	20	JUP

Norma Dolores Salaguero	41	
René Rufino Salamanca	35	PCR
Angela Alicia Salamone	28	
Nilda Susana Salamone	27	
Jorge Eduardo Salde	21	
Mario Enrique Salerno	24	
Nicolás Oscar Salerno	25	OCPO
Luis Rodney Salinas	21	
Victor Berman Salinas	26	Montoneros
Carlos Angel Salles	25	
María Luisa Salto	20	
Ruben Humberto Salvadeo	24	OCPO
José Eliseo Sanabria	23	
Beatriz Susana Sánchez	19	
Enrique Alberto Sánchez	23	
Francisco Isodoro Sánchez	28	
Jorge Elvio Sánchez	23	PRT
Mario Gustavo Sánchez	17	
Matias Sánchez	37	
Máximo Sánchez	27	
Daniel Horacio Sanmartin	19	
Juan Carlos Santamarina	22	
Luis Agustin Santillán	27	JUP
Luis Eduardo Santillán	22	JUP
Ricardo Daniel Santilli	30	JP/Montoneros
Mercedes Elmina Santucho	24	PRT
Teresa Elena Santucho		
Simon Angel Sapag	27	
Juan Saquilan		
Estela Rosario Sarmiento	48	
Luis Pablo Sarmiento		
José Alberto Scabuzzo	23	
Jorge Marcelo Scelso	26	PRT
Eduardo José Schiavoni	33	
Catalina Schiuma	39	
Miguel Angel Schlatter	26	Montoneros
Pablo Hipólito Schmucler	19	
Perla Elizabeth Schneider	22	PCML
Alicia Noemi Sciutto	22	
Eduardo Luis Scocco	20	PRT
Daniel Armando Segura	29	
Reineri Oscar Segura	41	
Olga Inés Sestares	28	ERP
Carlos Alberto Sgandurra	29	PRT/ERP
Ingrid Sidaravicius	37	OCPO
Juan Salvador Silvidio		
Alberto Luis Del Valle Simonazzi	23	
Alfredo Luis Sinopoli	22	JUP

(continued)

(continued)

Name	Age	Known Political Affiliation*
Daniel Antonio Sintora	24	
Norma Sintora	25	PRT/ERP
Horacio América Siriani	25	
Eduardo Adolfo Soares	50	
Daniel Oscar Sonzini	22	
Cesar Roberto Soria	22	OCPO
Claudio Soria		
Horacio Humberto Soria	38	
José Oreste Sorzana	32	
María Del Carmen Sosa	32	Montoneros
Juan Carlos Soulier	23	FAL
Luis Roberto Soulier	25	
Adriana Claudia Spaccavento	24	
Silvia Gloria Speranza	22	
Ana María Stiefkens	30	Montoneros
Eduardo Miguel Streger	32	
Susana Inés Strelzik	25	PRT
Osvaldo Ramón Suárez	28	
Raúl Ernesto Suarez	28	
Silvia Graciela Suarez	25	
Victorio Romero Suarez		
Raúl José Suffi	30	
José Alberto Svagusa	27	Montoneros
Juan Del Valle Taborda	24	PRT/ERP
Silvia Del Valle Taborda	23	
Roberto Tauil	30	
José Esteban Tello	31	
Marcelo Rodolfo Tello	25	
Rodolfo Tenreyro	64	
Isabel Olga Terraf	28	
Aníbal Carlos Testa	23	JG
María Ana Catalina Testa	20	Montoneros
Raúl Hector Tissera	27	OCPO
Ricardo Leandro Tissera	25	
Sergio Julio Tissera	32	
Daniel Alberto Toninetti	25	
Eduardo José Toniolli	21	Montoneros
Arnaldo Higinio Toranzo	20	JP/Montoneros
Graciela Haydee Torres	22	PRT
Gustavo Daniel Torres	16	JG
Hernán Lindor Torres	22	
Hilda Ramona Torres	18	PRT/ERP
Luis Eduardo Torres	22	PRT
Miguel Angel Torres		
Dardo José Tosetto	25	PRT/ERP
Victor Hugo Tosoratto		

Ana María Tossetti	31	
Ricardo Daniel Tramontini	21	
Hilda Teresa Trejo	39	
María Esther Trejo	27	
Diana Miriam Triay	30	PRT/ERP
Raúl Horacio Trigo	28	FJC
Sergio Pedro Trod	20	
Emilce Magdalena Trucco	23	
Carlos Alberto Tuda	25	Montoneros
Eugenia Francisca Turri	51	
Inés Magdalena Uhalde	20	
Jorge Alejandro Ulla		
Silvia Inés Urdampilleta	28	PRT/ERP
Francisco Reynaldo Urondo	46	FAR/Montoneros
Benito Alberto Urquia	39	
Miguel Hugo Vaca Narvaja (junior)	35	Montoneros
Miguel Hugo Vaca Narvaja (senior)	60	
Raúl Alberto Vaca	22	
Olga Vaccarini	22	Montoneros
Eduardo Enrique Vadillo	20	
Luis Enrique Valdes	24	Montoneros
Cristina Elena Vallejo	24	
Eduardo Jorge Valverde	36	
Adriana Vera Vanella	19	PRT/ERP
María Del Carmen Vanella	23	PRT/ERP
Alberto Segundo Varas	31	
Jorge Vargas	22	
Angel Fabian Vázquez	24	
Hector Raúl Vázquez	57	
Hugo Eduardo Vázquez		
Jorge Oscar Vázquez	24	
Hector Hugo Vedia	25	
Raúl Alberto Vega	29	Montoneros
Carlos Alberto Velazquez	25	
Victor Julio Velez	37	
Edith Vera	33	
Victor Hugo Vera	28	PRT/ERP
Wenceslao Vera	27	
José Enrique Verdiell	30	
Beatriz Virginia Verdura	36	
Edgardo Justino Vergara	27	PRT/ERP
Rodolfo José Vergara	25	PRT
Estela Beatriz Verolez	32	
Luis Ricardo Veron	27	JTP/Montoneros
Osvaldo Veron	19	
Raúl Francisco Viajande	27	
Maria Elma Viale	29	
Margarita Vich	47	

(continued)

(continued)

Name	Age	Known Political Affiliation*
Enrique Justo Viega	22	
Juan De Dios Vila	23	
Laura Vilches		
Federico Viles		
José Osvaldo Villada		
Juan Carlos Villafañe	22	
Silverio Fortunato Villagra	46	
Romelia Alicia Villalba	24	
Luis Villalba	26	
Ana María Villanueva	23	
Nestor Villarreal	46	
Aida Inés Villegas	23	
Jorge Villegas	20	
José María Villegas	20	
Carmen Rosa Vilte	30	
María Elena Beatriz Viola	26	PRT
Graciela Vitale	20	JG
Hector Antonio Vitantonio	22	PRT/ERP
Hernán Andrés Vives	34	PC
Gloria Isabel Waquim	23	
Norma Elinor Waquim	22	JUP
Osvaldo Mauricio Weldmann	32	
Eva Weinstein	18	PC
Margarita Susana Weiss	25	Montoneros
Juan Carlos Yabbur	23	
Raúl Clemente Yager	38	Montoneros
Miguel Angel Yanes		
Julio César Yañez	26	JP/Montoneros
Ricardo Manuel Yavcoli	24	JP/Montoneros
Gabriela Yofre	24	
Roberto Julio Yornet	30	OCPO
Ricardo Alberto Yung	32	Montoneros
Armando Agustin Zacari	31	JUP
Francisco Isidoro Zamora	32	PRT
Hugo Antonio Zárate	27	PRT
María Angelica Zárate	43	
David Oscar Zarco	22	FJC/PC
Claudio Manfredo Zieschank	24	
Claudio Aníbal Zorrilla	21	OCPO
Ricardo José Zucaria	24	JUP
Osvaldo Zun		PRT
Enzo Rafael Domingo Zunino	19	JUP/Montoneros
Julio Oscar Zurita	20	
Ricardo Alfredo Zurschmitten	46	

SOURCES: Archivo Provincial de la Memoria (Córdoba). Database on deaths and disappearances; Parque de la Memoria http://parquedelamemoria.org.ar/ "Registro de Víctimas," Dossier del Juicio.

Political Affiliations

ERP	Ejército Revolucionario del Pueblo
FAL	Frente Argentino de Liberación
FIP	Frente de Izquierda Popular
FJC	Federación Juvenil Comunista
FR 17	Frente Revolucionario 17 de Octubre
JG	Juventud Guevarista
JP	Juventud Peronista
JTP	Juventud Trabajadora Peronista
JUP	Juventud Universitaria Peronista
OCPO	Organización Comunista Poder Obrero
PC	Partido Comunista
PCML	Partido Comunista Marxista Leninista
PCR	Partido Comunista Revolucionario
PRT	Partido Revolucionario de los Trabajadores
PST	Partido Socialista de los Trabajadores
VC	Vanguardia Comunista

DECLARATION OF
GENERAL LUCIANO BENJAMIN MENÉNDEZ,
MENÉNDEZ IV TRIAL,
JUNE 1, 2015

I rebelled against my fellow officers in the military government. I did so because I wanted to see military rule end as soon as possible. That elections be called as soon as possible as prescribed by the 1853 constitution, and prior to that to have erased from the electoral rolls all those who had anything to do with subversive actions. I thought with such a framework we would return quickly to democracy and that it would be enduring, having eliminated the possibilities of interfering in our democratic life those who had conspired against these governments and who sought to impose and desired to impose an authoritarian system in Argentina.

There are some common themes in the declarations of the witnesses, of the plaintiffs, in these lawsuits, of the supposed victims, which are repeated over and over in all their testimony, even in their tears. One of the shared characteristics is that they all recognize having been members of one or another illegal organization in that period that were intent on seizing power. They were combatants, that is to say those who accuse us for having fought against them are those who yesterday fought against us. Of course those groups to which they belonged, which had the names of social and political organizations, they swear had charitable purposes. They were young folk who worked pacifically to transform us into a more socially just society. Yet all, or almost all the prisoners, at that time were tried by the federal courts. They were found guilty by the judges, yet none of them explain the reasons for their arrest, even though their very political activism put them in a state of illegality. Why are we being judged? When at that time it was a legally sanctioned matter. Now it all begins again, but the guerrillas of the 1970s are now judging us.

Another thing that all deponents do is conflate, misleadingly but skillfully, the counterrevolutionary war with the military government. This confusion allows them to at the same time discredit the military government while enhancing their own image, seeking to portray themselves as combatants against the military government and attributing to the military government the domestic persecution of the country's political parties. Our enemies were the Marxist terrorists. As has been demonstrated in all the trials as echoed in the words of all the witnesses, no one was ever persecuted for political ideas that had the best interests of the nation. The armed forces were completely preoccupied with the counterrevolutionary war. Nor were they persecuted by the military government, which simply aspired to govern.

I return to the subject of the peaceful sentiments that those organizations attribute to themselves, which paradoxically were charitable in nature yet they adopted names as if they were military ones. Aspirations that they must have had deep in their hearts. They called themselves the Ejército Revolucionario del Pueblo, the Fuerzas Armadas Revolucionarias, the Fuerzas Armadas Peronistas, etc. Despite the fact that now they tell us they were simply there to distribute welfare to the people. Che Guevara clarifies this subject. Their idol said that it was essential above all "to keep alive our hatred, to heighten it to the point of rage, an intransigent hatred toward the enemy, a hatred capable of lifting man beyond his natural limitations and transform him into a cold, selective, violent and efficient killing machine."

Now we know, moreover, that in 1964, I hope that no one has forgotten that date, precisely during the governments of Frondizi and Illia, both democratic governments, and not only by virtue of being elected by the people because democracy does not end with elections, it is only the start. Something that it would appear many do not understand. It was such for the exemplary exercise of power under which all institutions functioned and the citizenry was able to enjoy all its rights. The Marxist guerrillas cannot use as an excuse that they were peaceful citizens seeking to defend democracy, because democracy was well defended and they were the only ones who attacked it.

Continuing this brief summary of the war's chronology, let us remember that on August 19, 1964, the Gendarmería and police destroyed the recently established camp in Orán where the self-denominated Ejército Guerrillero del Pueblo trained. Once again I return to the military names such groups adopted. The guerrilla leader of the camp was Jorge Masetti, a journalist for the Cuban press agency, Prensa Latina. The Chamber of Deputies, functioning perfectly during the government of Dr. Illia, convoked Illia's ministers to inform them about the operation. The statements of the ministers of a democratically elected government are very revealing. Dr. Suárez, the minister of defense, explained: "The Communist Party of 1957 begins to concern itself fundamentally with Africa, with Latin America, and a part of Asia. When Fidel Castro declares himself a communist there begins a period of great disturbance in all of Latin America."

Zabala Ortiz, minister of foreign affairs in that government, declared on that same occasion: "The existence of a power so extraordinary as that of an atomic bomb has determined that conflict arises by other means, that of

revolutionary war, an undeclared war, silent but inexorable, total and permanent. That is the state of affairs that has taken root in Latin America. Communism establishes itself in Cuba with a permanent organization of a revolutionary nature. A revolutionary war is declared against governments, democracies
and otherwise. The prevailing Latin American democracies and nondemocra-
cies must respond to this situation and we must take the appropriate means."

This was the revolutionary war, an international war where on one side
fought the Russians and their servants and on the other sides was us, the
national forces who wanted to preserve our way of life and our independence.
The Argentine nation, to defend itself from the Marxist aggression, employed
all available means after 1964. Thus it applied against its aggressors the laws of
the land. Faced with the failure of such laws, the Federal Penal Chamber was
created, which prosecuted 1,600 guerrillas but was shut down and its sentences annulled on May 25, 1973, by the former attorney general, Dr. Regui,
who was then Cámpora's minister of the interior, and who granted an amnesty
to all the subversive prisoners, both those convicted and on trial. The government then returned to passing laws, without results. It declared illegal the ERP
[Ejército Revolucionario del Pueblo] and the PRT [Partido Revolucionario de
los Trabajadores] by presidential decree 1.474 of 1973. In 1974 Lastiri amended
the Penal Code, allowing a harsher repression, as it said in its reasoning, of
conduct that was creating anxiety among the population. The bombings, the
attacks that were taking place. Despite this strengthening of the Penal Code,
no judge managed to sentence any guerrilla between 1974 and 1975. It then
resorted to state terrorism through the AAA [Alianza Anticomunista Argen-
tina], a sinister organization disbanded on the demands of the army. Later, the
government entrusted to the armed forces the task of annihilating the subversion in Tucumán through decree 291 in 1975. It declared the Montoneros "an
unlawful association of a terrorist nature" by presidential decree 2.452 in 1975.

The Marxist terrorism overwhelmed all the national government's peaceful
measures. Thus the subversion grew and ended up constituting true clandestine armies. The military aspirations of the guerrillas were becoming realized.
They were veritable clandestine armies with a political leadership that had
international connections and support, their fighters organized in commandos and units in imitation of the country's armed forces, so also with their
intelligence services, their logistical support in health, materials, transport,
and munitions. In their practices of recruitment, their propaganda, their programs of political indoctrination and military training in the country and
abroad, their own system of furlough and deployment. It comprised the entire
structure of a true army.

Faced with growth and danger of these terrorist groups that ended up
recruiting 40,000 men, Argentina through a 1975 presidential decree created
the Council of Internal Security, presided over by the president of the nation
and composed of all the government ministers and commanders of the armed
forces in order to direct the nation's efforts in the struggle against subversion,
and ordered its armed forces through another 1975 presidential decree, both

decrees signed by the constitutional President Luder, to proceed to undertake military and security operations that would be necessary to crush the actions of the subversive enemy throughout the country. This expression "to crush the actions" has served as a pretext for the terrorists to claim that we went beyond the law, because we were only authorized to crush their actions. As if actions could be separated from the men who commit them.

We fought against an enemy who, when defeated, would disappear and join up with others, or continue to act individually. The Security Council that was established to direct the war sensed the flawed nature of this phrase and sought to correct the mission and to perfect it, saying that the armed forces and police should operate in the entire national territory in order to annihilate the subversive organizations. To clarify further, it added, "the actions should aim toward the crushing of the essential components of the subversive organizations." Argentina in the end employing military principles in light of this presidential decree, rejected the armed Marxist aggression.

The subversive forces bloodied the country for ten years. In that time they murdered 1,500 people of whom 60 percent were members of the armed and police forces, another 40 percent were civilians, businessmen, trade union leaders, politicians, employees, and priests. And they wounded many more. They wounded 1,700 people. They committed 21,600 terrorist attacks, six per day. I am tempted to ask, if all they engaged in were acts of charity, those organizations with the military names in which they participated undertook social and political work solely, who then wielded the arms that produced those 21,600 attacks and those 1,600 deaths and kidnappings?

It would be interesting to research. The armed forces enforced the laws and the military legislation in force, they fulfilled in just a few years the mission they were assigned by the nation, to vanquish the enemy. And by shortening the war they prevented further crimes. And they prevented the fatherland further suffering.

Let us compare our situation to Colombia's, which for sixty years has suffered the scourge of terrorism and which it has still been unable to defeat. Let us compare the situation to that we ended up living in Tucumán, where you could not go down Route 307 because the guerrillas came out of the jungle, detained travelers, and they demanded that they pay tolls and other things. And we are the ones being judged? We are the first country in the history of the world to judge its victorious soldiers who struggled and prevailed for the stability of its fellow citizens. We witness the sad spectacle of judging our military for the simple reason, and no one disputes me, that this outlandish spectacle is rigged. There is no country in the world that complains about its military doing what it was ordered to do.

Now the federal court system judges us for supposed crimes committed by armed forces in the counterrevolutionary war. It is also pointed out to us in a moreover pedantic way that we should have employed the Penal Code instead of resorting to arms. But it fails to remember that the Argentine nation used the law and the justice system in order to combat the actions of Marxist terrorism, before ordering the armed forces the use of arms. I have just enumerated the creation of federal tribunals, the strengthening of the Penal Code, the decrees consigning the guerrillas to an illegal status. All those efforts were undertaken peacefully, attempting to halt the march to the communist abysm. And that, despite the atrocious crimes by Marxist terrorism between 1960 and 1970. The nation tolerated so much before deciding to resort to arms that I remember a snide remark from the period reproaching us that the military we knew how to die but we did not know how to kill.

Why did the methods change and the legally constituted authorities finally order the armed forces to begin military operations to crush the subversion? Those judges assigned today to try us accepted their task of dealing with the actions of the subversives through the enforcement of the Penal Code and assigned this responsibility to the armed forces.

Let us remember once again that the armed forces combated Marxist terrorism for more than a year in Tucumán and for another six months in the rest of the country. From 1974 until 1975 and from 1975 until March 1976 we fought under the control and command of a legal, constitutional government. How is it then that between February 1975 and March 1976, no judge, no politician, no government functionary, no journalist raised his voice for the supposed excesses of the armed forces? Could it be that in 1975 no one in the country, not the president, not the legislative nor judicial branches, at that time thoroughly legitimate and chosen by a popular vote in full exercise of their authority, neither government officials nor journalists imagined it necessary to curb the onslaught of Marxist terrorism by another means than resorting to arms? Could it be that it was understood, as is proven by many newspaper stories at time, that we were at war, and neither the judiciary nor the Penal Code could wage that war?

It is appropriate to remember a speech of Isabel Perón on December 17, 1975, where it was said: "The Armed Forces in fulfillment of their constitutional duties and called upon by the government, have together with the security forces, responsibility for direct action against the subversion. To them we render the government's gratitude and homage, calling upon them from the hallowed principles of the fatherland."

At that time, those behaving illegally were in illegality. That was their status. And the legal forces were in legality. And no one disputed it, because the circumstances were very difficult and few were determined and capable of confronting them, given the level they had reached, thanks above all to international aid they had received. Terrorist crimes were occurring and triumphant statements made, ones that the young of today will have read. It is ridiculous that those who were unable to undertake the task, because it is not the responsibility of the judiciary to wage war, should intervene and convene, thirty years later after having put an end to the violence, thanks to the determination of the nation's armed forces and of the security and police forces, with the argument, among others, of not having applied the Penal Code. Behind this crude and ridiculous maneuver are the same guerrillas of that period, occupying positions in the government and attempting to kill two birds with one stone. On the one hand, to discredit the nation's judicial system. In order to judge us, they have violated numerous juridical norms and applied the law in an arbitrary and illegal way. And at the same time, they seek to discredit the armed forces, presenting as crimes its actions of counterrevolutionary war. We did not commit a single crime because crimes against humanity are defined as those committed against a civilian population. And we fought against military combatants. They identified themselves as such. They used insignias, badges, they manufactured uniforms for such purposes.

The guerrillas abandoned armed struggle and blended into society, pretending to be peaceful citizens. But they did not abandon their struggle. Revolutionary war did not end; it was simply transferred to other areas, following Gramsci's doctrine, who preached that it was necessary to take control of education, culture, and the means of communication, and from there to take political power to dominate civil society. Precisely what is happening now. Once they feel that the ability of Argentines to react is destroyed, that they are strong enough to squash that ability, then abandoning their peaceful disguise, just as Che Guevara and Fidel Castro did there in Cuba, they will use all manner of violence to change our way of life.

I trust that we Argentines will come together to halt this march towards the abyss and return to our institutions. We have been suffering with ten years of authoritarianism in which we have been steamrolled and insulted by a despotic government that has violated the constitution and the law. Its ultimate aspiration is to impose an authoritarian system. Right now it is being discovered that these trials, clearly unconstitutional, that nonetheless there are a number of players involved, playing their roles as if they were legal.

I hope these shameful years may serve so the citizens of our republic, both the governed and those who govern, respect and have respected the constitution. Let us not depart whatever our rank in society, from these institutional norms. Let us inaugurate a democratic stage again, and this time may it be genuine and long lasting. I am convinced that this experience we are living will serve us in the future to reject arbitrary whims of a caudillo as soon as they become apparent. To adhere unequivocally to constitutional principles. Only in this way the constitution, justice, and liberty will rule. The fatherland of liberty and democracy will guide the path of Argentines in their destiny of greatness. A path that we undertook successfully as we operated with total freedom within the framework of the constitution, and on various occasions was thwarted.

NOTES

INTRODUCTION

1. Equipo Argentino de Antropología Forense, "Cementerio de San Vicente. Informe 2003" (Córdoba: Ferreyra Editor, 2005).

2. On the history of the EAAF, see Patricia Bernardi and Luis Fondebrider, "Forensic Archaeology and the Scientific Documentation of Human Rights Violations: An Argentinian Example from the Early 1980s," in *Forensic Archaeology and Human Rights Violations*, ed. Roxana Ferllini (Springfield: Charles C. Thomas Publishers, 2007), 205–32; Mercedes Doretti and L. Fondebrider, "Perspectives and Recommendations from the Field: Forensic Anthropology and Human Rights in Argentina," Proceedings of the 56th Annual Meeting of the American Academy of Forensic Sciences, Dallas, 1984; Mercedes Doretti and Clyde C. Snow, "Forensic Anthropology and Human Rights: the Argentine Experience," in *Hard Evidence: Case Studies in Forensic Anthropology* (Upper Saddle River, NJ: Prentice Hall, 2003), 290–310.

3. Informe, Comisión Nacional sobre la Desaparición de Personas (CONADEP), Delegación Córdoba 1984/1999.

4. Despite herculean efforts, as of 2008 the EAAF had only been able to recover the remains of approximately 1,000 *desaparecidos* throughout the country, and of those some 320 have been identified. Equipo Argentino de Antropología Forense (EAAF), "Latin American Initiative for the Identification of the Disappeared: Genetics and Human Rights" Argentine Section, Report (2008): 15.

5. Charles S. Maier, "Doing History, Doing Justice: The Narrative of the Historian and of the Truth Commission," in *Truth vs. Justice: The Morality of Truth Commissions*, ed. Robert I. Rotberg and Dennis Thompson (Princeton, NJ: Princeton University Press, 2000), 266.

6. The list of such works is long and I will mention only some of the more notable examples: In English, Ian Guest, *Behind the Disappearances* (Philadelphia: University of

Pennsylvania Press, 1990); Martin E. Andersen, *Dossier Secreto: Argentina's Desaparecidos and the Myth of the "Dirty War"* (Boulder, CO: Westview, 1993); Marguerite Feitlowitz, *A Lexicon of Terror: Argentina and the Legacies of Terror*, rev ed. (New York: Oxford University Press, 1998). In Spanish, María Seoane and Vicente Muleiro, *El Dictador: la historia secreta y pública de Jorge Rafael Videla* (Buenos Aires: Editorial Sudamericana, 2001); Horacio Verbitsky, *El vuelo* (Buenos Aires: Editorial Planeta, 1996). The period of the 1976–83 dictatorship and state terrorism has also been a favorite subject of Argentine novelists and filmmakers.

7. Of these, the most significant contribution is Gabriela Aguila, *Dictadura, represión y sociedad en Rosario, 1976/1983: Un estudio sobre la represión y los comportamientos y actitudes sociales en dictadura* (Buenos Aires: Prometeo Libros, 2008). Two political scientists have also written a valuable comprehensive history of the military regime: Marcos Novaro and Vicente Palermo, *La dictadura militar 1976/1983: Del golpe a la restauración democrática* (Buenos Aires: Paidós, 2003).

8. One of the better examples of this genre is María Maneiro, *Como el árbol talado: Memorias del genocidio en La Plata, Berissso y Ensenada* (La Plata: Ediciones al Margen, 2005).

9. Donald Hodges, *Argentina's "Dirty War": An Intellectual Biography* (Austin: University of Texas Press, 1991).

10. David Sheinin, *Consent of the Damned. Ordinary Argentines in the Dirty War* (Gainesville: University of Florida Press, 2012), 49–56.

11. I conducted some preliminary research in Mexico on the collaboration between the Argentine and Mexican intelligence services and their monitoring of the large Argentine exile community there, especially in Mexico City. My findings were by no means conclusive but did suggest such cooperation existed and was ongoing. Given the prominence of *cordobeses* in that community, figures like political philosopher and Marxist intellectual Pancho Aricó, writer Antonio Marimón, and Peronist politician Ricardo Obregón Cano, I suspect that they may have been a particular source of interest for the military government. The subject merits its own study. On the Argentine exile experience generally in Mexico, see Pablo Yankelvich, *Ráfagas de un exilio. Argentinos en México* (Mexico City: El Colegio de México, 2009).

12. Thomas R. Mockaitis, *British Counterinsurgency, 1919–60* (London: Macmillan, 1990); Richard Bennett, *The Black and Tans* (London: Severn House, 1976): Richard English, *Armed Struggle: A History of the IRA* (London: Macmillan, 2003).

13. Richard Evans, *The Third Reich at War* (New York: Penguin, 2009); Eric A. Johnson, *Nazi Terror: The Gestapo, Jews, and Ordinary Citizens* (New York: Basic Books, 1999).

14. Raphaëlle Branche, *La torture et l'armée pendant la guerre d'Algerie* (Paris: Gallimard, 2001); Alistair Horne, *A Savage War of Peace: Algeria 1954–1962* (London: Macmillan, 1977).

15. Caroline Elkins, *Imperial Reckoning: The Untold Story of Britain's Gulag in Kenya* (New York: Henry Holt, 2005).

16. Death by disappearance makes it enormously difficult to provide precise numbers, complicated even more by the politics surrounding disputed figures. See Alison Brysk, "The Politics of Measurement: The Contested Count of the Disappeared in Argentina," *Human Rights Quarterly* 16 (1994): 677–92. These figures, moreover, reflect only the number of

"disappeared" and do not include those killed in confrontations, real or staged, with the security forces and for whom no public death certificate exists; nor the great numbers captured, tortured, and then released; nor the illicit adoption of children of political prisoners. Combining all categories of victims, the extent of the military's campaign of state terrorism becomes even more appalling.

17. In all these ways, Argentina's experience with state-directed mass murder stands apart from the mainstream in the twentieth century. Where it falls within that woeful tradition is in the state's willingness to employ violence against its own citizens and that its perpetrators were the country's military. See Mark Mazower, "Violence and the State in the Twentieth Century," *American Historical Review* 107, no. 4 (October 2002): 1158–78.

18. Greg Grandin, *Empire's Workshop: Latin America, the United States and the Rise of the New Imperialism* (New York: Henry Holt, 2006).

19. For a recent representative statement of this predominant view of the Cold War in Latin America see Stephen G. Rabe, *The Killing Zone: The United States Wages the Cold War in Latin America* (New York: Oxford University Press, 2012). As a counterpoint, see Hal Brands, *Latin America's Cold War* (Cambridge, MA: Harvard University Press, 2012).

CHAPTER ONE. THREATS: APOSTLES OF THE NEW ORDER

1. On the youth culture of the period generally, see Valeria Manzano, *The Age of Youth in Argentina: Culture, Politics and Sexuality* (Chapel Hill: University of North Carolina Press, 2014).

2. Antonius Robben rejects the rationale of the military's adoption of extreme measures, based as they were on an total absence of credible threats: "There was not an immediate threat because the ERP and Montoneros had been largely defeated by early 1976, nor was there a serious threat because neither guerrilla organizations nor revolutionary thought had sustained popular support. The moral gravity of the dirty war became thus quadrupled. The rhetorically erected state of urgency was an excuse to justify the elimination of an entire social sector believed to constitute an eventual threat." See Antonius C. G. M. Robben, *Political Violence and Trauma in Argentina* (Philadelphia: University of Pennsylvania Press, 2005), 173. I am not in full agreement with this assessment on several grounds. At least in Córdoba, the Montoneros for several months after the coup were still capable of and did engage in some small-scale operations. More importantly, though I agree with this assessment on the proposition of a credible *military* threat, one could argue that the guerrilla organizations had never been a serious military adversary, demonstrated by the army's swiftness in suppressing both the Tucumán *foco* and the urban guerrilla. However, the military's perception of the threat was above all its presence, extant not eventual, in the workplace, the university, and the Catholic Church. The military government did not assume a "defeat" of the Left in these sites at the time of the coup, and indeed one had not yet taken place. For the military, the outcome of this "cultural war" was still in the balance for several years after assuming power. Such a calculation of course does not attenuate its guilt for the egregious crimes committed, but it does provide an explanation.

3. On the subject of the youth as agents of change in these years see: Sergio Pujol, *La década rebelde: los sesenta en la Argentina* (Buenos Aires: Emecé, 2000); Alejandro Cataruzza, "Un mundo por hacer: una propuesta para el análisis de la cultura juvenil en la

Argentina de los años setenta," *Entrepasados*, no. 13 (1997); and Manzano, *The Age of Youth in Argentina*. On the specific case of Córdoba, see James Brennan, "Rebelión y Revolución: Los estudiantes de la Universidad Nacional de Córdoba en el contexto transnacional," in *Universidad Nacional de Córdoba. Cuatrocientos años de historia*, ed. Daniel Saur and Alicia Servetto (Córdoba: Editorial de la Universidad Nacional de Córdoba, 2013).

4. Pablo Buchbinder, *Historia de las universidades argentinas* (Buenos Aires: Editorial Sudamericana, 2005), 170–71; For a detailed if rather encyclopedic study of the student movement in Córdoba in these years, see Roberto A. Ferrero, *Historia crítica del Movimiento Estudiantil en Córdoba* tomo III (1955–1973) (Córdoba: Alción Editora, 2009).

5. I discuss all these episodes in detail in my book, *The Labor Wars in Córdoba*. Harsh, even illegal methods of repression were of course not confined to Córdoba. Accusations of torture of political prisoners elsewhere had become widespread by the early 1970s. See "Fueron dados a publicidad testimonios donde se denuncian casos de torturas," *La Opinión*, January 12, 1972, 10–11. The most infamous example of all was the 1972 Trelew massacre in which sixteen political prisoners who had attempted to escape the Trelew prison were summarily executed.

6. Daniel Mazzei, *Bajo el poder de la caballería: El ejército argentino (1962–1973)* (Buenos Aires, Editorial Universitaria de Buenos Aires, 2012), 234–35.

7. Mazzei, *Bajo el poder de la caballería*, 279.

8. By way of example, "El valor político del fusil," *El Descamisado*, Año 1, no. 17 (September 1973); "La participación del pueblo en la guerra," *Evita Montonera*, Año 1, no. 7 (September 1975): 9; and "Los militares cipayos. Una nueva etapa de la guerra," *Evita Montonera*, Año 2, no. 11 (January 1976): 16–20. Only after the coup did the guerrillas change their vocabulary and drop talk of " revolutionary war" in favor of that of "resistance." For the military, only late in the military government and especially after its fall did the military commanders begin to characterize publicly the campaign against the Left as a "dirty war." See María José Moyano, "The 'Dirty War' in Argentina: Was It a War and How Dirty Was It?" in *Staatliche und Parastaatliche Gewalt in Lateinamerika*, ed. Hans Werner Tobler and Peter Waldmann (Frankfurt: Veruvert Verlag, 1991), 54.

9. Archivo Provincial de la Memoria (henceforth APM), "Manual de Instrucción de las Milicias Montoneras," circa 1974. Córdoba was the site of some dramatic and well-publicized actions by the Left in the years leading up to the 1973 elections. The list included: the Montoneros' occupation of La Calera, the Banco de la Provincia, police commissary, and central post office and a shootout with police leading to the death of Montonero leader Emilio Maza (1970); the ERP's storming of the Channel 10 television station, occupation of the women's prison, the "Buen Pastor" and the Bolivian consulate, and kidnapping and murder of Fiat executive Oberdan Sallustro (1971); the FAP's kidnapping of business executive Aldo Benito Roggio (1972); the ERP's assault on the barracks of the Batallón de Comunicaciones 141 in the Parque Sarmiento and the Montoneros' assassination of the Army Third Corps head of intelligence, Col. Hector Iribarren (April 1973).

10. Marina Franco, *Un enemigo para la nación. Orden interno, violencia y "subversión,"* *1973–1976* (Buenos Aires: Fondo de Cultura Económica, 2012), 157–61.

11. The historiography on the revolutionary Left is now deep. Among others see Eduardo Anguita and Martín Caparrós, *La voluntad* (Buenos Aires, Norma, 1996); Richard Gillespie, *Soldiers of Perón: Argentina's Montoneros* (New York: Oxford University Press, 1982); María

José Moyano, *Argentina's Lost Patrol: Armed Struggle, 1969–1979* (New Haven, CT: Yale University Press, 1995); María Matilde Ollier, *La creencia y la pasión: Privado, público y político en la izquierda revolucionaria* (Buenos Aires: Ariel, 1998); Pablo Pozzi, *Por las sendas argentinas: El PRT-ERP. La guerrilla marxista* (Buenos Aires: EUDEBA, 2001). On the history of the Left in Córdoba specifically, see my *The Labor Wars in Córdoba* and "Rebelión y revolución: Los estudiantes de la Universidad Nacional de Córdoba en un contexto transnacional."

12. Robben, *Political Violence and Trauma in Argentina*, 125–27.

13. Grassroots activism rather than armed struggle characterized the Montoneros' efforts even more in other parts of the country. See Javier Salcedo, *Los Montoneros del barrio* (Buenos Aires: EDUTREF 2011).

14. On university youth and the Left in Córdoba in these years see Mónica Gordillo, "La revolución en la universidad" and James Brennan, "Rebelión y revolución: los estudiantes de la Universidad Nacional de Córdoba en un contexto transnacional," both in *Universidad Nacional de Córdoba: Cuatrocientos años de historia*, vol. II , ed. Daniel Saur and Alicia Servetto (Córdoba: Universidad Nacional de Córdoba, 2013).

15. Alicia Servetto, *73/76. El gobierno peronista contra las "provincias montoneras"* (Buenos Aires: Siglo XXI, 2010), 83–84, 91–98.

16. Shortly after assuming his functions, Lacabbane's words gave a chilling foretaste of the military dictatorship's totalizing logic: " 'Subversion'—an aberration—is not only found in the armed revolutionary organizations, it also exists in public administration, in factories, within the business class, in the province's very economy." Servetto, *73/76. El gobierno peronista*, 229. Lacabbane's denunciation of subversion within the business class was in reference to the pro-Peronist Confederación General Económica.

17. Melisa Paiaro, "La forma legal de lo ilegal. La legislación represiva nacional y su incidencia en la provincia de Córdoba (1973–1976)," *Boletín Bibliográfico Electrónico del Programa Buenos Aires de Historia Política*, Año 6 no. 12 (2013): 111.

18. Marcos Novaro and Vicente Palermo, *La dictadura militar 1976/1983: Del golpe de estado a la restauración democrática* (Buenos Aires: Paidós, 2003), 80–81. Members of this death squad would reputedly later comprise some of the personnel at the La Perla detention center/death camp. Pilar Calveiro, *Política y/o violencia: Una aproximación a la guerrilla de los años 70* (Buenos Aires: Editorial Norma, 2005), 97.

19. Equipo Argentino de Antropología Forense (EAAF), "Latin American Initiative for the Identification of the Disappeared: Genetics and Human Rights" Argentine Section, Report (2008), 15. Novaro and Palermo put the figure even higher, at some nine hundred victims of the death squads. Novaro and Palermo, *La dictadura militar 1976/1983*, 81.

20. On this union election and its importance, see Brennan, *Labor Wars in Córdoba*, 209–22.

21. See Victoria Basualdo, "Contribution to the Analysis of the Role of Labor Leadership in Worker Repression in the 1970s," in *The Economic Accomplices to the Argentine Dictatorship: Outstanding Debts*, ed. Horacio Verbitsky and Juan Pablo Bohoslavsky (Cambridge: Cambridge University Press, 2016), 201–16.

22. Brennan, *Labor Wars in Córdoba*, chapters 6–11. On the OCPO specifically, see Gabriel Montali, "Estrategia y táctica de la izquierda revolucionaria argentina," in *Córdoba a los 40 años del golpe. Estudios sobre la dictadura en clave local*, ed. Ana Carol Solís and Pablo Ponza (Córdoba: Editorial de la Universidad Nacional de Córdoba, 2016), 53–73.

23. Claudio Tognonato, "The Hidden Italy Connection," in Horacio Verbitsky and Juan Pablo Bohoslavsky, *The Economic Accomplices to the Argentine Dictatorship: Outstanding Debts*, ed. Horacio Verbitsky and Juan Pablo Bohoslavsky (Cambridge: Cambridge University Press, 2016), 249–50.

24. Gustavo Morello, *The Catholic Church and Argentina's Dirty War* (Oxford: Oxford University Press, 2015), 12–13. Morello, a Jesuit sociologist from Córdoba, is the foremost authority on the history of the Church and Catholicism during the dictatorship. His numerous publications on the subject are cited throughout this book.

25. Morello, *The Catholic Church and Argentina's Dirty War*, 26.

CHAPTER TWO. DICTATORSHIP: TERRORIZING CÓRDOBA

1. Hugo Quiroga, *El tiempo del Proceso: Conflictos y coincidencias entre civiles y militares (1976–1983)* (Rosario: Editorial Fundación Ross, 1994); Marcos Novaro and Vicente Palermo, *La dictadura militar, 1976/1983: Del golpe de estado a la restauración democrática* (Buenos Aires: Paidós, 2003).

2. According to Calveiro, because of their comparatively smaller size, Córdoba and Tucumán were the cities where the practices of abduction, torture, and disappearances were first essayed. Their size made possible the practice of the "dedo," (fingering) in which the kidnapped in police cars were forced to identify fellow party members and activists on the street, a practice only later adopted in Buenos Aires. Pilar Calveiro, *Política y/o violencia. Una aproximación a la guerrilla de los años 70* (Buenos Aires: Editorial Norma, 2005), 98, 128. The ERP's fate in the city was especially grim. By mid-April, just weeks after the coup, the army had dismantled one hundred of the estimated 120 party cells in the city. Antonius C.G.M. Robben, *Political Violence and Trauma in Argentina* (Philadelphia: University of Pennsylvania Press, 2005), 201. More importantly, the military's perception of the "defeat" of the armed Left would delay a year following the coup.

3. EAAF, "Latin American Initiative for the Identification of the Disappeared: Genetics and Human Rights," (2008): 15, 50. Most of the remains exhumed by the EAAF have been in municipal cemeteries in Buenos Aires and, more recently with the San Vicente discovery, in Córdoba. New exhumations have been undertaken by the team in Chaco province.

4. Frank Graziano, *Divine Violence: Spectacle, Psychosexuality and Radical Christianity in the Argentine "Dirty War"* (Boulder, CO: Westview, 1982).

5. Comité de Defensa de Derechos Humanos en el Cono Sur, Report "Desaparecidos en la Argentina," São Paulo (1982).

6. Ceferino Reato, *Disposición Final: La confesión de Videla sobre los desaparecidos* (Buenos Aires: Editorial Sudamericana, 2012), 43–44, 51–52.

7. Reato, *Disposición final*, 2012, 64–65.

8. Within weeks of the coup, the ambitions of the local military rulers was demonstrated in a public burning of books, presided over by Lieutenant Colonel Jorge Gorleri, who denounced "pernicious literature that disturbs the intellect and our Christian way of life . . . deceiving our youth regarding the true worth of our national symbols, our family, our Church, our most traditional values encapsulated in God, Fatherland, and Home." Among the authors of this pernicious literature figured Pablo Neruda, Marcel Proust, and Mario Vargas Llosa. Novaro Palermo, *La dictadura militar, 1976/1983*, 140.

9. Reato, *Disposición Final*, 107.

10. Reato, *Disposición Final*, 285–90. Both documents are reproduced in their entirety by Reato. The Policía Federal's failure to destroy them was an unusual oversight. Few such documents by any of the intelligence or security forces remain.

11. Robben, *Political Violence and Trauma in Argentina*, 395n100.

12. Camilo Ratti, *Cachorro. Vida y muerte de Luciano Benjamín Menéndez* (Córdoba: Editorial Raíz de Dos, 2013), 228–29.

13. Marta Philp, *Memoria y política en la historia argentina reciente: una mirada desde Córdoba* (Córdoba: Editorial de la Universidad Nacional de Córdoba, 2009), 451.

14. Reading material was, for example, closely monitored. All political literature was strictly forbidden and the penitentiaries were even provided the titles of specific books and magazines that the prisoners were permitted to read. Most magazines off the banned list were *historietas* (comic books), though not those of a political nature such as the Montoneros' *Camote* that had appeared in a few issues of the Montonero publication, *Evita Montonera* . Archivo Provincial de la Memoria, Servicio Penitenciario Provincial, "Disposiciones-Ordenes sobre Tratamiento y Traslado de Detenidos Subversivos," Legajo 7, Folios 7–110. On the Left's political cartoons see Fernando Reati, "Argentina's *Montoneros*: Comics, Cartoons, and Images as Political Propaganda in the Underground Guerrilla Press of the 1970s," in *Redrawing the Nation: National Identity in Latin American Comics*, ed. Hector Fernández L'Hoeste and Juan Poblete (New York: Palgrave McMillan 2009), 97–110. In Córdoba, unlike the situation in other federal penitentiaries, even the minor comfort provided by a closely monitored reading list was denied and prisoners were only permitted some very limited access to letters from friends and families.

15. Santiago Garaño, "El 'tratamiento' penitenciario y su dimensión productiva de identidades entre los presos políticos (1974–1983)," *Revista Iberoamericana* 10, no. 40 (2010): 122–25.

16. Juan Corradi, "The Mode of Destruction: Terror in Argentina," *Telos*, no. 54 (1982–83): 61–76.

17. Emilio Crenzel, *La historia política del Nunca Más: la memoria de las desapariciones en la Argentina* Buenos Aires: Siglo XXI, 2008), 203–4, n30.

18. Informe CONADEP, Delegación Córdoba 1984/1989. Second edition (1999): 160–61. This would make the percentage of working-class victims much higher than the national average, which was only slightly more than 30 percent according to the CONADEP report.

19. Informe, Comité de Defensa de Derechos Humanos en el Cono Sur (São Paulo, 1982)

20. Marta Philp, "La Universidad Nacional de Córdoba y 'la formación de almas': La dictadura de 1976," in *Universidad Nacional de Córdoba. Cuatrocientos años de historia* (Córdoba: Editorial de la Universidad Nacional de Córdoba, 2013), 276.

21. Philp, *Memoria y política*, 189, 206, 211. The letter was published as a *solicitada* in *La Voz del Interior* on October 14, 1978, with the signatories' names and their university affiliation.

22. Philp, "La Universidad Nacional de Córdoba," 281–82.

23. Edy Kaufman, "Jewish Victims of Repression in Argentina under Military Rule, 1976–1983," *Holocaust and Genocide Studies* 4 (1989).

24. Kaufman, "Jewish Victims ," 407; Miguel Galante and Adrián Jmelnizky, "Sobre el antisemitismo en el terrorismo de Estado en la Argentina, 1976–1983. Algunas hipótesis explicativas," in *Genocidio del siglo XX y formas de la negación. Actas del III Encuentro sobre*

Genocidio, Buenos Aires, ed. N. Boulgourdjian-Toufeksian, J.C. Toufkesian, and Carlos Alemian (Buenos Aires: Edición del Centro Armenio,, 2003), 84–107.

25. Report CO.SO.FAM, "La violación de los Derechos Humanos de Argentinos Judios Bajo el Régimen Militar (1976–1983)," Barcelona, March 1999.

26. See the testimony of Burton S. Levinson, chairman of the Latin American Affairs Committee of B'Nai B'rith in "Human Rights in Argentina" Hearings before the Subcommittee on International Organizations of the Committee on International Relations. House of Representatives. Ninety-fourth Congress, Second Session, September 28 and 29, 1976, 7–10.

27. *Será Justicia* 6, no. 42 (October 2014): 3–6, Mariano Saravia, *La sombra azul* (Rosario: Ediciones del Boulevard, 2005), 53–54. The greatest examples of such spoliation was the military's expropriation of the industrial empires of Perón's last minister of economy, José Ber Gelbard, and Julio Broner, Gelbard's close collaborator and former president of the Confederación General Económica. As with Mackentor, Gelbard and Broner were also associated with an economic model and nationalist policies, leading spokespersons of the so-called *burguesía nacional,* at odds with the dictatorship's guiding economic philosophy.

28. Organization of American States, Inter-American Commission on Human Rights, "Report on the Situation of Human Rights in Argentina," April 1980.

29. "El plus antisemita de la represión," *Será Justicia* 5, no. 26 (July 2013): 3.

30. Jewish Telegraph Agency, April 4, 1978.

31. APM, "Expedientes de la Casa de Gobierno," Caja 1. Of the forty-one files/individual petitions in this collection, in only one case did the government acknowledge the individual in question was under arrest and in custody. All the other names belong to those of *desaparecidos.*

32. Victoria Crespo, "Legalidad y dictadura," in *Argentina, 1976: Estudios en torno al golpe de estado,* ed. C. Lida, H. Crespo, and P. Yankelevich (Mexico City: El Colegio de México, 2007), 178–82. The ineffectiveness of habeas corpus efforts in Córdoba specifically is widely known. See for example the detailed testimony of María Elena Mercado from the 1985 trials of the junta. Mercado's husband was abducted on March 24, 1976, the day of the coup. Multiple habeas corpus efforts by her in Córdoba's courts were stonewalled and produced no information. Poder Judicial de la Nación, Actas de los testigos, Expediente 494, Testimony of María Elena Mercado, June 28, 1985.

33. See the testimony of Cordoban lawyer Gustavo Roca in "Human Rights in Argentina" Hearings before the Subcommittee on International Organizations of the Committee on International Relations. House of Representatives, Ninety-fourth Congress, Second Session, September 28 and 29, 1976, 10–23.

34. *La Voz del Interior,* March 27, 1976, 8.

35. *La Voz del Interior,* April 8, 1976, 12; April 22, 1976, 9, 13; April 25, 1976, 19; April 30, 1976, 6; Ratti, *Cachorro,* 310–11.

36. Gustavo Morello, *The Catholic Church and Argentina's Dirty War* (Oxford: Oxford University Press, 2015), 43.

37. Reato, *Disposición Final,* 254–55.

38. Morello, *The Catholic Church and Argentina's Dirty War,* 43.

39. Novaro and Palermo, *La dictadura militar 1976/1983,* 99. Despite insistent requests from the Archivo Provincial de la Memoria in Córdoba, the Church hierarchy has stoutly

refused to hand over internal Church documents from the period. Only one archival file has been donated, a dossier related to the Church's attempt to intercede on behalf of a progressive American priest, James Weeks, briefly imprisoned by the dictatorship, an episode examined in detail in Gustavo Morello's *The Catholic Church and Argentina's Dirty War.* This singular and unexpected generosity was not innocent. It was an obvious attempt to cast the Church in a positive light in one of the very few incidents in which it, no doubt influenced by the nationality of the priest involved, behaved honorably.

40. Novaro and Palermo, *La dictadura militar, 1976/1983,* 115–16. Novaro and Palermo contend that in Ford's plant in General Pacheco, on the outskirts of Buenos Aires, a detention and torture center operated for several months. They also point to the removal of shop floor steward commissions in numerous firms and even the assassination of a number of leading union leaders elsewhere, including Oscar Smith of the light and powers workers' union and Jorge Di Pasquale of the pharmaceutical workers union.

41. Victoria Basualdo, "Complicidad patronal-militar en la última dictadura argentina: Los casos de Acindar, Astarsa, Dálmine Siderca, Ford, Ledesma y Mercedes Benz," *Revista Engranajes,* No. 5 (March 2006).

42. Reato, *Disposición Final,* 129–30.

43. The two-volume report sponsored by the Secretaría de Derechos Humanos documents some twenty-five cases of company complicity in the state terrorism. On the specific case of Fiat, see *Responsabilidad empresarial en delitos de lesa humanidad. Represión a trabajadores durante el terrorismo de Estado* (Buenos Aires: Editorial Ministerio de Justicia y Derechos Humanos de la Nación, 2015), vol. II, 211–68, http://www.saij.gob.ar/docs-f/ediciones/libros/Responsabilidad_empresarial_delitos_lesa_humanidad_t.2.pdf.

44. In their memoir of captivity in La Perla, the Contepomis relate that there was widespread belief in the camp that major employers such as Renault and Fiat had assembled lists of activists and made them available to the military, even donating cars from their factories to the military to be used in their abductions. Gustavo Contepomi and Patricia Contepomi, *Sobrevivientes de La Perla* (Córdoba: El Cid Editor, 1984), 105, 107. Worker testimony in the human rights trials between 2007 and 2016 echoed such accusations. "Los automotrices que entregaron a sus obreros a la represión dictatorial," *Será Justicia* 5, no. 33 (November 2013): 3.

45. On the failure of the Social Pact and its consequences in Córdoba, see James P. Brennan and Marcelo Rougier, *The Politics of National Capitalism: Peronism and the Argentine Bourgeoisie, 1946–1976* (State College, PA: Penn State University Press, 2009).

46. For a succinct, insightful analysis of the military government's economic program, see Martin Schorr, "La desindustrialización como eje del proyecto refundacional de la economía y la sociedad argentina, 1976–1983," *América Latina Historia Económica* 19, no. 3 (September–December 2012): 31–56. On Luz y Fuerza, see Ana Elisa Arriaga, "Represión sindical y disciplinamiento laboral: La violencia en el dispositivo de control del conflicto en EPEC (1973–1978)," in *Córdoba a los 40 años del golpe. Estudios sobre la dictadura en clave local,* ed. Ana Carol Solís and Pablo Ponza (Córdoba: Editorial de la Universidad Nacional de Córdoba, 2016), 75–104.

47. *SITRAP: Boletín Informativo del Sindicato de Trabajadores de Perkins,* no. 3 (April 1973): 3; no. 4 (August 1973): 2; no. 5 (October1973): 1.

CHAPTER THREE. DEATH CAMP: LA PERLA

1. The 1984 CONADEP report listed 340 secret detention centers, later estimates revised the number to more than 600. Most, however, were small, police stations being the most common, and held few prisoners. I use the term *death camp* in reference to the handful of detention centers that held large numbers of prisoners, the vast majority of whom were murdered there and entered the ranks of the disappeared.

2. The five large detention centers and their estimated number of detainees under the dictatorship as asserted both in print and by some human rights groups were as follows: Campo de Mayo and Vesubio (in greater Buenos Aires with 4,000 and 2,000 detainees respectively), ESMA and Club Atlético (in the federal capital with 4,500 and 1.500 detainees), and La Perla (Córdoba, with 2,500 detainees). Given the downwardly revised figures of the total number of disappeared by the EAAF and other researchers in recent years, I believe all these numbers are substantial overestimations. They certainly are for La Perla. There could have been no more than 1,000 total detainees in Córdoba's death camp. There has simply been too much careful data collection by the EAAF and the APM to reasonably believe that there are upward of a 1,500 unaccounted-for *desaparecidos* in La Perla. The bureaucratic reach of the Argentine state with all citizens possessing a national identity card and other identifiers make most improbable the vanishing without a trace of more than a thousand former detainees. I discuss the issue of total numbers of victims in subsequent chapters.

3. Pilar Calveiro, "La experiencia concentracionaria," in *Argentina, 1976. Estudios en torno al golpe de estado*, ed. C. Lida, H. Crespo, and P. Yankelevich (Mexico City: El Colegio de México, 2007), 188–90; Marcos Novaro and Vicente Palermo, *La dictadura militar, 1976/1983: Del golpe de estado a la restauración democrática* (Buenos Aires: Paidós, 2003), 88n20; Wolfgang S. Heinz and Hugo Frühling, *Determinants of Gross Human Rights Violations by State and State-Sponsored Actors in Brazil, Uruguay, Chile and Argentina 1960–1980* (The Hague: Martinus Nijhoff Publishers, 1999), 692. In another study of the camps, Calveiro notes evidence that this practice was enhanced over time in La Perla by decreasing the numbers killed in executions while increasing the frequency of these firing squads, thereby providing all a chance to participate in the killings. See Pilar Calveiro, *Poder y desaparición: Los campos de concentración en Argentina* (Buenos Aires: Ediciones Colihue, 1998), 33.

4. Calveiro, *Poder y desaparición*, 63.

5. Calveiro, *Poder y desaparición*, 68–69.

6. Feitlowitz notes the Contepomis' estimates of survivors: seventeen prisoners were freed after one or two years, twenty after one or two days, and some one hundred were officially charged, registered, and transferred to the Campo de la Ribera detention center, surviving, one would assume, because formal charges made them publicly visible. According to the Contepomis, nearly all the survivors were of middle-class and upper-middle-class background. Marguerite Feitlowitz, *A Lexicon of Terror: Argentina and the Legacies of Torture* (New York: Oxford University Press, 1998), 63–64.

7. Vergez was accused by former La Perla detainees of running a store in downtown Cordoba that sold the furniture and other household possessions of those who had been abducted and imprisoned in the detention center. See Feitlowitz, *Lexicon of Terror*, 213–15.

8. The layout of La Perla was thus very different from the compartmentalized design at another large detention center, ESMA, so well described by Antonius Robben. At ESMA, the passage from section to section, each with its own purpose, including the prospect of rehabilitation, was absent in the cavernous open space of the *cuadra* in La Perla. There the only passage was, for a lucky few, release from the camp, and for the others, execution. See Antonius C. G. M. Robben, *Political Violence and Trauma in Argentina* (Philadelphia: University of Pennsylvania Press, 2005), 250–55. Pilar Calveiro also describes a layout in which prisoners in the death camps were physically separated by partition walls in cells or tubes, an accurate description of ESMA but not of La Perla where bunks lay side-by-side. In La Perla, the isolation was not physical but achieved through handcuffs, blindfolds, and hooding. See Pilar Calveiro, "Spatialities of Exception," in *Space and the Memories of Violence. Landscapes of Erasure, Disappearances and Exception*, ed. Estela Schindel and Pamela Colombo (New York: Palgrave-Macmillan, 2014), 211.

9. Comisión Provincial de la Memoria, "Centros Clandestinos de Detención en Córdoba," 2009; Gustavo Contepomi and Patricia Contepomi, *Sobrevivientes de La Perla* (Córdoba: El Cid Editor, 1984), 27–29. Because of the camp's elevation, in the barracks jargon it was also called simply "arriba" (up there) or alternately the "Universidad," (University), in the military's dark humor to distinguish it from the Campo de la Ribera detention center, called the "Escuelita" (Little School). To be transferred to the University implied a recognized importance as a prisoner and assignment to the death camp that was La Perla, slated for execution.

10. Feitlowitz, *Lexicon of Terror*, 65.

11. Ana Mariani and Alejo Gómez Jacobo, *La Perla: Historia y testimonios de un campo de concentración* (Buenos Aires: Aguilar, 2012), 425–26.

12. The trucks were Mercedes Benz models, dubbed by the prisoners, in the gallows humor of the camp, the Menéndez Benz, in reference to the camp commandant.

13. Comisión Provincial de la Memoria, "Megacausa 'La Perla.' Informe sobre el juicio al terrorismo de estado en Córdoba," (2012), 95–96.

14. Calveiro, *Poder y desaparición*, 38.

15. Contepomi and Contepomi, *Sobrevivientes de La Perla*, 83.

16. Contepomi and Contepomi, *Sobrevivientes de La Perla*, 105–6.

17. The army's uncontested supervision of the antisubversive campaign in Córdoba contrasts with the experience of Rosario where conduct for the dirty war fell more heavily on the local police forces, especially during the first two years of the dictatorship, and police chief, Agustín Feced, enjoyed greater autonomy than his counterparts in Córdoba. Though technically under the command of the army's Second Corps, the police in Rosario exercised a great deal of independence. Most political prisoners were detained in police stations and no large camp such as La Perla existed in Rosario. The largest detention center there was in fact the central police station. See Gabriela Águila, *Dictadura, represión y sociedad en Rosario, 1976/1983* (Buenos Aires: Prometeo Libros, 2008), 49, 64–67, 86–89, 176.

18. Águila, *Dictadura*, 82. Survivor testimonies concur that at the large detention centers such as La Perla careful records were kept by the military of the prisoners, complete with photos, fingerprints, and bulky files including the date of capture and torture sessions, work histories, and political antecedents on each detainee. A few scattered files have been recovered for La Perla and other camps such as ESMA.

19. Feitlowitz, *Lexicon of Terror*, 64–65.

20. Hugo Vanzetti, *Pasado y presente: Guerra, dictadura y sociedad en la Argentina* (Buenos Aires: Siglo XXI, 2002), 176–77. As Pilar Calveiro notes, the clandestine Argentine death camp also viewed and handled the prisoners differently from the only semihidden, teeming Nazi concentration camp, its prisoners "animalized," branded, and housed in saturated places, with its daily work routines and final herding for the gas chambers. In contrast, in Argentina, "Internally the camp is not organized in accordance with the productive industrial model, but rather as a deposit for dangerous waste. For nothing other than useful information is expected to be extracted from the prisoners. Once this objective has been achieved they are deposited, like toxic material, until the time of their elimination . . . prisoners are treated as objects or 'packages' rather than animalized . . . It is a biopolitical experience based on the selection-isolation-casting aside of a dysfunctional Other who is understood to be 'dangerous material.'" Calveiro, "Spatialities of Exception," 213.

21. Calveiro, *Poder y desaparición*, 41.

22. Calveiro, *Poder y desaparición*, 56.

23. Calveiro, *Poder y desaparición*, 79.

24. Poder Judicial de la Nación, Actas de los testigos, Expediente 464, Testimony of Susana Sastre, June 14, 1985.

25. Ana Mariani and Alejo Gómez Jacobo, *La Perla. Historia y testimonios de un campo de concentración* (Buenos Aires: Aguilar, 2012), 252–53.

26. Poder Judicial de la Nación, Actas de los testigos, Expediente 490, Testimony of Susan Deutsch, June 28, 1985.

27. Mariani and Jacobo, *La Perla*, 224–25.

28. Contepomi and Contepomi, *Sobrevivientes de La Perla*, 120–21.

29. It has been suggested that for elsewhere in the country, the army was assigned responsibility for eliminating the Marxist ERP and the navy, perhaps due to its longstanding anti-Peronist tradition, with annihilating the Montoneros. See Andrés Di Tella, "La vida privada en los campos de concentración," in *Historia de la vida privada en la Argentina*, ed. Fernando Devoto and Marta Madero (Buenos Aires: Taurus, 1999), 86–87, and María Seoane and Vicente Murillo, *El dictador: La historia secreta y pública de Jorge Rafael Videla* (Buenos Aires: Editorial Sudamericana, 2001), 66. The large presence of Montoneros in the navy's ESMA detention center lends some credence to such speculations. In landlocked Córdoba, there were no naval units to assign such a charge and the army had full responsibility for the repression of all so-called subversive groups.

30. Di Tella, "La vida privada en los campos de concentración," 87.

31. Dossier del Juicio. See appendix 1 for the full list.

32. Di Tella, "La vida privada en los campos de concentración," 88–89. Águila asserts that in Rosario a sizable number of prisoners survived, though she offers no reasons for their survival (Águila, *Dictadura*, 105).

33. Poder Judicial de la Nación, Actas de los Testigos, Expediente 463, Testimony of Gustavo Contepomi, June 24, 1985.

34. This is the compelling argument, for example, in Pilar Calveiro's *Poder y desaparición: Los campos de concentración en Argentina*.

35. Poder Judicial de la Nación, Actas de los Testigos, Expediente 482 Testimony of Ricardo Mora, June 27, 1985.

36. Emilio Crenzel, *La historia política del Nunca Más: La memoria de las desapariciones en la Argentina* (Buenos Aires: Siglo XXI, 2008), 77, 81.

37. *El Diario del Juicio*, no. 6 (July 2, 1985).

38. Poder Judicial de la Nación, Actas de los testigos, Expediente 485, testimony of José Julian Solanille, June 27, 1985. Solanille's recollections of mass executions would later be vindicated with the 2014–15 discovery of the remains of the JUP members by the EAAF mentioned in the Introduction.

39. Poder Judicial de la Nación, Actas de los testigos, Expediente 463, testimony of Gustavo Contepomi, June 24, 1985; Expediente 470, testimony of Margarita Elgoghen, June 25, 1985.

CHAPTER FOUR. INSTITUTIONAL DYNAMICS: THE THIRD ARMY CORPS

1. Daniel Mazzei, *Bajo el poder de la caballería: El ejército argentino (1962–1973)* (Buenos Aires, Editorial Universitaria de Buenos Aires, 2012), 280.

2. Wolfgang S. Heinz and Hugo Frühling, *Determinants of Gross Human Rights Violations by State and State-Sponsored Actors in Brazil, Uruguay, Chile and Argentina 1960–1980* (The Hague: Martinus Nijhoff Publishers, 1999), 644.

3. Heinz and Frühling, *Determinants of Gross Human Rights Violations*, 682.

4. Federico Mittelbach, *Informe sobre desaparecedores*, 9–12, 86. The designated zones and assignments were as follows: zone 1, Federal capital and parts of Buenos Aires province and La Pampa province (First Army Corps); zone 2, Santa Fe, Entre Ríos, Corrientes, Misiones, Chaco, Formosa provinces (Second Army Corps); zone 3, Córdoba, San Luis, Mendoza. San Juan, La Rioja, Catamarca, Santiago del Estero, Tucumán, Salta Jujuy provinces (Third Army Corps); zone 4, Greater Buenos Aires and surrounding industrial towns (no single commanding entity, responsibilities divided among army units and military institutes such as the Colegio Militar and Escuela de Guerra and commanded from the Campo de Mayo army base); zone 5, Buenos Aires province (southern districts), Río Negro, Neuquén, Chubut, Santa Cruz provinces (Fifth Army Corps). The navy was assigned jurisdiction over riverine and ocean coastal areas and two of the designated "areas" in greater Buenos Aires, and the air force over airports and their surrounding areas as well as one subzone and three areas, also in greater Buenos Aires. The Fourth Army Corps, abolished in 1964 and only reestablished during the dictatorship in 1982, initially had no territorial jurisdiction and was responsible solely for logistics. It would quickly be assigned jurisdiction over zone 4, but by this point the dirty war was largely over and it had little impact.

5. Marie-Monique Robin, *Escadrons de la mort, l'école française* (Paris: Éditions La Découverte, 2004), 209.

6. APM, Memo, DGI CD No. 61, May 5, 1976. Meeting presided over by III Cuerpo General Luciano Benjamín Menéndez with the presence of the commander of the Fourth Infantry Brigade, General Juan Sasiaiñ.

7. These were Regimiento Infantería Aerotransportada 2, Regimiento Infantería Aerotransportada 14, Grupo Artilleria 4, and Batallón Comunicaciones 141. Mittelbach, *Informe sobre desaparecedores*, 89.

8. Ceferino Reato, *Disposición Final: La confesión de Videla sobre los desaparecidos* (Buenos Aires: Editorial Sudamericana, 2012), 262–63.

9. Gustavo Contepomi and Patricia Contepomi, *Sobrevivientes de La Perla* (Córdoba: El Cid Editor, 1984), 123; Marcos Novaro and Vicente Palermo, *La dictadura militar, 1976/1983: Del golpe de estado a la restauración democrática* (Buenos Aires: Paidós, 2003), 185. The Argentine Communists went so far as to criticize the human rights policy of the Carter administration and the US arms embargo of Argentina for human rights violations.

10. Ariel C. Armony, *Argentina, the United States and the Anti-Communist Crusade in Central America, 1977–1984* (Athens: Ohio University Center for International Studies, 1997), 77.

11. Nora Kinzer Stewart, *Mates and Muchachos: Unit Cohesion in the Falklands/Malvinas War* (New York: Brassey's, 1991), 52.

12. In the specific case of the army, as Kinzer Stewart notes, "The social distance and lack of vertical bonding produced a rigid, hierarchically organized army which de facto is incapable of flexibility and creativity under stress." Kinzer Stewart, *Mates and Muchachos*, 53.

13. Centro de Estudios Legales y Sociales (CELS), Serie: Memoria y Justicia, no. 6 "Conscriptos Detenidos-Desaparecidos," 7–8.

14. Ministerio de Defensa. Digital Archive, Libro de Actas de la Junta Militar, volume I, Acta no. 34, August 30, 1977, 201–17. In the final months of the previous Peronist government, this right had been greatly restricted, but the military government suspended it outright.

15. Ministerio de Defensa. Digital Archive, Libro de Actas de la Junta Militar, volume III, Acta no. 68 (July 20, 1978), 16–20.

16. Pablo Pozzi, *Oposición obrera a la dictadura* (Buenos Aires: Editorial Contrapunto, 1988), 84; Ronaldo Munck, *Argentina: From Anarchism to Peronism, Workers, Unions and Politics, 1855–1985* (London: Zed Books, 1987), 212.

17. APM. Servicio Penitenciario Provincial (SPP). "Disposiciones–Ordenes sobre el Tratamiento y Traslados de Detenidos Subversivos." Legajo 7 Memorandum, "Orden Especial Nr. 23/80 Para Cambio de Situación de Detenidos a Disposición del PEN," March 1980, folio 256.

18. Archive of the Dirección de Inteligencia de la Policía de la Provincia de Buenos Aires (henceforth DIPBA) Mesa D (s) Carpetas Varias, Legajos 9994, 1184.

19. DIPBA Mesa D (s) Carpetas Varias, Legajo 4497: "Asunto: Procedimiento antisubversivo en Córdoba," January 29, 1976; Legajo 5948: "Asunto: Elementos extremistas abatidos en un efrentamiento con la Policía Córdoba," July 13, 1976; Legajo 8450: "Asunto: "Accionar Subversivo en Córdoba y Rosario," October 12, 1976.

20. There are multiple sources that confirm the role of the police in Córdoba's dirty war, but perhaps the best is the detailed testimony of a former ERP member and longtime D-2 detainee turned collaborator with the police, Carlos Raimundo ("Charlie") Moore. See Miguel Robles, *La búsqueda. Una entrevista con Charlie Moore* (Córdoba: Ediciones del Pasaje, 2010), especially pages 129–34, 232–34 and 247–49.

21. Jaime Malmud-Goti, *Game Without End: State Terror and the Politics of Justice* (Norman: University of Oklahoma Press, 1996), 113.

22. On the Chilean military, see John R. Bawden, *The Pinochet Generation: The Chilean Military in the Twentieth Century* (Tuscaloosa: University of Alabama Press, 2016).

CHAPTER FIVE. TRANSNATIONAL DYNAMICS: THE COLD WAR AND THE WAR AGAINST SUBVERSION

1. The studies that subscribe to this interpretation are legion. A classic statement is Eduardo L. Duhalde, *El estado terrorista argentino* (Buenos Aires: El Caballito, 1983).

2. Camilo Ratti, *Cachorro. Vida y muertes de Luciano Benjamín Menéndez* (Córdoba: Editorial Raíz de Dos, 2013), 404; Marta Philp, *Memoria y política en la historia argentina reciente: Una lectura desde Córdoba* (Córdoba: Editorial Nacional de Córdoba, 2009), 172.

3. Wolfgang S. Heinz and Hugo Frühling, *Determinants of Gross Human Rights Violations by State and State-Sponsored Actors in Brazil, Uruguay, Chile and Argentina 1960–1980* (The Hague: Martinus Nijhoff, 1999), 614, 694. Alain Rouquié, in his careful research in U.S. Defense Department sources, notes a relatively low participation of the Argentine officer corps compared to other Latin American countries, comparable in numbers to those of Guatemala and Bolivia with their much smaller armies while lagging far behind Brazil, Chile, Peru, Venezuela, and Ecuador. See Alain Rouquié, *Pouvoir militaire et societé politique en République argentine* (Paris: Presses de la Fondation Nationale des Sciences Politiques, 1977), 668–69.

4. Daniel Mazzei, *Bajo el poder de la caballería: El ejército argentino (1962–1973)* (Buenos Aires: Editorial Universitaria de Buenos Aires, 2012), 151.

5. Mazzei, *Bajo el poder de la caballería*, 209–11, 214–17.

6. See Martin E. Andersen, *Dossier Secreto: Argentina's Desaparecidos and the Myth of the "Dirty War"* (Boulder, CO: Westview, 1993), 248.

7. Marie-Monique Robin, *Escadrons de la mort, l'école française* (Paris: Éditions La Découverte, 2004), 235. U.S. counterinsurgency training manuals in the 1960s and 1970s did contain sections on "terrorism and urban guerrilla warfare" but given the overwhelmingly rural nature of Third World revolution, such subjects were never stressed. What was said on the subject was largely lifted from the writings of Algerian veteran and counterinsurgency theorist Col. Roger Trinquier, especially his highly influential *La Guerre moderne*. Robin writes of the manuals used at U.S. military training sites, "The similarity with Colonel Trinquier's prose is so stunning that one might legitimately wonder if he did not directly participate in the writing of these manuals" (270). More likely, they were simply plagiarized.

8. Robin, *Escadrons de la mort*, 38–43.

9. Robin, *Escadrons de la mort*, 52.

10. Antonius C. G. M. Robben, *Political Violence and Trauma in Argentina* (Philadelphia: University of Pennsylvania Press, 2005), 181.

11. Raphaëlle Branche, *La torture et l'armée pendant la guerre d'Algerie (1954–1962)* (Paris: Gallimard, 2001), 41–42.

12. Branche, *La torture et l'armée*, 76–80, Robin, *Escadrons de la mort*, 77–78.

13. Robin, *Escadrons de la mort*, 101–8.

14. Branche, *La torture et l'armée*, 137–46.

15. Branche, *La torture et l'armée*, 54–56, 126–31, 330–31. In those rare cases where electric shocks did leave incriminating marks, the French developed techniques to heal such wounds within a relatively short period of time. See Branche, 136–37, 338–39.

16. Branche, *La torture et l'armée*, 335–42.

17. Branche, *La torture et l'armée*, 63.

18. Branche, *La torture et l'armée*, 72–76; Robben, *Political Violence and Trauma*, 181.

19. Branche, *La torture et l'armée*, 107–11.

20. Irwin M. Wall, *France, the United States, and the Algerian War* (Berkeley: University of California Press, 2001), 15.

21. Matthew Connelly, *A Diplomatic Revolution: Algeria's Fight for Independence and the Origin of the Post-Cold War Era* (New York: Oxford University Press, 2002), 183–84, 224–26, 231–32, 277.

22. The French also first coined the term and developed the concept of "subversion," of revolutionary war being more than the attempted overthrow of a political order, but also of a moral order, of a threat to values and indeed of their favorite word, "civilization." See Marnia Lazreg, *Torture and the Twilight of Empire: From Algiers to Baghdad* (Princeton, NJ: Princeton University Press, 2008), 20–23.

23. Heinz and Frühling, *Determinants of Gross Human Rights Violations*, 642–43.

24. Robin, *Escadrons de la mort*, 308–10.

25. Despite initially following in Tucumán the French and later American strategy of separating the civilian population from the guerrillas, the specific tactics adopted were closer to the French school than the American "strategic hamlet" policy. As Robben correctly notes, "The French taught the Argentines that an urban insurgency was fought best through intelligence gathering, not through territorial control" (*Political Violence and Trauma*, 182, 197).

26. Andrew J. Birtle, *U.S. Army Counterinsurgency and Contingency Operations Doctrine 1942–1976* (Washington, DC: Center of Military History, 2006), 133. Irregular warfare and tactics to defeat it were, of course, as old as war itself. The U.S. Army had adopted what essentially amounted to counterinsurgency tactics as early as the nineteenth century against the Comanche and other Native American tribes. In the twentieth century, there were numerous antecedents: the U.S. suppression of the Philippine independence movement, the British campaign after World War I to subdue the Irish rebellion, the Nazis' "night and fog" tactics against partisan and resistance fighters, the British again in the campaign against the Mau Mau insurgents in Kenya. On the latter, see Caroline Elkins, *Imperial Reckoning: The Untold Story of Britain's Gulag in Kenya* (New York: Henry Holt, 2005).

27. Birtle, *U.S. Army Counterinsurgency and Contingency Operations Doctrine*, 151.

28. Birtle, *U.S. Army Counterinsurgency and Contingency Operations Doctrine*, 161–62.

29. Robben attributes the coining of the term *dirty war* in Argentina to the country's guerrilla organizations, but the term had long been a part of French military parlance and more likely entered the Argentine military's lexicon through their French tutors (*Political Violence and Trauma*, 171–72, 389n77).

30. Birtle, *U.S. Army Counterinsurgency and Contingency Operations Doctrine*, 291–304. On the Alliance's increased emphasis on military aid and counterinsurgency, see Stephen C. Rabe, *The Most Dangerous Area in the World: John F. Kennedy Confronts Communist Revolution in Latin America* (Chapel Hill: University of North Carolina Press, 1999).

31. Birtle, *U.S. Army Counterinsurgency and Contingency Operations Doctrine*, 230.

32. Birtle, *U.S. Army Counterinsurgency and Contingency Operations Doctrine*, 241–43.

33. Michael McClintock, *Instruments of Statecraft: U.S. Guerrilla Warfare, Counter-Insurgency and Counter-Terrorism, 1940–1990* (New York: Pantheon Books, 1992), 428–29.

34. Birtle, *U.S. Army Counterinsurgency and Contingency Operations Doctrine*, 300.

35. It is interesting to note that one of the few scholars who has undertaken extensive interviews with former military commanders relates their denial of any direct influence by

the United States on their worldview. See Mark J. Osiel, *Mass Atrocity, Ordinary Evil, and Hannah Arendt: Criminal Consciousness in Argentina's Dirty War* (New Haven, CT: Yale University Press, 2001), 110.

36. Marcos Novaro and Vicente Palermo, *La dictadura militar, 1976/1983: Del golpe de estado a la restauración democrática* (Buenos Aires: Paidós, 2003), 84–85; Robin, *Escadrons de la mort*, 201–2.

37. Ariel C. Armony, *Argentina, the United States and the Anti-Communist Crusade in Central America, 1977–1984* (Athens: Ohio University Center for International Studies, 1997); McClintock, *Instruments of Statecraft*, 319, 414, 416.

38. The Colegio Militar is Argentina's equivalent of West Point, the Escuela Superior de Guerra of the U.S. Army War College.

39. Daniel H. Mazzei, "La misión militar francesa en la Escuela Superior de Guerra y los orígenes de la Guerra Sucia, 1957–1962," *Revista de Ciencias Sociales*, no. 13 (November 2002): 111–13. Videla himself acknowledged the greater influence of the French than the Americans, see *Disposición Final*, 76–77.

40. Heinz and Frühling, *Determinants of Gross Human Rights Violations,*, 677–80; The French ambassador at the time went so far as to claim that the U.S. military representatives in Argentina were "jealous" of the French expertise in counterrevolutionary war and the influence that the latter had acquired among the Argentine officer corps. Argentine officers at the time confirmed the ambassador's reading of the American attitude and their unfamiliarity with counterrevolutionary warfare. See Robin, *Escadrons de la mort*, 212–14.

41. Mazzei, "La misión militar francesa," 117.

42. Mazzei, "La misión militar francesa," 129–30.

43. The leading historian of the Argentine military during this period summarizes the French influence as this: "As a final assessment of the military mission in Buenos Aires between 1957 and 1961 it is possible to assert that it established the tactical, methodological, and even semantic foundation that would guide the Argentine army's repressive actions in the 1970s. It contributed to a vision that justified the use of torture, instilled the ideology of counterrevolutionary war, provided reading materials in support of such theories, and helped redefine the 'enemy.' During that five-year period, the Argentine army developed an entire structure to implement the 'antisubversive' struggle and established the mechanisms for the elaboration and dissemination of the Doctrine of the Internal Enemy" (Mazzei, *Bajo el poder de la caballería*, 143).

44. Leslie Gill, *The School of the Americas: Military Training and Political Violence* (Durham, NC: Duke University Press, 2004), 54–56, 108.

45. Robben, *Political Violence and Trauma in Argentina*, 182, 188.

46. Heinz and Frühling, *Determinants of Gross Human Rights Violations*, 638; Robin, *Escadrons de la mort*, 316–17.

47. As Heinz and Frühling note, the working class, generally not fertile recruiting ground for any of the guerrilla organizations, accounted for more of the *desaparecidos* than any other group (*Determinants of Gross Human Rights Violations*, 713–14).

48. Mark Osiel, "Constructing Subversion in Argentina's Dirty War," *Representations* 75 (Summer 2001): 120–21; Prudencio García, *El drama de la autonomía militar: Argentina bajo las Juntas Militares* (Madrid: Alianza Editorial, 1995), 67–73, Donald Hodges, *Argentina's*

"Dirty War": An Intellectual Biography (Austin: University of Texas Press, 1991), 157–71, Robben, *Political Violence and Trauma,*, 178–79.

49. García, *El drama de la autonomía militar*, 65–72, Novaro and Palermo, *La dictadura militar*, 83. Cité Catolique was the name of both a conservative nationalist movement based on traditional Catholic values and its eponymous publication. It played an important role in the Algerian War as an advocate of counterrevolutionary war, including methods of torture. Its "flexible, capillary methods" of establishing study groups and small cells to indoctrinate troops was later adopted in Argentina. On its role in Algeria see Lazreg, *Torture and the Twilight of Empire*, 206–8.

50. Mario Ranalletti, "Aux origenes du terrorisme d'Etat en Argentine. Les influences françaises dans la formation des militaires argentins (1955–1976)," *Vingtième Siecle. Revue d'histoire*, no. 105 (January–March 2010): 53–54.

51. Federico Finchelstein, *The Ideological Origins of the Dirty War: Fascism, Populism, and Dictatorship in Twentieth Century Argentina* (New York: Oxford University Press, 2014). In a particularly bold assertion Finchelstein states, "The dictatorship's radical brand of political violence was less a result of French and North American concerns about national security—these concerns provided the dictatorship with an international framework and even legitimized it—than a product of the historical genealogy of fascist Argentine *nacionalismo*" (97). Finchelstein traces diverse ideological influences of this Christian fascist tradition on the dictatorship, especially the conflation of Catholicism with an exclusionary national essence combined with authoritarian political practices, though fascism understood as a movement and a regime, as he acknowledges, certainly did not characterize the 1976–83 military dictatorship. Finchelstein's argument is persuasive for the most part in ideological terms, less so in the dirty war's methods and tactics, the ones responsible for the thousands of disappeared and murdered.

52. As Mark Osiel has noted, the discourse of the Argentine military government, with its emphasis on ethical issues of moral community and national integrity, contrasted sharply with its Brazilian counterpart that employed a technocratic language exalting economic development. Osiel, "Constructing Subversion in Argentina's Dirty War," 129.

53. Osiel's provocative article and Finchelstein's interesting if polemical book do overstate the case a bit. Certainly in Córdoba, working-class militancy and what this meant for Argentina's fractious political economy were considerations in the dirty war there, as the high number of working-class *desaparecidos* demonstrates. A Cold War ethos was also more present than they both acknowledge; the military junta's dirty war ideology appears to be an amalgam of diverse influences and obsessions.

54. Loris Zanatta, "La dictadure militaire argentine (1976–1983): Une interpretation à la lumière du mythe da la nation catholique," *Vingtième Siecle. Revue d'histoire*, no. 105 (January–March 2010): 150–53.

55. Gustavo Morello, *Donde estaba Dios. Católicos y terrorismo de Estado en la Argentina de los setenta* (Buenos Aires: Ediciones B Argentina, 2014), 279–80.

56. Marta Philp, "El orden natural como fortaleza. Continuidades y rupturas en las bases ideológicas de la dictadura," in *Córdoba a los 40 años del golpe*, ed. Ana Carol Solís and Pablo Ponza (Córdoba: Editorial de la UNC, 2016), 193.

57. Mazzei, *Bajo el poder de la caballería*, 79.

58. Osiel, "Constructing Subversion in Argentina's Dirty War," 139.

59. The most accomplished example of this line of reasoning is David Pion-Berlin, *The Ideology of State Terror: Economic Doctrine and Political Repression in Argentina and Peru* (Boulder, CO: Lynne Rienner, 1989).

60. On this point, see Klaus Friedrich Vogel, *Dictatorship, Democracy, and Globalization: Argentina and the Cost of Paralysis, 1973–2001* (University Park: Pennsylvania State Press, 2009), chapter 3.

61. Carina Perelli, "La percepción de la amenaza y el pensamiento politico de los militares en América del Sur," in *Los militares y la democracia*, ed. Luis W. Goodman, Johanna S. R. Mendelson and Juan Rial (Montevideo: Peitho, 1990), 143–55.

62. Ministerio de Defensa (Argentina), Libros de Actas de la Junta Militar, Tomo V, Acta no. 255 (April 6, 1983), 283–311, 336–64.

63. Ministerio de Defensa (Argentina), Libros de Actas de la Junta Militar, Tomo VI, Acta no. 256 (April 13, 1983), 13–25.

64. Ministerio de Defensa (Argentina), Libros de Actas de la Junta Militar, Tomo VI, Acta 261 (May 19, 1983), 128–34.

CHAPTER SIX. FIVE TRIALS: PUBLIC RECKONINGS OF A VIOLENT PAST

1. On the history of the French judicial process following the Algerian war, see Raphaëlle Branche, *La torture et l'armée pendant la guerre d'Algerie (1954–1962)* (Paris: Gallimard, 2001), 362–421.

2. By international law, "crimes against humanity" (*lesa humanidad*) are those defined by a general or systematic attack against a civilian population as part of a plan devised by a state or some other organization. By that definition, there can be little doubt of the applicability of the category to the Argentine case. See Ricardo Luis Lorenzetti and Alfredo Jorge Kraut, *Derechos humanos: Justicia y reparación, La experiencia de los juicios en la Argentina. Crímenes de lesa humanidad* (Buenos Aires: Editorial Sudamericana, 2011), 44.

3. M. Cherif Bassiouni, *Crimes Against Humanity: Historical Evolution and Contemporary Application* (Cambridge: Cambridge University Press, 2011), 684–92.

4. Bassiouni, *Crimes Against Humanity*, 692.

5. Rodolfo Yanzon, "The Trials from the End of the Dictatorship until Today," in *Desaparición. Argentina's Human Rights Trials*, ed. Gabriele Andreozzi (Oxford: Peter Lang, 2014), 157; Ana Oberlin, "The Process of Justice for State Crimes Committed in Argentina During the Last Civil-Military Dictatorship: The View of a Lawyer Representing Victims and Militants in HIJOS," in *Desaparición. Argentina's Human Rights Trials*, ed. Gabriele Andreozzi (Oxford: Peter Lang, 2014), 231.

6. Oberlin, "Process of Justice for State Crimes," 224.

7. Oberlin, "Process of Justice for State," 233.

8. David M. K. Sheinin, *Consent of the Damned: Ordinary Argentines in the Dirty War* (Gainesville: University of Florida Press, 2012), 137.

9. "Entrevista a Claudio Orosz y Martín Fresnada en su Tercer Juicio," *Será Justicia. El Diario del Juicio* 2, no. 15 (October 2010): 4–5.

10. *Será Justicia* 1, no. 7 (December 2009): 1.

11. Such rights were, however, not absolute. In the case of the UP1 prisoners, from March 1976 to October 1978 when the UP1 was emptied of all political prisoners, there were exactly two visitations granted each prisoner, of one-hour duration, at Christmas 1976 and Christmas 1977. Except for those two visits, the UP1 prisoners were held incommunicado.

12. For background on the trial, see Comisión Provincial de la Memoria, "Un recorrido sobre las Causas UP 1 y Gontero," 2010. Lorenzetti and Kraut provide a good summary of the trial (*Derechos humanos*, 208–34).

13. *La Voz del Interior*, May 28, 2009; December 1, 2009; and December 15, 2009.

14. *La Voz del Interior*, July 7, 2010; July 12, 2010; July 13, 2010; July 14. 2010; July 15, 2010; and July 21, 2010.

15. *La Voz del Interior*, August 10, 2010, and August 11, 2010.

16. *La Voz del Interior*, December 10, 2010; December 16, 2010; and December 21, 2010.

17. *Será Justicia* 7, no. 45 (March 2014): 7.

18. *Será Justicia* 7, no. 48 (June 2015): 3.

19. *Será Justicia* 7, no. 36 (April 2014): 3, 7.

20. Comisión Provincial de la Memoria. "Megacausa 'La Perla.' Informe sobre el juicio al terrorismo de estado en Córdoba," (2012), 22.

21. *Será Justicia* 5, no. 29 (September 2013): 3.

22. Mark J. Osiel, *Obeying Orders: Atrocity, Military Discipline and the Law of War* (New Brunswick, NJ: Transaction, 1999), 139.

23. Osiel, *Obeying Orders*, 190, 309.

24. Luis Alberto Romero, "El teatro de los juicios," *La Nación*, September 29, 2015.

CHAPTER SEVEN. REMEMBERING: MEMORIES OF VIOLENCE AND TERROR

1. Steve Stern's trilogy has been the most nuanced and insightful of these studies on such themes. See *Remembering Pinochet's Chile: On the Eve of London, 1998* (Durham, NC: Duke University Press, 2004); *Battling for Hearts and Minds: Memory Struggles in Pinochet's Chile, 1973–1988* (Durham, NC: Duke University Press, 2006); *Reckoning with Pinochet: The Memory Question in Democratic Chile, 1989—2006* (Durham, NC: Duke University Press, 2010).

2. Antonius C. G. M. Robben, "Seduction and Persuasion: The Politics of Truth and Emotion among Victims and Perpetrators of Violence," in *Fieldwork under Fire: Contemporary Studies of Violence and Survival*, ed. Carolyn Nordstrum and Antonius C. G. M. Robben (Berkeley: University of California Press, 1995), 83–87.

3. Marcelo Suárez-Orozco, "A Grammar of Terror: Psychocultural Responses to State Terrorism in Dirty War and Post-Dirty War Argentina," in *The Paths to Domination, Resistance, and Terror*, ed. Carolyn Nordstrom and JoAnn Martin (Berkeley: University of California Press, 1992), 220.

4. Suárez-Orozco, "A Grammar of Terror," 243.

5. Antonius C. G. M. Robben and Carolyn Nordstrom, "The Anthropology and Ethnography of Violence and Sociopolitical Conflict," in *Fieldwork under Fire: Contemporary Studies of Violence and Survival*, ed. Carolyn Nordstrom and Antonius C. G. M. Robben

(Berkeley: University of California Press, 1995), 1–23; Jeffrey A. Sluka, "The Anthropology of Conflict," in *The Paths to Domination, Resistance, and Terror*, ed. Carolyn Nordstrom and JoAnn Martin (Berkeley: University of California Press, 1992), 18–36.

6. See for example Macarena Gomez-Barris, *Where Memory Dwells: Culture and State Violence in Chile* (Berkeley: University of California Press, 2008); Leslie Jo Frazier, *Salt in the Sand: Memory, Violence, and the Nation-State in Chile, 1890-Present* (Durham, NC: Duke University Press, 2007).

7. Elizabeth Jelin, "¿Víctimas, familiares, o ciudadanos/as? Las luchas por la legitimidad de la palabra," in *Los desaparecidos en la Argentina: Memorias, representaciones, e ideas, 1983-2008*, ed. Ernesto Crenzel (Buenos Aires: Biblos, 2010), 227–49. Jelin argues that it is groups like the Mothers of the Plaza de Mayo, HIJOS, and the survivors of the clandestine detention centers who have provided what has become the virtually canonized official memory of the dictatorship, thereby crowding out the alternative memories of those not directly affected by the violence., the vast majority of the population.

8. Lucía S. Garay et al., *Vivencias frente al límite* (Córdoba, Universidad Nacional de Córdoba, 2006).

9. Ana Mariani and Alejo Gómez Jacobo, eds., *La Perla. Historia y testimonios de uno de los más grandes campos de concentración de la Argentina* (Buenos Aires: Aguilar, 2012).

10. Mariani and Gómez Jacobo, *La Perla*, 40.

11. Mariani and Gómez Jacobo, *La Perla*, 69–70.

12. Mariani and Gómez Jacobo, *La Perla*, 221–22.

13. Mariani and Gómez Jacobo, *La Perla*, 81.

14. Mariani and Gómez Jacobo, *La Perla*, 217.

15. Mariani and Gómez Jacobo, *La Perla*, 132–33.

16. Mariani and Gómez Jacobo, *La Perla*, 366.

17. Mariani and Gómez Jacobo, *La Perla*, 186.

18. Mariani and Gómez Jacobo, *La Perla*, 256.

19. On the trials of the juntas, see Carlos Nino, *Radical Evil on Trial* (New Haven, CT: Yale University Press, 1996). Most military witnesses refused to testify, but some, such as former army commander and president General Alejandro Lanusse and military subordinates to the junta, did testify.

20. *Será Justicia. El Diario del Juicio de Videla en Córdoba*, no. 20 (December 27, 2010): 2.

21. Marta Philp, *Memoria y política en la historia argentina reciente: Una lectura desde Córdoba* (Córdoba: Editorial Nacional de Córdoba, 2009), 249.

22. President Nestor Kirchner presented at the 2006 National Book Fair an "updated" version of the *Nunca más* truth commission report that included a new annex and the names of an additional 1,169 victims, thereby broadening the charge of the original truth report commission that had been to document only the cases of the disappeared.

23. APM, *Un recorrido histórico sobre las Causas UP1 y Gontero*, 16–17.

24. Jenny Edkins, *Trauma and the Memory of Politics* (Cambridge: Cambridge University Press, 2003), 111–74.

25. On the South African case see Christopher J. Cobin, "Brothers and Sisters, Do Not be Afraid of Me. Trauma, History and the Therapeutic Imagination in the New South Africa," in *Contested Pasts. The Politics of Memory*, ed. Katherine Hodgkin and Susannah Radstone (London: Routledge, 2003).

26. The 1985 *Brasil: Nunca mais* report, taking its name from the official Argentine truth commission report, was not sanctioned by the government but by a private initiative, a collaboration between human rights lawyers and the Archdiocese of São Paulo.

27. On the Brazilian experience, see Rebecca J. Atencio, *Memory's Turn: Reckoning with Dictatorship in Brazil* (Madison: University of Wisconsin Press, 2014). In Brazil, writers and artists helped to keep alive a cultural memory of dictatorship, as happened in Argentina as well, but this was not complemented by either state policy or the large and diverse human rights movement of the kind found in Argentina, a crucial distinction. Indeed, the political class in Brazil fretted about what they described as a possible "Argentinization" of the human rights question. Of course, the crimes of the Argentine dictatorship were on a different order from its counterpart in Brazil.

28. Alison Brysk, "The Politics of Measurement: The Contested Count of the Disappeared in Argentina," *Human Rights Quarterly* 16 (1994): 676–92.

29. Carlos Somigliana and Darío Olmo, "Los desaparecidos. La huella del genocidio," *Encrucijadas. Revista de la Universidad de Buenos Aires* 2, no. 15 (2002): 21–35. EAAF members Somigliana and Olmo note that the original CONADEP report had a number of duplicate entries for the disappeared persons as well as individuals reported as *desaparecidos* who later turned out not to be, hence their lower figure than the truth commission report, though even these lower figures they characterize as a "genocide." Their figures are, however, confined only to those cases that the EAAF can verify and document with certainty. The real figure of the disappeared is certainly higher; just how high remains a point of contention. The current Macri government has disputed the problematic 30,000 figure to discredit the human rights movement and withdraw government support for future litigation. Some human rights organizations such as the Madres and Abuelas in turn have reacted furiously to any suggestion of a lower figure as a sign of support for the dictatorship and its methods.

30. See Samuel Totten et al., *Genocide in the Twentieth Century: Critical Essays and Eyewitness Accounts* (New York: Garland, 1995); Eric D. Weitz, *A Century of Genocide: Utopias of Race and Nation* (Princeton, NJ: Princeton University Press, 2003); William D. Rubenstein, *Genocide. A History* (London: Pearson Longman, 2004).

31. For an alternative and largely legalistic perspective that argues the case for a genocide in Argentina, see Daniel Feierstein, "Political Violence in Argentina and Its Genocidal Characteristics," in *State Violence and Genocide in Latin America; the Cold War Years*, ed. Maria Esparza, Henry R. Huttenbach, and Daniel Feierstein (London: Routledge, 2010), 44–63.

32. Antonius C. G. M. Robben, "From Dirty War to Genocide: Argentina's Resistance to National Reconciliation," *Memory Studies* 5, no. 3 (2012): 306.

33. As Robben states, "Whereas the two-demon theory confined the responsibility for the escalating violence to the military and the insurgency, and state terrorism held the armed forces alone accountable, the term *genocide* hints at the complicity of most Argentines through active support or passive acceptance. . . . Genocide makes national reconciliation much harder than 'dirty war' because an armed confrontation between military and insurgents carries a certain war logic missing from the indiscriminate extermination of people" ("From Dirty War to Genocide," 313).

34. Martin Meredith, *The State of Africa* (London: Free Press, 2005), 660–61.

35. Many draw the distinction between the "retributive justice" of the kind practiced in Argentina with the "restorative justice" of the South African case, which demanded, among other things, the assumption of guilt, public shaming, and financial compensation for victims at the same time that it rejected a strictly punitive policy and legal redress. Such an approach to accountability does nonetheless prioritize a commitment to reconciliation. Societal dynamics influence greatly distinct approaches, in the case of South Africa the military stalemate between the apartheid and antiapartheid forces and the impossibility therefore of a "victors' justice" and the political imperative of a general amnesty. For a defense of South Africa's restorative justice, see Elizabeth Kiss, "Moral Ambition and Political Constraints. Reflections of Restorative Justice," in *Truth v. Justice, the Reality of Truth Commissions*, ed. Robert I. Rotberg and Dennis Thompson (Princeton, NJ: Princeton University Press, 2000), 68–97, and Dumisa B. Ntsebeza, "The Uses of Truth Commissions. Lessons for the World," in *Truth v. Justice, the Reality of Truth Commissions*, ed. Rotberg and Thompson, 158–69.

36. Hugo Vezzetti, "The Use of the Past and the Politics of the Present," in *Desaparición. Argentina's Human Rights Trials*, ed. Gabrielle Andreozzi (Bern: Peter Lang, 2014), 316–17.

37. Beatriz Sarlo, *La audacia y el cálculo. Kirchner 2003—2010* (Buenos Aires: Editorial Sudamericana, 2011), 180–98.

CHAPTER EIGHT. ASSIGNING BLAME: WHO WAS RESPONSIBLE FOR THE DIRTY WAR?

1. Ana Carol Solis, "Mostrar, ocultar y desligar frente al terror estatal. La prensa y la cuestión de los derechos humanos en Córdoba, 1976 1979," in *Córdoba a los 40 años del golpe. Estudios sobre la dictadura en clave local*, ed. Carol Solís and Pablo Ponza (Córdoba: Editorial de la Universidad Nacional de Córdoba, 2016), 149–89.

2. On the history of the human rights movement in Córdoba, see Silvina Verónica Oviedo and Ana Carol Solís, "Violencia Institucionalizada y Formas de Resistencia: Los organismos de Derechos Humanos en Córdoba Durante la Dictadura," M.A. thesis, Universidad Nacional de Córdoba, 2006.

3. Emilio Crenzel, *La historia política del Nunca Más: La memoria de las desapariciones en la Argentina* (Buenos Aires: Siglo XXI, 2008), 49, 87, 110.

4. Crenzel, *La historia política*, 102. The now infamous formula of the "dos demonios" of the military and leftist guerrilla organizations in the CONADEP report's prologue referred to the leadership of both, though the truth commission's charge was only to investigate the crimes of the military. A revised prologue to the report in the Kirchner years in 2006 (and again in 2016) similarly excluded involvement of any of the disappeared in guerrilla organizations or even in nonviolent political activism, stripping them of their historical role, creating in its stead what Crenzel calls an "abstract humanization" by presenting only their generic lives (age, occupation, gender) and their status as victims. See Crenzel, "The Memories of the Disappeared in Argentina," in *Desaparición. Argentina's Human Rights Trials*, ed. Gabrielle Andreozzi (Bern: Peter Lang, 2014), 288–89, 295.

5. Emilio Crenzel, "La victima inocente: de la lucha antidictatorial al relato de *Nunca más*," in *Los desaparecidos en la Argentina. Memorias, representaciones e ideas (1983-2008)*, ed. Emilio Crenzel (Buenos Aires: Editorial Biblos, 2010), 69–73; Emilio Crenzel, "Between

the Voices of the State and the Human Rights Movement: Never Again and the Memories of the Disappeared in Argentina," *Journal of Social History* 44, no. 4 (Summer 2011): 1071.

6. Emilio Crenzel, "The Memories of the Disappeared," in *Desaparición. Argentina's Human Rights Trials*, ed. Gabrielle Andreozzi (Bern: Peter Lang, 2014), 292; María Soledad Catoggio, *Los desaparecidos de la Iglesia. El clero contestatario frente a la dictadura* (Buenos Aires: Siglo XXI Editores, 2016), 239–40.

7. Fernando Oscar Reati, "Entre el amor y el reclamo: Las literatura de los hijos de militantes en la postdictadura argentina," *Alternativas*, no. 5 (2015): 1–45.

8. Marina Franco, *Un enemigo para la nación. Orden interno, violencia y "subversión"* 1973–1976 (Buenos Aires: Fondo de Cultura Económica, 2012).

9. Sebastián Carassai, *The Argentine Silent Majority: Middle Classes, Politics, Violence and Memory in the Seventies* (Durham, NC: Duke University Press, 2014), especially chapter 4. Society's complicity before and during the dictatorship, however, was certainly more a passive than an active one. Complicity during the 1973–76 Peronist government and the subsequent dictatorship did not involve the mass mobilization of the citizenry found in other examples of state terror such as Nazi Germany. The "ordinary men" of the SS and police battalions and not-so-ordinary Gestapo career officials who created a vast web of informers and collaborators among the citizenry in the Nazi genocide dwarfed anything found in the clandestine terrorist state that was Argentina. On Nazi state terrorism, see Christopher R. Browning, *Ordinary Men: Reserve Police Battalion 101 and the Final Solution in Poland* (New York: Harper, 1992), and Eric A. Johnson, *Nazi Terror: The Gestapo, the Jews, and Ordinary Germans* (New York: Basic Books, 1999).

10. Crenzel, "La victima inocente," 75. As Crenzel notes, even the frequent use of the word *compañero* (comrade) was stripped of its usual political meaning as a marker of political sympathies or militancy of any kind and used only as a common status of incarceration.

11. Crenzel, p. 139. Perhaps no better example exists for Charles Maier's point about the historian's need to interrogate the "truth" of truth commission reports than the CONADEP report. See Charles S. Maier, "Doing History, Doing Justice: The Narrative of the Historian and of the Truth Commission," in *Truth v. Justice; The Morality of Truth Commissions*, ed. Robert I. Rotberg and Dennis Thompson (Princeton. NJ: Princeton University Press, 2000), 261–78.

12. Greg Grandin, "The Instruction of Great Catastrophe: Truth Commissions, National History, and State Formation in Argentina, Chile, and Guatemala," *American Historical Review* 110, no. 1 (February 2005): 48.

13. Héctor Ricardo Leis, *Un testamento de los años 70. Terrorismo, política y verdad en Argentina* (Buenos Aires: Katz Editores, 2013), 42.

14. Fiction, especially the novel, has been far more discriminating and insightful on these questions than historical scholarship. For an overview of this literature, see Fernando Reati, "Culpables e inocentes, héroes y traidores, cómplices y espectadores: Representaciones de la violencia política en Argentina desde 1980 hasta el presente," in *Memorias en tinta. Ensayos sobre la representación de la violencia política en Argentina, Chile y Perú*, ed. Lucero de Vivanco Rey (Santiago: Ediciones Universidad Alberto Hurtado, 2014), 81–106, and "Entre el amor y el reclamo: la literatura de los hijos de militantes en la postdictadura argentina," *Alternativas*, no. 5 (2015): 1–45.

15. *Será Justicia* 7, no. 45 (March 2014): 4–5; *Será Justicia* 7, no. 46 (April 2015): 4–5.

16. National Security Archive, U.S. State Department Research Study, "Latin America: The Outlook for Arms Spending" (March 5, 1973).

17. Archdiocese of São Paulo, *Torture in Brazil. A Report by the Archdiocese of São Paulo*, ed. Joan Dassin, trans. Jaime Wright (New York: Vintage Books, 1986), Appendix III, 235–38.

18. See William M. Schmidli, *The Fate of Freedom Elsewhere: Human Rights and US Cold War Policy Toward Argentina* (Ithaca, NY: Cornell University Press, 2013). Schmidli's book is the definitive study on Carter's human rights policy in Argentina. The thousands of recently declassified documents made available by the Obama administration have strongly confirmed Schmidli's findings on Carter's human rights policy and tense relationship, not support of the military authorities in Argentina.

19. J. Patrice McSherry, *Predatory States: Operation Condor and Covert War in Latin America* (New York: Rowman and Littlefield, 2005), 128–32.

20. U.S. State Department, Argentina Declassified Collection. Cable from Ambassador Robert Hill to U.S. State Department, October 19, 1976.

21. The classic study on the Catholic Church's complicity is Emilio Mignone, *Iglesia y dictadura* (Buenos Aires: Ediciones Colihue 2006).

22. Horacio Verbitsky, "The Price of the Church's Blessing," in *The Economic Accomplices of the Argentine Dictatorship: Outstanding Debts*, ed. Horacio Verbitsky and Juan Pablo Bohoslavsky (New York: Cambridge University Press, 2016), 325–28.

23. Verbitsky, "The Price of the Church's Blessing," 331–33.

24. Victoria Basualdo, Tomás Ojea Quintana, and Carolina Varsky, "The Cases of Ford and Mercedes Benz," Victorio Paulón, "Acindar and Techint: Extreme Militarization of Labor Relations," and Alejandra Dandon and Hannah Franzki, "Between Historical Analysis and Legal Responsibility: The Ledesma Case," in *The Economic Accomplices of the Argentine Dictatorship: Outstanding Debts*, ed. Horacio Verbitsky and Juan Pablo Bohoslavsky (New York: Cambridge University Press, 2016), 159–200.

25. Gustavo Morello, *Dónde estaba Dios. Católicos y terrorismo de Estado en la Argentina de los setenta* (Buenos Aires: Ediciones B Argentina, 2014), 256.

26. Vera Carnovale, *Los combatientes. Historia del PRT–ERP* (Buenos Aires: Siglo XXI Editores, 2011), 143–55.

EPILOGUE

1. Horacio Verbitsky and Juan Pablo Bohoslavsky, eds. *The Economic Accomplices to the Argentine Dictatorship: Outstanding Debts* (New York: Cambridge University Press, 2016).

SELECTED BIBLIOGRAPHY

ARCHIVES AND LIBRARIES
Argentina

Buenos Aires
Archivo Nacional de la Memoria (ANM)
Círculo Militar
Memoria Abierta

Córdoba
Archivo Provincial de la Memoria (APM)

La Plata
Archivo Dirección de Inteligencia de la Policía de la Provincia de Buenos Aires (DIPBA)

United States
Benson Latin American Collection, University of Texas, Austin
Library of Congress

Digital Archives
Department of State: Argentina Declassification Collection (United States)
Diario del Juicio (Argentina)
Ministerio de Defensa (Argentina)
National Security Archive (United States)
Office of the Director of National Intelligence (United States)
Parque de la Memoria (Argentina)

SECONDARY SOURCES

The Military, Dictatorship, State Terrorism, and Memory

Atencio, Rebecca J. *Memory's Turn. Reckoning with Dictatorship in Brazil.* Madison: University of Wisconsin Press, 2014.

Bassiouni, M. Cherif. *Crimes Against Humanity: Historical Evolution and Contemporary Application.* Cambridge: Cambridge University Press, 2011.

Bawden, John R. *The Pinochet Generation. The Chilean Military in the Twentieth Century.* Tuscaloosa: University of Alabama Press, 2016.

Birtle, Andrew J. *U.S. Army Counterinsurgency and Contingency Operations Doctrine 1946–1976.* Washington, DC: Center of Military History, 2006.

Bloxham, Donald, and A. Dirk Moses, eds. *The Oxford Handbook of Genocide Studies.* New York: Oxford University Press, 2010.

Branche, Raphaëlle. *La torture et l'armée pendant la guerre d'Algérie (1954–1962).* Paris: Éditions Gallimard, 2001.

Brands, Hal. *Latin America's Cold War.* Cambridge, MA: Harvard University Press, 2010.

Browning, Christopher. *Ordinary Men: Reserve Police Battalion 101 and the Final Solution in Poland.* New York: Harper Perennial, 1998.

Cobin, Christopher J. "Brothers and Sisters, Do Not be Afraid of Me. Trauma, History and the Therapeutic Imagination in the New South Africa." In *Contested Pasts. The Politics of Memory,* edited by Katherine Hodgkin and Susannah Radstone. London: Routledge, 2003.

Conroy, John. *Unspeakable Acts, Ordinary People: The Dynamics of Torture.* New York: Alfred A. Knopf, 2000.

Curthoys, Ann, and John Docker. "Defining Genocide." In The *Historiography of Genocide,* edited by Dan Stone. New York: Palgrave Macmillan, 2008.

Davila, Jerry. *Dictatorship in South America.* Oxford: Wiley-Blackwell, 2013.

Della Porta, Donatella. *Social Movements, Political Violence and the State. A Comparative Analysis of Italy and Germany.* Cambridge: Cambridge University Press, 1995.

Edkins, Jenny. *Trauma and the Memory of Politics.* Cambridge: Cambridge University Press, 2008.

Evans, Richard J. *The Third Reich at War.* New York: Penguin, 2009.

Feierstein, Daniel. *El genocidio como práctica social : Entre el nazismo y la experiencia argentina,* Buenos Aires: Fondo de Cultura Económica, 2007.

Ferllini, Roxana, ed. *Forensic Archaeology and Human Rights Violations.* Springfield, IL: Charles C. Thomas, 2007.

Frazier, Lessie Jo. *Salt in the Sand: Memory, Violence, and the Nation-State in Chile, 1890-Present.* Durham, NC: Duke University Press, 2007.

Gill, Lesley. *The School of the Americas: Military Training and Political Violence in the Americas.* Durham, NC: Duke University Press, 2004.

Gomez-Barris, Macarena. *Where Memory Dwells: Culture and State Violence in Chile.* Berkeley: University of California Press, 2008.

Grandin, Greg. *Empire's Workshop: Latin America, the United States and the Rise of the New Imperialism.* New York: Henry Holt, 2006.

———. "The Instruction of Great Catastrophe: Truth Commissions, National History, and State Formation in Argentina, Chile, and Guatemala." *American Historical Review* 110, no. 1 (2005): 46–67.

Gutman, Daniel. *Somos derechos y humanos*. Buenos Aires: Editorial Sudamericana, 2015.

Johnson, Eric A. *Nazi Terror: The Gestapo, the Jews, and Ordinary Germans*. New York: Basic Books, 1999.

Kiss, Elizabeth. "Moral Ambition and Political Constraints. Reflections of Restorative Justice." In *Truth v. Justice, the Reality of Truth Commissions*, edited by Robert I. Rotberg and Dennis Thompson, 68–97. Princeton, NJ: Princeton University Press, 2000.

Koonings, K., and Dirk Krujit, eds. *Societies of Fear: The Legacy of Civil War, Violence and Terror in Latin America*. New York: St. Martin's, 1999.

La Capra, Dominick. *Writing History, Writing Trauma*. Baltimore, MD: John Hopkins University Press, 2000.

Lazreg, Marina. *Torture and the Twilight of Empire: From Algiers to Baghdad*. Princeton, NJ: Princeton University Press, 2008.

Maier, Charles S. "Doing History, Doing Justice: The Narrative of the Historian and of the Truth Commission." In *Truth v. Justice, the Reality of Truth Commissions*, edited by Robert I. Rotberg and Dennis Thompson, 261–78. Princeton, NJ: Princeton University Press, 2000.

Mazower, Mark. *Dark Continent: Europe's Twentieth Century*. New York: Alfred A. Knopf, 1999.

———. "Violence and the State in the Twentieth Century." *American Historical Review* 107, no. 4 (October 2002): 1158–78.

McSherry, J. Patrice. *Predatory States: Operation Condor and Covert War in Latin America*. New York: Rowman and Littlefield, 2005.

Olick, Jeffrey. *States of Memory: Continuities, Conflicts, and Transformations in National Retrospection*. Durham, NC: Duke University Press, 2003.

Osiel, Mark J. *Mass Atrocity, Ordinary Evil, and Hannah Arendt: Criminal Consciousness in Argentina's Dirty War*. New Haven, CT: Yale University Press, 2001.

———. *Obeying Orders: Atrocity, Military Discipline, and the Laws of War*. New Brunswick, NJ: Transaction, 1999.

Rabe, Stephen G. *The Killing Zone: The United States Wages the Cold War in Latin America*. New York: Oxford University Press, 2012.

Robben, Antonius C.G.M. "Seduction and Persuasion: The Politics of Truth and Emotion among Victims and Perpetrators of Violence." In *Fieldwork under Fire: Contemporary Studies of Violence and Survival*, edited by Carolyn Nordstrum and Antonius C.G.M. Robben. Berkeley: University of California Press, 1995.

Robin, Marie-Monique. *Escuadrons de la mort, l'école française*. Paris: Éditions La Découverte, 2004.

Rubinstein, William D. *Genocide: A History*. London: Pearson Longman, 2004.

Scheper-Hughes, Nancy, and Philippe Bourgois. "Introduction: Making Sense of Violence." In *Violence in War and Peace: An Anthology*, edited by Nancy Scheper-Hughes and Philippe Bourgois. Oxford: Blackwell Publishing, 2004.

Sluka, Jeffrey A. *Death Squad: The Anthropology of State Terror*. Philadelphia: University of Pennsylvania Press, 2000.

Stepan, Alfred. "The New Professionalism of Internal Warfare and Military Role Expansion." In *Armies and Politics in Latin America*, edited by Abraham Lowenthal. New York: Holmes and Meier, 1976.

Stern, Steve. *Battling for Hearts and Minds: Memory Struggles in Pinochet's Chile, 1973–1988.* Durham, NC: Duke University Press, 2006.

———. *Reckoning with Pinochet. The Memory Question in Democratic Chile, 1989—2006.* Durham, NC: Duke University Press, 2010.

Totten, Samuel et al. *Genocide in the Twentieth Century. Critical Essays and Eyewitness Accounts.* New York: Garland, 1995.

Weitz, Eric D. 2003. *A Century of Genocide: Utopias of Race and Nation.* Princeton, NJ: Princeton University Press, 2003.

Weld, Kirsten. *Paper Cadavers: The Archives of the Dictatorship in Guatemala.* Durham, NC: Duke University Press, 2014.

Wolf. Eric R. *Envisioning Power: Ideologies of Dominance and Crisis.* Berkeley: University of California Press, 1998.

Zoglin, Katie. "Paraguay's Archive of Terror: International Cooperation and Operation Condor." *Inter-American Law Review* 32, no. 1 (Winter–Spring, 2004).

Argentina: Political Violence, the Dirty War, and Human Rights

Águila, Gabriela. *Dictadura, represión y sociedad en Rosario, 1976/1983.* Buenos Aires: Prometeo Libros, 2008.

Andersen, Martin E. *Dossier Secreto: Argentina's Desaparecidos and the Myth of the "Dirty War."* Boulder, CO: Westview, 1993.

Andreozzi, Gabriele, ed. *Desaparición: Argentina's Human Rights Trials.* Bern: Peter Lang, 2014.

Anguita, Eduardo, and Martín Caparrós. *La Voluntad: Una historia de militancia revolucionaria en la Argentina.* 3 vols. Buenos Aires: Grupo Editorial Norma, 1997 and 1998.

Arditti, Ruth. *Searching for Life: The Grandmothers of the Plaza de Mayo and the Disappeared of Argentina.* Berkeley: University of California Press, 1999.

Armony, Ariel C. *Argentina, the United States, and the Anti-Communist Crusade in Central America, 1977–1984.* Athens: Ohio University Center for International Affairs, 1997.

Arriaga, Ana Elisa. "Represión sindical y disciplinamiento laboral: La violencia en el dispositivo de control del conflicto en EPEC (1973–1978)." In *Córdoba a los 40 años del golpe. Estudios sobre la dictadura en clave local,* edited by Ana Carol Solís and Pablo Ponza, 75–104. Córdoba: Editorial de la Universidad Nacional de Córdoba, 2016.

Basualdo, Victoria. "Complicidad patronal-militar en la última dictadura argentina: Los casos de Acindar, Astarsa, Dálmine Siderca, Ford, Ledesma y Mercedes Benz." *Revista Engranaje,* no. 5 (March 2006).

———. "Contribution to the Analysis of the Role of Labor Leadership in Worker Repression in the 1970s." In *The Economic Accomplices to the Argentine Dictatorship: Outstanding Debts,* edited by Horacio Verbitsky and Juan Pablo Bohoslavsky. New York: Cambridge University Press, 2016.

Bernardi , Patricia, and Luis Fondebrider. "Forensic Archaeology and the Scientific Documentation of Human Rights Violations: An Argentinian Example from the Early 1980s." In *Forensic Archaeology and Human Rights violations,* edited by Roxanna Ferllini, 205–32. Springfield, IL: Charles C. Thomas, 2007.

Brennan, James P. *The Labor Wars in Córdoba, 1965–76: Ideology, Work, and Labor Politics in an Argentine Industrial City.* Cambridge, MA: Harvard University Press, 1994.

————. "Rebelión y Revolución: Los estudiantes de la Universidad Nacional de Córdoba en el contexto transnacional." In *Universidad Nacional de Córdoba. Cuatrocientos años de historia*, edited by Daniel Saur and Alicia Servetto, 255–73. Córdoba: Editorial de la Universidad Nacional de Córdoba, 2013.

Brysk, Alison. "The Politics of Measurement: The Contested Count of the Disappeared in Argentina." *Human Rights Quarterly* 16 (1994): 676–92.

Burdick, Michael. *For God and Fatherland: Religion and Politics in Argentina*. Albany: State University of New York Press, 1995.

Calveiro, Pilar. "Antiguos y nuevos sentidos de la política y la violencia." *Lucha Armada* 1, no. 4 (2005).

————. *Poder y desaparición: Los campos de concentración en Argentina*. Buenos Aires: Ediciones Colihue, 1998.

————. *Política y violencia. Una aproximación a la guerrilla de los años 70*. Buenos Aires: Grupo Editorial Norma, 2005.

————. "Spatialities of Exception." In *Space and the Memories of Violence: Landscapes of Erasure, Disappearances and Exception*, edited by Estela Schindel and Pamela Colombo, 205–18. New York: Palgrave-Macmillan, 2014.

Carasai, Sebastián. *The Argentine Silent Majority: Middle Classes, Politics, Violence and Memory in the Seventies*. Durham, NC: Duke University Press, 2014.

Carnovale, Vera. *Los combatientes: historia del PRT-ERP*. Buenos Aires: Siglo XXI, 2011.

Cattoggio, María Soledad. *Los desaparecidos de la Iglesia. El clero contestatario frente a la dictadura*. Buenos Aires: Siglo XXI Editores, 2016.

Comisión Nacional sobre la Desaparición de Personas. Delegación Córdoba (CONADEP). *Informe.* 2nd ed. Córdoba: Familiares de Desaparecidos y Detenidos por Razones Políticas de Córdoba, 1999.

Contepomi, Gustavo, and Patricia Contepomi. *Sobrevivientes de La Perla*. Córdoba: El Cid Editor, 1984.

Crenzel, Emilio. "Between the Voices of the State and the Human Rights Movement: Never Again and the Memories of the Disappeared in Argentina." *Journal of Social History* 44, no. 4 (Summer 2011): 1063–76.

————. *La historia política del Nunca Más: La memoria de las desapariciones en la Argentina*. Buenos Aires: Siglo XXI, 2008.

————. "La víctima inocente: De la lucha antidictatorial al relato del Nunca Más." In *Los desaparecidos en la Argentina: Memorias, representaciones, e ideas, 1983–2008*, edited by Ernesto Crenzel. Buenos Aires: Biblos, 2010.

D'Andrea Mohr, José Luis. *Memoria De Vida*. Buenos Aires: Colihue, 1999.

da Silva Catela, Ludmila. "El mundo de los archivos." In *Los archivos de la represión: Documentos, memoria y verdad*, edited by Ludmila da Silva Catela and Elizabeth Jelin. Madrid: Siglo XXI, 2002.

Díaz Besone, Ramón Genaro. *Guerra Revolucionaria en la Argentina (1959–1978)*. Buenos Aires: Editorial Fraterna, 1986.

Di Stefano, Roberto, and Loris Zanatta. *Historia de la iglesia argentina: Desde la Conquista hasta fines del siglo XX*. Buenos Aires: Grijalbo, 2000.

Di Tella, Andrés. "La vida privada en los campos de concentración." In *Historia de la vida privada en la Argentina*, edited by Fernando Devoto and Marta Madero. Buenos Aires: Taurus, 1999.

Doretti, M., and Clyde Snow. "Forensic Anthropology and Human Rights: The Argentine Experience." In *Hard Evidence: Case Studies in Forensic Anthropology*, edited by Dawn Wolfe Steadman, 290–310. Upper Saddle River, NJ: Prentice Hall, 2003.

Doretti, M., and L. Fonderbrider. "Perspectives and Recommendations from the Field: Forensic Anthropology and Human Rights in Argentina." *Proceedings of the 56th Annual Meeting of the American Academy of Forensic Sciences*, Dallas, TX, 1984.

Duhalde, Edurdo Luis. *El estado terrorista argentino*. Barcelona: Argos Vergara, 1983.

Feierstein, Daniel. "Political Violence in Argentina and Its Genocidal Characteristics." In *State Violence and Genocide in Latin America. The Cold War Years*, edited by Maria Esparza, Henry R. Huttenbach, and Daniel Feiertsein. London: Routledge, 2010.

Feitlowitz, Marguerite. *A Lexicon of Terror: Argentina and the Legacies of Torture*. Rev. ed. New York: Oxford University Press, 2011.

Feldman, David. "Argentina, 1945–1971: Military Assistance, Military Spending, and the Political Activity of the Armed Forces." *Journal of Interamerican Studies and World Affairs* 24 (1982).

Filc, Judith. *Entre el parentesco y la política: Familia y dictadura, 1976–1983*. Buenos Aires: Editorial Biblos, 1997.

Finchelstein, Federico. *The Ideological Origins of the Dirty War: Fascism, Populism, and Dictatorship in Twentieth-Century Argentina*. New York: Oxford University Press, 2014.

Franco, Marina. *Un enemigo para la nación: orden interno, violencia y 'subversión.'* Buenos Aires: Fondo de Cultura Económica, 2012.

Galante, Miguel, and Adrián Jmelnizky. "Sobre el antisemitismo en el terrorismo de Estado en Argentina." In *Genocidio del siglo XX y formas de la negación. Actas del III Encuentro sobre Genocidio*, edited by N. Boulgourdjian-Toufeksian, J.C. Toufkesian, and Carlos Alemian. Buenos Aires: Edición del Centro Armenio, 2003.

García, Prudencio. *El drama de la autonomía militar: Argentina bajo las Juntas Militares*. Madrid: Alianza Editorial, 1995.

Garaño, Sebastián. "El 'tratamiento' penitenciario y su dimensión productiva de identidades entre los presos políticos (1974–1983)." *Revista Iberoamericana* 10, no. 40 (2010): 113–30.

Garay, Lucía S., et al. *Vivencias frente al límite*. Córdoba: Universidad Nacional de Córdoba, 2006.

Gillespie, Richard. *Soldiers of Perón: Argentina's Montoneros*. New York: Oxford University Press, 1982.

Gordillo, Mónica. "La revolución en la universidad." In *Universidad Nacional de Córdoba. Cuatrocientos años de historia*, edited by Daniel Saur and Alicia Servetto, 231–54. Córdoba: Editorial de la Universidad Nacional de Córdoba, 2013.

Guest, Ian. *Behind the Disappearances*. Philadelphia: University of Pennsylvania Press, 1990.

Heinz, Wolfgang S., and Hugo Frühling. *Determinants of Gross Human Rights Violations by the State and State Sponsored-Actors in Brazil, Uruguay, Chile and Argentina*. The Hague: M. Nijhoff, 1999.

Hodges, Donald C. *Argentina's "Dirty War": An Intellectual Biography*. Austin: University of Texas Press, 1991.

Huggins, Martha, et al. *Violence Workers: Police Torturers and Murderers Reconstruct Brazilian Atrocitie*. Berkeley: University of California Press, 2002.

Lewis, Paul H. *Guerrillas and Generals: The "Dirty War" in Argentina*. New York: Praeger, 2002.

Lorenzetti, Ricardo Luis, and Alfredo Jorge Kraut. *Derechos Humanos: Justicia y reparación. La experiencia de la Justicia en la Argentina. Crímenes de lesa humanidad*. Buenos Aires: Editorial Sudamericana, 2011.

Malmud-Goti, Jaime. *Game Without End: State Terror and the Politics of Justice*. Norman: University of Oklahoma Press, 1996.

Maneiro, María. *Como el árbol talado: Memorias del genocidio en La Plata, Berisso y Ensenada*. La Plata: Ediciones al Margen, 2006.

Manzano, Valeria. *The Age of Youth in Argentina: Culture, Politics and Sexuality*. Chapel Hill: University of North Carolina Press, 2014.

Marchak, Patricia. *God's Assassins: State Terrorism in Argentina in the 1970s*. Montreal: McGill-Queens University Press, 1999.

Mariani, Ana, and Alejo Gómez Jacobo. *La Perla: Historia y testimonios de uno de los más grandes campos de concentración de la Argentina*. Buenos Aires: Aguilar, 2012.

Mazzei, Daniel H. *Bajo el poder de la caballería: El ejército argentino (1962–1973)*. Buenos Aires: Editorial de la Universidad de Buenos Aires, 2012.

———. "La mision militar francesa en la Escuela Superior de Guerra y los orígenes de la Guerra Sucia, 1957–1962." *Revista de Ciencias Sociales*, no. 13 (November 2002): 105–37.

Morello, Gustavo. *The Catholic Church and Argentina's Dirty War*. Oxford: Oxford University Press, 2015.

———. *Dónde estaba Dios. Católicos y terrorismo de Estado en la Argentina de los setenta*. Buenos Aires: Ediciones B Argentina, 2014.

Moyano, María José. *Argentina's Lost Patrol: Armed Struggle, 1969–1979*. New Haven, CT: Yale University Press, 1995.

———. "The 'Dirty War' in Argentina: Was It a War and How Dirty Was it?" In *Staatliche und Parastaatliche Gewalt in Lateinamerika*, edited by Hans Werner Tobler and Peter Waldmann, 45–73. Frankfurt: Veruvert Verlag, 1991.

Munck, Gerardo L. *Authoritarianism and Democratization: Soldiers and Workers in Argentina, 1976–1983*. University Park: Pennsylvania State University Press, 1998.

Nino, Carlos. *Radical Evil on Trial*. New Haven, CT: Yale University Press, 1996.

Noguera, Ana, and Alicia Servetto. "De guerrilleros a subversivos. Hacia un perfil de los y las militantes de las organizaciones revolucionarias armadas de Córdoba." In *Córdoba a los 40 años del golpe. Estudios sobre la dictadura en clave local*, edited by Ana Carol Solís and Pablo Ponza. Córdoba: Editorial de la Universidad Nacional de Córdoba, 2016.

Ollier, María Matilde. *La creencia y la pasión: Privado, público y político en la izquierda revolucionaria*. Buenos Aires: Ariel, 1998.

———. *Golpe o revolución: La violencia legitimada, Argentina, 1966/1976*. Buenos Aires: EDUNTREF, 2005.

Olmo, Darío. "Reconstruir desde restos y fragmentos: El uso de archivos policiales en la antropología forense en Argentina." In *Los archivos de la represión: Documentos, memoria y verdad*, edited by Ludmila da Silva Catela and Elizabeth Jelin. Madrid: Siglo XXI, 2002.

Osiel, Mark J. "Constructing Subversion in Argentina's Dirty War." *Representations* 75 (Summer 2001): 119–58.

Paiaro, Melisa. "La forma legal de lo ilegal. La legislación represiva nacional y su incidencia en la provincia de Córdoba (1973–1976)." *Boletín Bibliográfico Electrónico del Programa Buenos Aires de Historia Política* 6, no. 12 (2013): 99–117.

Palermo, Vicente, and Marcos Novaro. *La dictadura militar, 1976–1983. Del golpe de Estado a la restauración democrática*. Buenos Aires: Paidós, 2003.

Perelli, Carina. "From Counterrevolutionary Warfare to Political Awakening: The Uruguayan and Argentine Armed Forces in the 1970s." *Armed Forces and Society* 20 (Fall 1979): 25–49.

———. "La percepción de la amenaza y el pensamiento político de los militares en América del Sur." In *Los militares y la democracia: El futuro de las relaciones civico-militares en América Latina*, edited by Louis Goodman, et al. Montevideo: PEITHO, 1990.

Philp, Marta. *Memoria y política en la historia argentina reciente: Una lectura desde Córdoba*. Córdoba: Universidad Nacional de Córdoba, 2009.

———. "El orden natural como fortaleza. Continuidades y rupturas en las bases ideológicas de la dictadura." In *Córdoba a los 40 años del golpe. Estudios sobre la dictadura en clave local*, edited by Ana Carol Solís and Pablo Ponza, Córdoba: Editorial de la UNC, 2016.

———. "La Universidad Nacional de Córdoba y 'la formación de almas': La dictadura de 1976." In *Universidad Nacional de Córdoba. Cuatrocientos años de historia*, edited by Daniel Saur and Alicia Servetto, 275–96. Córdoba: Editorial de la Universidad Nacional de Córdoba, 2013.

Piñeiro, Elena. *La tradición nacionalista ante el peronismo*. Buenos Aires: A-Z Editora, 1997.

Pion-Berlin, David. *The Ideology of State Terror. Economic Doctrine and Political Repression in Argentina and Peru*. Boulder, CO: Lynne Rienner, 1989.

Ranalletti, Mario. "Aux origines du terrorisme d'État en Argentine. Les influences françaises dans la formation des militaires argentins (1955–1976)." *Vingtième Siécle. Revue d'histoire*, no. 105 (January–March 2010): 45–56.

Ratti, Camilo. *Cachorro: Vida y Muertes de Luciano Benjamín Menéndez*. Córdoba: Editorial Raíz de Dos, 2013.

Reati, Fernando, and Mario Villani. *Desaparecidos: Memoria de un cautiverio*. Buenos Aires: Biblos, 2011.

Reati, Fernando Oscar. "Culpables e inocentes, héroes y traidores, cómplices y espectadores: Representaciones de la violencia política en Argentina desde 1980 hasta el presente." In *Memorias en tinta. Ensayos sobre la representación de la violencia política en Argentina, Chile y Perú*, edited by Lucero de Vivanco Rey, 81–106. Santiago: Ediciones Universidad Alberto Hurtado, 2014.

———. "Entre el amor y el reclamo: la literatura de los hijos de militantes en la postdictadura argentina." *Alternativas*, no. 5 (2015): 1–45.

Reato, Ceferino. *Disposición Final: La confesión de Videla sobre los desaparecidos*. Buenos Aires: Editorial Sudamericana, 2012.

Robben, Antonius C.G.M. "From Dirty War to Genocide: Argentina's Resistance to National Reconciliation." *Memory Studies* 5, no. 3 (2012): 305–15.

———. *Political Violence and Trauma in Argentina*. Philadelphia: University of Pennsylvania Press, 2005.

———. "The Politics of Truth and Emotion among Victims and Perpetrators of Violence." In *Fieldwork under Fire: Contemporary Studies of Violence and Survival*, edited by Carolyn

Nordstrom and Antonius C. G. M. Robben. Berkeley: University of California Press, 1995.

Robles, Miguel. *La búsqueda: Una entrevista con Charlie Moore.* Córdoba: Ediciones del Pasaje, 2010.

Rouquié, Alain. *Pouvoir militaire et societé politique en la Republique Argentine.* Paris: Presses de la Fondation Nationale des Sciences Politiques, 1977.

Salcedo, Javier. *Los montoneros del barrio.* Buenos Aires: EDUTREF, 2011.

Sarlo, Beatriz. *La audacia y el cálculo. Kirchner 2003–2010.* Buenos Aires: Sudamericana, 2011.

Schindel, Estela. "A Limitless Grave: Memory and Abjection of the Rio de la Plata." In *Space and the Memories of Violence: Landscapes of Erasure, Disappearances and Exception,* edited by Estela Schindel and Pamela Colombo, 188–218. New York: Palgrave-Macmillan, 2014.

Schmidli, William M. *The Fate of Freedom Elsewhere: Human Rights and US Cold War Policy Toward Argentina.* Ithaca, NY: Cornell University Press, 2013.

Schorr, Martin. "La desindustrialización como eje del proyecto refundacional de la economía y la sociedad argentina, 1976–1983." *América Latina Historia Económica* 19, no. 3 (September–December 2012): 31–56.

Servetto, Alicia. *73/76. El gobierno peronista contra las "provincias montoneras."* Buenos Aires: Siglo XXI, 2010.

Sheinin, David M. K. *Consent of the Damned: Ordinary Argentinians in the Dirty War.* Gainesville: University of Florida Press, 2012.

Solis, Ana Carol. "Mostrar, ocultar y desligar frente al terror estatal. La prensa y la cuestión de los derechos humanos en Córdoba, 1976 1979." In *Córdoba a los 40 años del golpe. Estudios sobre la dictadura en clave local,* edited by Ana Carol Solís and Pablo Ponza, 149–89. Córdoba: Editorial de la Universidad Nacional de Córdoba, 2016.

Somigliana, M., and Darío Olmo. "Los desaparecidos. La huella del genocidio." *Encrucijadas. Revista de la Universidad de Buenos Aires* 2, no. 15 (2002): 21–35.

Stewart, Kinzer Nora. *Mates and Muchachos: Unit Cohesion in the Falklands/Malvinas War.* New York: Brassey's, 1991.

Suárez-Orozco, Marcelo. "A Grammar of Terror: Psychocultural Responses to State Terrorism in Dirty War and Post-Dirty War Argentina." In *The Paths to Domination, Resistance, and Terror,* edited by Carolyn Nordstrom and JoAnn Martin. Berkeley: University of California Press, 1992.

———. "Speaking the Unspeakable: Towards a Psychosocial Understanding of Responses to Terror." *Ethos* 18, no. 3 (1990): 353–83.

Taylor, Diana. *Disappearing Acts: Spectacles of Gender and Nationalism in Argentina's "Dirty War."* Durham, NC: Duke University Press, 1997.

Tognonato, Claudio. "The Hidden Italy Connection." In *The Economic Accomplices to the Argentine Dictatorship: Outstanding Debts,* edited by Horacio Verbitsky and Juan Pablo Bohoslavsky. New York: Cambridge University Press, 2016.

Verbitsky, Horacio, and Juan Pablo Bohoslavsky, eds. *The Economic Accomplices to the Argentine Dictatorship: Outstanding Debts.* New York: Cambridge University Press, 2016.

Vergara, María. *Silence, Obedience, and Discipline: The Educational Discourse of the Argentine Military Regime (1976–1983).* Lund, Sweden: Lund University Press, 1997.

Villegas, Osiris Gen. *Guerra revolucionaria comunista*. Buenos Aires: Editorial Pleamar, 1963.

Vogel, Klaus Friedrich. *Dictatorship, Democracy, and Globalization: Argentina and the Cost of Paralysis, 1973–2001*. University Park: Pennsylvania State University Press, 2009.

Yankelvich, Pablo. *Ráfagas de un exilio. Argentinos en México*. Mexico City: El Colegio de México, 2009.

Zanatta, Loris, "La dictadure militaire argentine (1976–1983): Une interpretation à la lumière du mythe da la nation catholique." *Vingtième Siecle. Revue d'histoire*, no. 105 (January–March 2010): 145–53.

INDEX

air force, 15; intelligence services of, 22, 53; role in the dirty war, 46, 53–54
Alfonsín, Raúl, 11, 80, 90; and amnesty laws, 75–76; and the CONADEP truth commission report, 80–81, 107–109; and human rights policies, 1, 7, 78, 87, 104, 106; and trials of the junta, 7, 77–80
Algerian War: French counterrevolutionary tactics in, 4, 64–71, 77; postwar amnesty for the French military, 77
Alianza Argentina Anticomunista (AAA), 9, 151. *See also* death squads
anti-semitism, influence on state terrorism in Córdoba, 29–30, 55
APDH (Permanent Assembly on Human Rights), 4, 105, 112
Archivo de la Dirección de Inteligencia de la Policía de la Provincia de Buenos Aires (DIPBA), 99
Archivo Provincial de la Memoria (APM), ix–x, 95*fig.*, 96*fig.*; archive of, 97–99; and memory construction, 97–100, 117
army: anti-Peronism in, 62, 72–73; counterinsurgency training in, 62–71, 169n7; counterrevolutionary theories in, 62–71; ethnic and class composition of, 55–56; factionalism in, 74; French influence on Catholic nationalism, 72–73; French influence on strategic thinking, 62–71; national traditions in, 72–75; responsibility for conducting the dirty war in Córdoba, 51–61; US influence on, 62–64, 69–71, 169n3

Barreiro, Ernesto, 33–34; as a defendant in the La Perla–Campo de la Ribera trial, 85, 88; and the dirty war in Córdoba, 42, 45, 54
Bignone, Reynaldo, 4, 67, 97
black market, in babies, 49
Bonafini, Hebe, 102
Brazil: human rights and justice in, 101, 176n27; US influence on the military in, 63
Buen Pastor (Good Shepherd) women's prison, 25–26, 25*fig.*, 26*fig.*, 92
business, and collaboration with the dictatorship, 9, 33–35, 114, 116–117. *See also* Fiat
Bussi, Antonio Domingo, 58

Campo de la Ribera, x, 3, 56*fig.*, 57*fig.*; establishment of, 16, 23–24, 56–57; and human rights trials, 84–88; as a memory site, 110; as a site of detention, 39, 92, 95
Cardozo, Cesáreo, 72
Carter, James, human rights policy of and Argentina, 29, 46, 57, 111–112
Castro, Fidel, 150, 154
Catholic Church, 13–14; complicity with the dictatorship, 32–33, 114; conflicts within, 8, 73; reforms and political activism in Córdoba, 17–18. *See also* Third World Priests Movement (Sacerdotes del Tercer Mundo)

CPSIA information can be obtained
at www.ICGtesting.com
Printed in the USA
BVHW031709301220
596757BV00003B/37